Input Trade and Production Networks in East Asia

Input Trade and Production Networks in East Asia

Edited by

Daisuke Hiratsuka

Director-General, Research Planning Department, Institute of Developing Economies (IDE), JETRO, Japan

Yoko Uchida

Associate Senior Research Fellow, Microeconomic Analysis Group, Development Studies Center, Institute of Developing Economies (IDE), JETRO, Japan

INSTITUTE OF DEVELOPING ECONOMIES (IDE), JETRO

Edward Elgar

Cheltenham, UK • Northampton, MA, USA

Published by
Edward Elgar Publishing Limited
The Lypiatts
15 Lansdown Road
Cheltenham
Glos GL50 2JA
UK

Edward Elgar Publishing, Inc.
William Pratt House
9 Dewey Court
Northampton
Massachusetts 01060
USA

A catalogue record for this book
is available from the British Library

Library of Congress Control Number: 2009941265

Mixed Sources
Product group from well-managed
forests and other controlled sources
www.fsc.org Cert no. SA-COC-1565
© 1996 Forest Stewardship Council

ISBN 978 1 84980 069 3

Printed and bound by MPG Books Group, UK

Contents

Contributors

Kazunobu Hayakawa, Research Fellow, Economic Integration Studies Group, Inter-disciplinary Studies Center, Institute of Developing Economies, Japan External Trade Organization.

Daisuke Hiratsuka, Director-General, Research Planning Department, Institute of Developing Economies, Japan External Trade Organization.

David Hummels, Professor of Economics, Department of Economics, Krannert School of Management, Purdue University, Indiana, USA.

Fukunari Kimura, Professor, Faculty of Economics, Keio University, Tokyo, Japan and Chief Economist, Economic Research Institute for ASEAN and East Asia (ERIA), Jakarta, Indonesia.

Toshiyuki Matsuura, Senior Assistant Professor, Institute for Economic and Industrial Studies, Keio University, Tokyo, Japan.

Hiromichi Ozeki, Senior Research Fellow, Development Studies Center, Institute of Developing Economies, Japan External Trade Organization.

Laura Puzzello, Lecturer, Department of Economics, Monash University, Caulfield, Australia.

Keola Souknilanh, Associate Senior Research Fellow, Development Strategies Studies Group, Development Studies Center, Institute of Developing Economies, Japan External Trade Organization.

Yoko Uchida, Associate Senior Research Fellow, Microeconomic Analysis Group, Development Studies Center, Institute of Developing Economies, Japan External Trade Organization.

Kazuhiko Yokota, Associate Professor, School of Commerce, Waseda University, Tokyo, Japan.

Preface

One of the most prominent features of world trade in recent decades has been a rapid growth in trade in intermediate goods. In East Asia, intermediate input trade has grown markedly and at a rate much faster than that of the world average. It follows that this has led to an increase in East Asia's share of world intermediate input trade.

In the context of this remarkable growth, since the early 1990s East Asia as a region has developed production networks in the manufacture of various products where production processes are divided into several stages, and the outcome has been the emergence of sequential production blocks that are separately located across countries, according to comparative advantage in various factors. As a consequence of the development of sequential production, intermediate goods are traded among the countries in the region so as to produce final products. This mechanism has brought about a notable expansion of intermediate trade in East Asia.

Yet despite this phenomenon, so far there have been no rigorous studies on intermediate input trade and production networks within the region. In particular, the causes and extent of intermediate input trade and the resulting production networks in East Asia remain unclear. In 2006, the Institute of Developing Economies (IDE) initiated a two-year project, entitled 'Vertical Specialization and Economic Integration in East Asia'. Its aim is to undertake for the first time rigorous empirical analyses of the growth of intermediate input trade as well as detailed studies that capture the main features and characteristics of production networks in East Asia. To this end, we have used various sources such as trade statistics, firm-level data in the form of basic surveys on Japanese Overseas Business Activities, and data derived from the Asian Input–Output tables. This book is one of the outcomes of the project. It investigates to what extent intermediate input trade has developed within the East Asian region, and it attempts to identify the determinants of intermediate input trade and the formation of associated production networks within the region. We also investigate what kinds of production operations are undertaken by multinational enterprises (MNEs) in East Asia and we show how an understanding of these operations can inform predictions of what is likely to happen in the East

Asian less-developed countries (LDCs) in the years ahead. We thank all the contributors for their support and for their helpful cooperation in the project.

The editors

1. The development of input trade and production networks in East Asia

Daisuke Hiratsuka and Yoko Uchida

1.1 INTRODUCTION

As noted in the preface, East Asia's rapid growth in intermediate input trade, and the associated emergence of sequential production blocks that are separately located across countries, according to comparative advantage in factors such as technology, factor endowment, trade and investment promotion measures, and market size, has resulted in a huge expansion of intermediate trade in the region. Yet despite this phenomenon, apart from contributions by Kimura and Ando (2005) and Ng and Yeats (1999), so far there have been no rigorous studies, and the causes and extent of intermediate input trade and the resulting production networks in East Asia remain unclear. This book aims to make good this deficiency by presenting rigorous empirical analyses of the growth of intermediate input trade and by capturing the main features and characteristics of production networks in East Asia. We separate the question: 'why and to what extent have intermediate input trade and resulting production networks developed in East Asia?' into three stages, because the subject is too large and complicated to answer otherwise.

First we examine to what extent intermediate input trade has developed within the East Asian region. Several scholars have examined production networks in East Asia. Kimura and Ando (2005), using microdata relating to Japanese firms as well as trade statistics, claim that production networks have developed to a greater extent in East Asia than in any other major region of the world. Ng and Yeats (1999) used parts and components data derived from trade statistics to assess the magnitude of production sharing in East Asia. They showed that production sharing in East Asia has deepened over the years. However, since these studies used a definition that classifies any particular product as either an intermediate or a final good, their findings are not always accurate and they tend to be somewhat limited in scope. In this book, we quantitatively measure to what extent intermediate input trade has increased within East Asia.

Second, we attempt to identify the determinants of intermediate input trade and the formation of associated production networks within the region. During the last few decades, economists, employing various technical advances, have made substantial progress in areas such as increasing returns to scale, the possibility of product differentiation and imperfect competition, theoretical studies of international trade, the location of industry, and multinational enterprises (MNEs). Taking these and other theoretical developments into account, we empirically explore the causes of intermediate input trade and production networks in East Asia, and in doing so, hope that our empirical evidence will provide useful feedback concerning the validity of recently developed theories.

Third, we explore what kinds of production operations are undertaken by MNEs in East Asia. It is widely recognized that MNEs have played an important role in the increase in input trade and in the formation of production networks. We explore how MNEs contribute to the development of production networks in East Asia, with particular reference to the procurement and locational patterns of Japanese affiliates operating within the region.

We find that intermediate trade in East Asia is undergoing a conspicuous growth, especially in electronic and chemical products. It is widely recognized that any increase in intermediate trade is brought about by a decrease in trade costs. We provide confirmation of this phenomenon and we also find that factor endowment differences across the countries of the region are important in explaining East Asia's intermediate trade growth.

In East Asia, sequential production stages are located across the various countries of the region, with each country specializing in each of the production stages concerned, depending on the nature of its particular comparative advantage. Countries that are well endowed with labor produce low-value-added parts whose production requires a relatively low level of technology, while countries well endowed with capital produce high-value-added parts that are based on high technology. This is the production mechanism that has led to an expansion of intermediate trade in East Asia.

Using micro-level analyses of the behavior of Japanese affiliates that operate in East Asia, we empirically confirm that Japanese affiliates procure intermediate goods not only from Japan but also from other East Asian countries and export finished goods to third countries after processing them. In this way, the presence of Japanese affiliates in East Asia helps to foster new industries in third countries of the region. East Asia's production networks are expanding into industrial sectors and across national borders through the diffusion of know-how from Japanese affiliates that have been established within the region. Indeed, regional production networks can be seen not only in electronics but also in other industries such as garment manufacture and automobile assembly. Even less-developed countries (LDCs), which have not belonged to industrial production networks hitherto, have recently begun to be drawn into the production process.

The following section reviews the existing theoretical and empirical literature relevant to the above three research questions and clarifies the significance of our own contributions. In the third section, we provide a summary of our findings and comment on the implications of each of the book's chapters. In the final section of this introductory survey, we offer our thoughts concerning the future possibility of East Asia's economic integration, taking into account the conclusions arrived at by each of the chapters that make up the book.

1.2 PREVIOUS THEORETICAL AND EMPIRICAL STUDIES AND OUR OWN CONTRIBUTIONS

1.2.1 Development of Intermediate Input Trade

Sequential production across countries has been investigated from a theoretical standpoint by many authors and has been referred to variously as fragmentation (Jones and Kierzkowski, 1990), slicing up the value chain (Krugman, 1996), vertical specialization (Hummels et al., 2001), and the production network (Hanson et al., 2005).

Several studies have attempted to investigate to what extent fragmentation has developed in East Asia. Among them, the contribution by Hummels et al. (2001) has attracted widespread attention, as it provides a measurement of the vertically fragmented production process. The authors of this study calculated a vertical specialization index, which measures the imported inputs that are embodied in another country's exports, using Input–Output tables from the OECD. We ourselves used a similar methodology, but in order to calculate a vertical specialization index for East Asia, we have used the Asian Input–Output tables compiled by the Institute of Developing Economies (IDE).

We have obtained some interesting findings. First, with the exception of Singapore, between 1975 and 2000 most of the East Asian countries increased their vertical specialization export share within the region. Second, vertical specialization export shares in 2000 were higher in Malaysia (0.33), the Philippines (0.28), Singapore (0.31) and Thailand (0.24), compared with the OECD country average of 0.21, as measured by Hummels et al. (2001). Third, vertical specialization has developed especially in the electronic products and chemical products industries. This study confirms the widespread impression that within East Asia, intermediate input trade increased significantly from 1975 to 2000, especially in electronics and chemical products industries. Moreover, the share of input trade to total trade is larger in East Asia than in the OECD as a whole.

1.2.2 Determinants of Intermediate Input Trade and Production Networks

Why has intermediate input trade and the resulting formation of international fragmentation (production networks) developed in East Asia? In broad terms, there are two explanations for this. One emphasizes trade costs. New economic geography (NEG), or spatial economics, argues that the location of manufacturing changes over time according to trade costs. Krugman and Venables (1995), for example, have examined the location of intermediate goods and final goods output, but they have not explicitly analyzed the location of intermediate goods production. It was Amiti (2005) who extended the literature in NEG by embedding a model with vertical linked industries involving upstream and downstream types of manufacturing. Amiti (2005) argues that the location of upstream and downstream production changes in accordance with trade costs and market sizes. Yi (2003) has discussed to what extent the reduction of trade costs affects intermediate trade, and has predicted that a one-percentage-point reduction in tariffs leads to a multiple of one-percentage-point decline in costs and prices due to at least a doubling of border controls where tariffs are incurred. Amiti suggests that intermediate trade would be encouraged by a small reduction of trade costs.

Other studies have emphasized factor endowment differences. Using a simple two-country trade model, Jones and Kierzkowski (1990) and Deardorff (2001a, 2001b) discussed how, with growth of its output level, a firm was able to promote a switch to a production process characterized by fragmented production blocks. They concluded that fragmentation increases the value of output of any country where it occurs as well as that of the world in general.

Differences in factor endowment and in trade costs seem to be important for East Asia's formation of production networks, but which of the two has been the most important within the region? We investigate the determinants of intermediate input trade in several ways: by using trade data, input–output tables and information derived from fieldwork. We find that the reduction of trade costs primarily affects the expansion of intermediate trade, and that intermediate input trade is highly sensitive to it. This result is consistent with the findings of Yi (2003). Moreover, we find that differences in factor prices affect bilateral trade among the countries in the region, especially in the electronics industry where production networks are especially well developed. The implication of our study, therefore, is that the reduction of trade costs will be effective in East Asia in circumstances where large differences in factor prices exist.

1.2.3 Main Features of Production Operations by Multinational Enterprises

It is often assumed that MNEs have played a significant role in the growth of international input trade and in the development of production networks. One of our concerns has been to test the validity of this assumption. Ever since the work of Markusen (1984) and Helpman (1984), theoretical studies of MNEs have examined various features of production operation. Markusen (1984) argues that the horizontal production operations by MNEs in foreign countries are similar to those of firms whose objective is to produce goods for the home market. By contrast, Helpman (1984) claims that in vertical production operations, the production process is geographically fragmented by stages of production. Two theoretical models of horizontal and vertical operations are presented in the knowledge-capital (KK) model devised by Markusen (see Markusen et al., 1996; Markusen, 1997, 2002). These models posit two countries, namely the home and host countries. However, since foreign affiliates are nowadays increasing their export ratio to third countries, the model needs to include third countries, too. Ekholm et al. (2007) propose the concept of export-platform FDI (PFDI): a parent country invests in a particular host country with the intention of serving 'third' markets by importing from its home country and exporting final goods from the affiliate in the host country.

In the analysis of the operations of MNEs, because relevant data have been either absent or hard to find, far more attention has been given to theory than to empirical approaches. The data on the operations of MNEs are often not publicly available because they relate to sensitive areas of corporate strategy. Despite this difficulty, some useful empirical studies have been carried out. An example is the work of Hanson et al. (2005) who examined the vertical production relations by which US affiliates import materials and parts from the USA; and export finished products back to the home country. Belderbos et al. (2001) and Kiyota et al. (2008) have examined the determinants of local content so far as Japanese affiliates are concerned. These studies, however, focused on the production relationship between home and host countries, and did not investigate production relations with third countries.

Our own empirical studies have paid attention to the tendency of MNEs to import from third countries and export to third countries, and have been carried out at firm level, using microdata analysis. Using the Basic Survey of Overseas Business Activities by Japanese Firms, we have found that procurement from third countries in terms of value is about 20 percent of the whole, including 15 percent from Asia, as against 60 percent locally and 20 percent from the home base of Japan in the case of firms not procuring items from third countries. This figure is not low if we take border barriers into account. Moreover, we found that procurement by origin is affected by sales by destination: procurement from abroad (Japan or a third country) tends to be sent back abroad. However, at firm level, there is a growing tendency for procurement from third countries as well as from the home country to be replaced by procurement from the host country. On the other hand, in terms of the number of affiliates, procurement from, and sales to, third countries is more widespread than the kind of operation envisaged by Ekholm et al., whereby items are procured from home countries and finished products sold to third countries. Our findings indicate that Japanese affiliates have been deeply engaged in international fragmentation and in production networks within East Asia.

1.3   SUMMARY OF THE CHAPTERS AND THEIR FINDINGS

Chapters 2 and 3 use IDE's Asian Input–Output tables, which provide precise data on intermediate inputs and final goods by destination and by industry. This data set is unique in that it categorizes goods into intermediate and final inputs, and it shows the share of each industry's output that is absorbed by other industries and by final consumers.

Chapter 2, by Hummels and Uchida, is the first study to calculate a vertical specialization index (the import input share that is embodied in the country's exports) for East Asia. Three interesting findings have emerged. First, the degree of vertical specialization varies according to country and is high in Malaysia, the Philippines and Thailand, in which the values range from 0.2 to 0.37. By contrast, China and Indonesia exhibit relatively low vertical specialization shares of less than 0.1. This may reflect the fact that in a large country, a wider range of intermediate inputs can be produced. Second, with the exception of Singapore, the vertical specialization index has been increasing everywhere in the region over time. In particular, between 1990 and 2000, the vertical specialization index increased in Indonesia, Malaysia and the Philippines, all of which are countries where the electronics industry has developed. Third, the degree varies according to industry: the electronics industry shows the highest vertical specialization index, increasing most between 1990 and 2000. This indicates that vertical specialization has been more advanced in the electronics industry than in other kinds of manufacturing, and that the electronics industry is amenable to fragmentation.

Why does input trade take place? Chapter 3, by Hummels and Puzzello, examines the country- and industry-level determinants of the sourcing of intermediate goods and the extent of vertical specialization. Surprisingly, the chapter concludes that input trade is more likely than final goods trade to be characterized by features that are less sensitive to differences in factor endowment and more sensitive to differences in trade costs. The result is consistent with the argument that input trade may be driven by trade costs and is influenced by the balance between scale economies and trade costs (as in Krugman and Venables, 1995, 1996; Venables, 1996). Our finding suggests that policy efforts to reduce trade costs can encourage fragmentation and the emergence of production networks.

The question arises as to what extent the argument that input trade may be driven by factor endowment differences (as in Arndt, 1997, 1998; Deardorff, 2001a, 2001b) is a valid one. Chapter 4, by Hiratsuka, investigates the determinants of bilateral trade including intermediate trade for the 14 countries of the East Asian region. East Asia is well on the way to becoming the world's factory: its world export shares are very high, amounting in 2006 to about 40 percent for parts and components, 40 percent for capital goods and 30 percent for consumer goods. This chapter investigates the determinants of East Asia's trade, focusing on the relationship between skill differences (factor prices) and bilateral trade. Differences in skill levels have a positive effect on bilateral trade with partners for intra-East Asia trade, and on the other hand, a negative effect so far as interregional trade is concerned. The positive relationship between the skill-level difference and bilateral trade for intra-East Asian regional trade implies that skill- and labor-abundant countries produce skilled-labor-intensive products while unskilled-labor-abundant countries produce unskilled-labor-intensive products. This indicates that vertical production characterized by separated production blocks, which require different levels of skill and technology for the manufacture of a final product, is intensively operated within the region.

Vertical production is mainly operated by MNEs in East Asia and, in particular, in ASEAN (Association of South East Asian Nations). It follows that the relationship between MNEs and trade is an issue that needs investigation. Chapter 5, by Yokota, investigates the relationship between Japanese foreign direct investment (FDI) and the parts and components trade in East Asia. As the econometric analysis clearly indicates, there is a positive relationship between Japanese FDI and Japanese exports. In other words, Japanese outward FDI may also promote domestic production of parts and components for export, resulting from a vertical linkage structure among Japanese firms. The complementary effect of FDI on parts and components exports is largest in electrical machinery, the size of the impact on electrical machinery being 16 times larger than that on the textile industry. These facts suggest that fragmentation brings about positive effects on production, as theory has predicted (Jones and Kierzkowski, 1990; Deardorff, 2001a, 2001b). At an empirical level, too, it is clear that fragmentation occurs to a greater degree in electronics than in any other industry.

So far, we have examined the extent and determinants of the intermediate input trade in East Asia, but what can be said regarding the actual operations of MNEs in the region? It is widely assumed that fragmentation is mainly the work of MNEs, and the nature of production by MNEs forms the next research issue discussed by the book's authors. Any attempt to analyze MNE behavior must rest on micro-analysis at firm level. Chapters 6 and 7 investigate the behavior of affiliates of Japanese MNEs operating in East Asia. Both chapters use the Basic Survey of Overseas Business Activities, an annual survey of the business activities of overseas Japanese affiliates and parent companies conducted by the Ministry of Economy, Trade and Industry (METI), Government of Japan.

Chapter 6, by Hayakawa and Matsuura investigates the motivations of Japanese MNEs with particular reference to their procurement by origin and their affiliate sales by destination. This study distinguishes three types of affiliate (home, host and third country) according to the origin of their procurements and the destinations of their sales, and we further divide each Japanese affiliate into nine types. In terms of numbers of firms, Japanese affiliates operating in East Asia mainly export abroad (to Japan or third countries). This is quite different from Japanese affiliates operating in North America, whose products are sold mainly in the market of the host country. Furthermore, affiliates supplying overseas markets with exports of final goods from an affiliate in the host country, while procuring from abroad, account for a large proportion of the firms operating in the electronics, information and technology, and precision machinery industries. These observations are consistent with the view that Japanese affiliates have expanded their production and distribution networks in East Asia.

Do Japanese affiliates operating in East Asia procure mainly from the home country, as the vertical production operation theory would lead us to expect? Or do they, like their counterparts in North America, tend to procure more from their host countries? Chapter 7, by Ozeki, investigates procurement by Japanese multinational affiliates operating in East Asia. An empirical analysis finds that the operating period, share of local sales and degree of agglomeration of Japanese manufacturers have a positive effect on local procurement and a negative effect on purchasing from a third country or from Japan. Another finding is that such determinants have different effects on intra-firm and inter-firm (arm's-length) purchasing activities; agglomeration has a positive effect on arm's-length local procurement and a negative effect on intra-firm purchasing from the home country. These empirical results suggest in particular that the share of local procurement from arm's-length transactions will probably continue to increase, while the share of international procurement and especially from Japan is likely to decrease in the future.

Of course, this must not be taken to mean that production networks in East Asia will disappear in the future. The study results simply mean that when an affiliate is established, it has to procure from abroad. But as time goes by, the affiliate procures increasingly from the host country. That said, the rapid development of intermediate input trade and production networks indicates that the East Asian factory is growing as the international market expands. And in response to the expansion of the market, MNEs continue to expand their production bases, with the result that materials and parts are traded between these new bases and existing production bases and/or the home country.

With the expansion of purchasing from host countries, production of intermediate input goods may to some extent move to lower-income counties. Such a dispersion depends on to what extent low-income countries can reduce trade costs. This leads us to ask whether or not East Asian LDCs such as Cambodia, Laos and Myanmar are likely to become involved in production networks. In relation to this and other related questions, the last two chapters discuss the future development of production networks in East Asia.

Chapter 8, by Kimura, argues that a variety of firm specificity supported by sophisticated inter-firm relationships is essential to an understanding of the mechanics and spatial structure of international production and distribution networks in East Asia. By mapping geographically a two-dimensional fragmentation framework (Kimura and Ando, 2005), the study distinguishes four layers of transactions within production and distribution networks: (i) local; (ii) sub-regional; (iii) regional, and (iv) global. This concept effectively bridges the geographical extensions of production and distribution networks and the nature of transactions in terms of intra-firm versus inter-firm (arm's-length) transactions, as well as technological and managerial conditions. The geographical structure of production and distribution networks for technology transfers and spillovers suggests that sub-regional production networks can develop together with other production networks such as local and regional production networks.

Chapter 9, by Souknilanh, seeks to answer the question of whether or not the East Asian LDCs will become involved in production networks. The study investigates all manufacturing affiliates in Laos, and categorizes the country's production network into three groups, according to the type of driver involved: (i) those driven by preferential trade arrangements (including the Generalized System of Preferences or GSP); (ii) those driven by tariff barriers; and (iii) those driven by factor endowments. Types (i) and (ii) developed in Laos almost immediately after the country opened its doors to FDI in 1988. Many companies hitherto based in Thailand either relocated garment factories to Laos or set up branches there so as to benefit from the preferential trade arrangements granted to Laos, mainly by the European Union (henceforth EU). On a smaller scale, motorcycle assembly factories were also set up by local and foreign-affiliated manufacturing firms in neighboring countries, in order to overcome high tariffs. Approximately ten years later, from 1997 onwards, networks driven by factor endowments also started to appear, with some Japanese-affiliated factories in Thailand beginning to take advantage of Laos's relative lower wage rates. Other attractions included the almost complete absence of language and currency barriers, and decreasing transport costs, broadly defined. These factors led firms based in Thailand to establish so-called second factories in Laos. A similar kind of fragmentation has appeared in the electronics industry.

1.4   GLOBAL AND REGIONAL PERSPECTIVES ON INTERMEDIATE INPUT TRADE AND INTRA-EAST ASIA TRADE

Our empirical studies confirmed that intermediate input trade is increasing, and that East Asia's production structure is becoming more dependent on intermediate inputs and is becoming fragmented. The expansion of intermediate input trade has been stimulated by the reduction of trade costs in East Asia where there are large differences in factor endowment among the countries that make up the region. In East Asia, sequential production stages are located across countries, with each country specializing in production stages in areas where it enjoys comparative advantage. Labor-abundant countries specialize in producing low-value-added parts, the manufacture of which requires relatively low technology, while capital-abundant countries produce high-value-added parts that incorporate high technology. This production mechanism has led to a sustained expansion of intermediate trade in East Asia.

The development of international fragmentation or production networks is perhaps mainly the result of zero-tariff scheme arrangements in East Asia. The investment schemes that are in operation exempt firms from import taxes on production for export purposes, while Information Technology Agreements (ITAs) permit participants to completely eliminate duties on IT products. In addition, logistic networks have developed in the region.

MNEs are closely involved with the rapid growth in intermediate input trade and production networks because of their participation in the sequential production system. MNEs have exploited differences in skill and factor prices, and have taken advantage of the variety of policies offered by the various countries of the region. In fact, Japanese MNEs behave as export platforms, both in ASEAN and in China. Meanwhile, procurement from third countries has prevailed, especially in the electronics, information and technology, and precision machinery industries, and in particular in ASEAN.

Given the background of rapid growth in intermediate goods trade and the development of sequential production systems, what kind of perspective can we obtain on the possible contribution of LDCs such as Cambodia, Laos and Myanmar to East Asia's production networks?

According to fragmentation theory and vertical multinational theory, the development of sequential production systems leads to increases in production in both home and host countries. Our empirical studies have confirmed that, over time, Japanese affiliates tend to increase procurements from local sources rather than from their parent country of Japan. On the other hand, Japanese FDI has promoted exports through vertical production networks. These findings indicate that affiliates procure mainly from their host countries, while obtaining some parts from host and third countries, and this in turn suggests that the home country of Japan should move increasingly to more skills-based activities.

Another important issue is whether or not East Asian LDCs can participate in the sequential production system. Theoretically, due to congestion in advanced countries, we can expect some manufacturing products and processes to disperse from higher-wage countries to lower-wage countries. Our own perspective is that with the growth of intermediate trade and the development of production networks, the Asian LDCs can achieve faster development by participating in sub-regional transactions.

REFERENCES

Amiti, Mary (2005), 'Location of vertically linked industries: agglomeration versus comparative advantage', *European Economic Review*, **49** (4), 809–32.

Arndt, Sven (1997), 'Globalization and open economy', *North American Journal of Economics and Finance*, **8** (1), 71–9.

Arndt, Sven (1998), 'Super-specialization and the gains from trade', Working Paper 9801, Lowe Institute of Political Economy.

Belderbos, Bene, Giovanni Capannelli and Kyoji Fukao (2001), 'Backward vertical linkages of foreign manufacturing affiliates: evidence from Japanese multinationals', *World Development*, **29** (1), 189–208.

Deardorff, Alan V. (2001a), 'Fragmentation in simple trade model', *North American Journal of Economics and Finance*, **12**, 121–37.

Deardorff, Alan V. (2001b), 'Fragmentation across cones,' in S. Arndt and H. Kierzkowski (eds), *Fragmentation: New Production Patterns in the World Economy*, Oxford: Oxford University Press, pp. 35–51.

Ekholm, Karoline, Rikard Forslid and James Markusen (2007), 'Export-platform foreign direct investment', *Journal of the European Economic Association*, **5** (4), 776–95.

Hanson, Gordon, Raymond Mataloni Jr and Matthew Slaughter (2005), 'Vertical production networks in multinational firms', *Review of Economics and Statistics*, **87** (4), 664–78.

Helpman, Elhanan (1984), 'A simple theory of trade with multinational corporations', *Journal of Political Economy*, **92**, 451–71.

Hummels, David, Jun Ishii and Kei-Mu Yi (2001), 'The nature and growth of vertical specialization in world trade', *Journal of International Economics*, **54**, 75–96.

Jones, Ronald W. and Henryk Kierzkowski (1990), 'The role of services in production and international trade: a theoretical framework', in Ronald W. Jones and Anne O. Krueger (eds), *The Political Economy of International Trade: Essays in Honor of Robert E. Baldwin*, Cambridge, MA: Blackwell, pp. 31–48.

Kimura, Fukunari and Mitsuyo Ando (2005), 'Two-dimensional fragmentation in East Asia: conceptual framework and empirics', special issue edited by Henryk Kierzkowski, 'Outsourcing and Fragmentation: Blessing or Threat', *International Review of Economics and Finance*, **14** (3), 317–48.

Kiyota, Kozo, Toshiyuki Matsuura, Shujiro Urata and Yuhong Wei (2008), 'Reconsidering the backward vertical linkages of foreign affiliates: evidence from Japanese multinationals', *World Development*, **36** (8), 1398–414.

Krugman, Paul R. (1996), 'Does Third World growth hurt First World prosperity?', *Harvard Business Review*, **72**, 113–21.

Krugman, Paul and Anthony J. Venables (1995), 'Globalization and the inequality of nations', *Quarterly Journal of Economics*, **110** (4), 857–80.

Krugman, P. and A.J. Venables (1996), 'Integration, specialization and adjustment', *European Economic Review*, **40**, 959–67.

Markusen, James R. (1984), 'Multinationals, multi-plant economies, and the gains from trade', *Journal of International Economics*, **16**, 205–26.

Markusen, James R. (1997), 'Trade versus investment liberalization', NBER Working Paper no. 6231.

Markusen, James R. (2002), *Multinational Firms and the Theory of International Trade*, Cambridge, MA: MIT Press.

Markusen, James R., Anthony J Venables, Denise Eby-Konan and Kevin Honglin Zhang (1996), 'A unified treatment of horizontal direct investment, vertical direct investment, and the pattern of trade in goods and services', NBER Working Paper no. 5696.

Ng, Francis and Alexander J. Yeats (1999), 'Production sharing in East Asia: who does what for whom, and why?', Policy Research Working Paper no. 2197, World Bank.

Venables, A. (1996), 'Equilibrium location of vertically linked industries', *International Economic Review*, **37** (2), 341–59.

Yi, Kei-Mu (2003), 'Can vertical specialization explain the growth of world trade?', *Journal of Political Economy*, **111** (1), 52–102.

2. Vertical specialization: some evidence from East Asia from 1975 to 2000

David Hummels and Yoko Uchida

2.1 INTRODUCTION

In recent years, economists have focused on the importance of intermediate input trade and production fragmentation in explaining a wide range of facts about trade, including: the growth in world trade; magnification of trade cost shocks; the effect of trade on wages; and productivity growth within firms. International fragmentation of production and the resulting intermediate input trade is not a new phenomenon (Jones et al., 2005, dating back to the early 1960s), but it is widely perceived that its magnitude and impact have grown substantially in recent decades.

There are many excellent theoretical papers exploring the causes and consequences of input trade, beginning with Sanyal and Jones (1982) and Ethier (1982), and continuing with Jones and Kierzkowski (1990), Deardorff (2001), Arndt and Kierzkowski (2001) and Yi (2003). However, empirical work has lagged behind theory due to difficulties with data. The literature contains three basic approaches to studying input trade.

The first approach (see Ng and Yeats, 1998, 1999, 2003 for examples) classifies particular products as intermediates or final goods using product definitions.[1] The advantage of this approach is that it maximizes geographic and time-series coverage. The disadvantages are two-fold. First, it is not possible to determine which industries in the importing country are using the input and therefore not possible to determine the effects it has, industry by industry, on wages, productivity and so on. Second, any such division between intermediate and non-intermediate goods is arbitrary. The second approach relies on firm-level data that report the usage of imported inputs into the production process (Amiti and Konings, 2007). These data are ideal for assessing the impact of input trade on firm productivity, and definitively solve the classification problem. However, they are very limited in scope, typically covering a single country for a limited number of years. This makes them of limited use for understanding if input trade has grown, why, and how that varies across countries.

The final approach employs input–output data with international input coverage to assess input trade and fragmentation. Examples include Campa and Goldberg (1997), who study Canada, the UK and the USA from 1974 to 1995; Hummels et al. (2001), who study ten OECD countries and a handful of East Asian nations from 1970 to 1990, and Koopman et al. (2008), who study the share of foreign value added in Chinese manufacturing exports in 1997, 2002 and 2006.

We add to this last literature in three ways. First, we extend the country and time-series coverage explored in the previous literature by employing the Asian Input–Output database, which offers a broad country and time-series coverage of input–output relationships within the Asia-Pacific region. These data allow us to show whether the extent of vertical specialization and its importance for the growth in world trade are similar to those in the OECD.

Second, the nature of the Asian IO data allows us to substantially improve on calculations of the bilateral pattern of input trade. Hummels et al. (2001) examine whether fragmentation is a North–North or a North–South phenomenon, which has implications for why fragmentation occurs and its effect on factor returns. However, they do not directly observe the bilateral pattern of sourcing and sales. Instead, they use an *ad hoc* procedure in which imports of each input are assigned to particular source countries, and then describe the geographic orientation of vertical specialization. We also offer calculations on the geographic orientation of vertical specialization, but do not rely on an *ad hoc* imputation procedure. The Asian IO data already include information on which inputs are purchased from particular source countries and we employ these data to more carefully assess orientation.

Third, the bilateral nature of the Asian IO data allows us to perform a calculation that other authors cannot provide. Consider the definition of vertical specialization contained in Hummels et al. (2001).

Vertical Specialization occurs when:
A.   a good is produced in two or more sequential stages,
B.   two or more countries provides value-added during the production process of the goods,
C.   at least one country must use imported inputs in its stage of the production process and some of the resulting output must be exported.

This definition was closely tied to these authors' abilities to trace the chain of input flows using single country IO tables. However, the definition neglects the case of the 'first' country in the chain, that is, the case where a country produces an input using only domestic value added[2] and subsequently exports it to another country for further processing and export. The country providing the initial input is also participating in a fragmented production chain, and is in fact critical to the process. Identifying its role requires bilateral details on sources and destinations of product flows as in the Asian IO data. We also provide a new calculation designed to capture the complexity of fragmentation. Vertical specialization might involve a very simple input–output process. Country 1 provides iron ore, which country 2 processes into steel, and country 3 uses steel to produce automobiles. The first two inputs are reasonably homogeneous goods, requiring a simple form of transaction and logistics for distribution. Vertical specialization might also involve an extremely complicated input–output process involving hundreds of components sourced from dozens of countries. An example is hard-disk drives, as described in the case study by Daisuke Hiratsuka in Chapter 4 of this volume. In this instance firms face significant issues of transactions and logistics for distribution, quality assurance and hold-up problems.

To shed some light on the complexity of vertical specialization, we provide indices designed to calculate the distribution of input purchases, whether they are of the simple form of the first type described above or the complex form of the second type. This approach is similar to that employed by Blanchard and Kremer (1997) in assessing the complexity of input–output relationships within the former Soviet Union. They showed that more complex goods suffered the greatest output declines in the economic collapse following the break-up of the Soviet Union.

The chapter is organized as follows. Section 2.2 introduces the Asian International Input–Output tables. Section 2.3 provides the concept and calculation method of vertical specialization (VS). In section 2.3, we also present VS calculation results and growth accounting. The index of vertical specialization is decomposed geographically. Section 2.4 introduces a new calculation of fragmentation. Concluding remarks are finally provided.

2.2   ASIAN INTERNATIONAL INPUT–OUTPUT TABLES

In order to examine the extent of vertical specialization in East Asia, we utilize Asian International Input–Output tables (AIO) for the reference years 1975, 1985, 1990, 1995 and 2000.[3] The AIO contains ten national input–output tables, namely tables from China, Indonesia, Japan, Korea, Malaysia, the Philippines, Singapore, Taiwan, Thailand and the USA.[4] It

Table 2.1   Sector classification

Code	Description
AX001	Agriculture
AX002	Fishery and forestry
AX003	Crude oil and natural gas
AX004	Coal and other mining
AX005	Food product
AX006	Beverage and tobacco
AX007	Manufacture of textile product
AX008	Manufacture of wearing apparel
AX009	Manufacture of leather products
AX010	Manufacture of timber, wooden products and furniture
AX011	Manufacture of chemical products
AX012	Manufacture of petroleum products
AX013	Manufacture of rubber products
AX014	Manufacture of ceramics and mineral products
AX015	Manufacture of glass and glass products
AX016	Manufacture of steel and steel products
AX017	Manufacture of non-ferrous metal products
AX018	Manufacture of metal products
AX019	Manufacture of industrial machinery
AX020	Manufacture of electronic products
AX021	Manufacture of motor vehicles
AX022	Manufacture of other transport equipment
AX023	Manufacture of precision machines
AX024	Manufacture of plastic products
AX025	Other manufacturing
AX026	Electricity, gas and water supply
AX027	Construction
AX028	Trade and transportation
AX029	Telephone and telecommunication
AX030	Other services

is constructed by linking each national table of ten countries, using bilateral trade flows.[5] The AIO depicts each domestic industry with its input composition from, and output distribution to, home industries as well as industries overseas. Industrial sectors of each AIO are aggregated into 30 sectors in order to make comparisons among tables of different years. The sector classification is shown in Table 2.1. There are three primary sectors, 21 secondary sectors and six service sectors.

An overview of the AIO table for 2000 is shown in Table 2.2. It can be read in the same manner as a national input–output table. The

Table 2.2   Overview of the AIO

code	Intermediate demand (A)												
	1 (AI)	2 (AM)	3 (AP)	4 (AS)	5 (AT)	6 (AC)	7 (AN)	8 (AK)	9 (AJ)	10 (AU)	1 (FI)	2 (FM)	3 (FP)
Indonesia (AI)	A^{II}	A^{IM}	A^{IP}	A^{IS}	A^{IT}	A^{IC}	A^{IN}	A^{IK}	A^{IJ}	A^{IU}	F^{II}	F^{IM}	F^{IP}
Malaysia (AM)	A^{MI}	A^{MM}	A^{MP}	A^{MS}	A^{MT}	A^{MC}	A^{MN}	A^{MK}	A^{MJ}	A^{MU}	F^{MI}	F^{MM}	F^{MP}
Philippines (AP)	A^{PI}	A^{PM}	A^{PP}	A^{PS}	A^{PT}	A^{PC}	A^{PN}	A^{PK}	A^{PJ}	A^{PU}	F^{PI}	F^{PM}	F^{PP}
Singapore (AS)	A^{SI}	A^{SM}	A^{SP}	A^{SS}	A^{ST}	A^{SC}	A^{SN}	A^{SK}	A^{SJ}	A^{SU}	F^{SI}	F^{SM}	F^{SP}
Thailand (AT)	A^{TI}	A^{TM}	A^{TP}	A^{TS}	A^{TT}	A^{TC}	A^{TN}	A^{TK}	A^{TJ}	A^{TU}	F^{TI}	F^{TM}	F^{TP}
China (AC)	A^{CI}	A^{CM}	A^{CP}	A^{CS}	A^{CT}	A^{CC}	A^{CN}	A^{CK}	A^{CJ}	A^{CU}	F^{CI}	F^{CM}	F^{CP}
Taiwan (AN)	A^{NI}	A^{NM}	A^{NP}	A^{NS}	A^{NT}	A^{NC}	A^{NN}	A^{NK}	A^{NJ}	A^{NU}	F^{NI}	F^{NM}	F^{NP}
Korea (AK)	A^{KI}	A^{KM}	A^{KP}	A^{KS}	A^{KT}	A^{KC}	A^{KN}	A^{KK}	A^{KJ}	A^{KU}	F^{KI}	F^{KM}	F^{KP}
Japan (AJ)	A^{JI}	A^{JM}	A^{JP}	A^{JS}	A^{JT}	A^{JC}	A^{JN}	A^{JK}	A^{JJ}	A^{JU}	F^{JI}	F^{JM}	F^{JP}
USA (AU)	A^{UI}	A^{UM}	A^{UP}	A^{US}	A^{UT}	A^{UC}	A^{UN}	A^{UK}	A^{UJ}	A^{UU}	F^{UI}	F^{UM}	F^{UP}
(BF)	BA^{I}	BA^{M}	BA^{P}	BA^{S}	BA^{T}	BA^{C}	BA^{N}	BA^{K}	BA^{J}	BA^{U}	BF^{I}	BF^{M}	BF^{P}
(CH)	A^{HI}	A^{HM}	A^{HP}	A^{HS}	A^{HT}	A^{HC}	A^{HN}	A^{HK}	A^{HJ}	A^{HU}	F^{HI}	F^{HM}	F^{HP}
(CO)	A^{OI}	A^{OM}	A^{OP}	A^{OS}	A^{OT}	A^{OC}	A^{ON}	A^{OK}	A^{OJ}	A^{OU}	F^{OI}	F^{OM}	F^{OP}
(CW)	A^{W}	A^{WM}	A^{WP}	A^{WS}	A^{WT}	A^{WC}	A^{WN}	A^{WK}	A^{WJ}	A^{WU}	F^{WI}	F^{WM}	F^{WP}
(DT)	DA^{I}	DA^{M}	DA^{P}	DA^{S}	DA^{T}	DA^{C}	DA^{N}	DA^{K}	DA^{J}	DA^{U}	DF^{I}	DF^{M}	DF^{P}
(VV)	V^{I}	V^{M}	V^{P}	V^{S}	V^{T}	V^{C}	V^{N}	V^{K}	V^{J}	V^{U}			
(XX)	X^{I}	X^{M}	X^{P}	X^{S}	X^{T}	X^{C}	X^{N}	X^{K}	X^{J}	X^{U}			

Key: 1 = Indonesia; 2 = Malaysia; 3 = Philippines; 4= Singapore; 5 = Thailand;
6 = China; 7 = Taiwan; 8 = Korea; 9 = Japan; 10 = USA.

demand-side information is shown in columns, and the supply-side information in rows. Each 'cell' in the table shows the input compositions of the industries of respective countries. A^{II} in Table 2.2, for instance, shows input compositions of Indonesia *vis-à-vis* domestically produced goods and services. Also, A^{MI} shows imported input composition from Malaysia to Indonesia. The rest of the cells, A^{PI}, A^{SI}, A^{TI}, A^{CI}, A^{NI}, A^{KI}, A^{JI} and A^{UI}, can be read in the same manner. Those cells are all valued at producer's price. The international freight and insurance amounts paid by Indonesian industry for imported inputs from the rest of the nine countries are all aggregated into a row vector and recorded in the cell BA^{I}. A^{HI}, A^{OI} and A^{WI} are imported input goods from Hong Kong, the EU and the rest of the world respectively, and valued at c.i.f. (cost, insurance, freight) price. The import duty and sales tax levied

Final demand (F)							Export (L)			Stat. discr. (QX)	Total output (XX)
4 (FS)	5 (FT)	6 (FC)	7 (FN)	8 (FK)	9 (FJ)	10 (FU)	To Hong Kong (LH)	To EU (LE)	To R.O.W (LW)		
F^{IS}	F^{IT}	F^{IC}	F^{IN}	F^{IK}	F^{IJ}	F^{IU}	LH^I	LE^I	LW^I	Q^I	X^I
F^{MS}	F^{MT}	F^{MC}	F^{MN}	F^{MK}	F^{MJ}	F^{MU}	LH^M	LE^M	LW^M	Q^M	X^M
F^{PS}	F^{PT}	F^{PC}	F^{PN}	F^{PK}	F^{PJ}	F^{PU}	LH^P	LE^P	LW^P	Q^P	X^P
F^{SS}	F^{ST}	F^{SC}	F^{SN}	F^{SK}	F^{SJ}	F^{SU}	LH^S	LE^S	LW^S	Q^S	X^S
F^{TS}	F^{TT}	F^{TC}	F^{TN}	F^{TK}	F^{TJ}	F^{TU}	LH^T	LE^T	LW^T	Q^T	X^T
F^{CS}	F^{CT}	F^{CC}	F^{CN}	F^{CK}	F^{CJ}	F^{CU}	LH^C	LE^C	LW^C	Q^C	X^C
F^{NS}	F^{NT}	F^{NC}	F^{NN}	F^{NK}	F^{NJ}	F^{NU}	LH^N	LE^N	LW^N	Q^N	X^N
F^{KS}	F^{KT}	F^{KC}	F^{KN}	F^{KK}	F^{KJ}	F^{KU}	LH^K	LE^K	LW^K	Q^K	X^K
F^{JS}	F^{JT}	F^{JC}	F^{JN}	F^{JK}	F^{JJ}	F^{JU}	LH^J	LE^J	LW^J	Q^J	X^J
F^{US}	F^{UT}	F^{UC}	F^{UN}	F^{UK}	F^{UJ}	F^{UU}	LH^U	LE^U	LW^U	Q^U	X^U
BF^S	BF^T	BF^C	BF^N	BF^K	BF^J	BF^U					
F^{HS}	F^{HT}	F^{HC}	F^{HN}	F^{HK}	F^{HJ}	F^{HU}					
F^{OS}	F^{OT}	F^{OC}	F^{ON}	F^{OK}	F^{OJ}	F^{OU}					
F^{WS}	F^{WT}	F^{WC}	F^{WN}	F^{WK}	F^{WJ}	F^{WU}					
DF^S	DF^T	DF^C	DF^N	DF^K	DF^J	DF^U					

on Indonesian imported inputs are entered in row vector DA^I. V^I is the value added of Indonesian industries and X^I is the total output of Indonesian industries.

Final demand of Indonesia to domestically produce goods is shown in F^{II} at the center of the table. In contrast, F^{MI} is final demand of Indonesia for the imported goods from Malaysia. The rest of the cell can be read column-wise in the same manner as input composition.

As can be seen from the rows, the table shows the output distribution of the commodities produced by domestic industries. A^{IM}, for instance, shows the distribution of Indonesia's output to Malaysia. F^{IM}, on the other hand, shows the flow of Indonesian commodities to Malaysia to meet Malaysia's final demand. These are valued at producer's price. L^{IH}, L^{IO} and L^{IW} are Indonesia's goods export to Hong Kong, the EU and the rest of the world, respectively. The statistical discrepancy is entered in Q^I. The right-hand cell, X^I, represents the total output of Indonesia.

There are no other data that describe trade flows divided into intermediate and final goods transaction than the AIO. These detailed trade data are obtained by conducting surveys. Moreover, the AIO tells us that inputs from which industry and of which country are used to produce final goods. The AIO has been utilized mainly to analyze industrial interdependence in East Asia since the first table was published. It is, however, now regarded as an important data source for investigating research questions on international trade.

2.3 GROWING VERTICAL SPECIALIZATION IN EAST ASIA

2.3.1 Vertical Specialization: Concept and Measurement

Recalling the conceptual definition of vertical specialization provided by Hummels et al. (2001) as noted in the introduction, we can use the Asian IO tables to track the use of imported inputs in producing a good that is subsequently exported. We can also track additional instances of international fragmentation chain For example, Figure 2.1 shows a vertical specialization chain involving five countries. Countries 1 and 2 produce intermediate inputs that are exported. Country 3 combines imported intermediate goods, domestic intermediate inputs, and capital and labor to produce the new product. Some portion of Country 3 output is consumed in the domestic market, while the rest is exported as an intermediate or final goods to Country 4.

Hummels et al. calculate Country 3's participation in the vertical specialization chain as a whole, while the AIO enable us to calculate more detailed participation of Country 3. We separate the measure of *VS* employed in Hummels et al. into two parts. *VS_i* measures the use of imported inputs in producing intermediate goods that are exported. *VS_f* measures the use of imported inputs in producing goods that are exported as a final good. That is, *VS_f* shows final stage of the goods circulation, while *VS_i* describes the middle stage of the vertical specialization. We are able to provide this calculation because we see Country 3's IO structure as well as the production linkage of Countries 4 and 5 from Country 3, showing how they use Country 3's products.

We calculate these measures as follows.

$$VS = (\text{imported intermediates/gross output}) * \text{exports} \qquad (2.1)$$

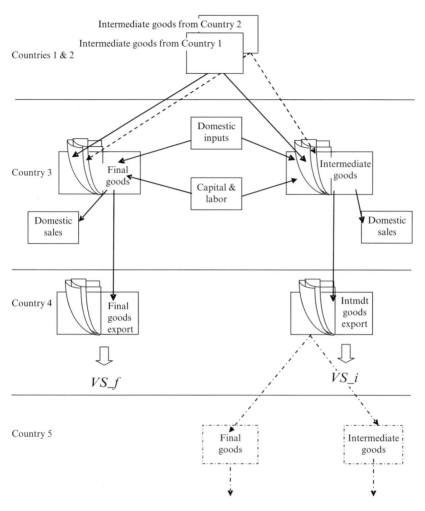

Figure 2.1   Vertical specialization chain involving five countries

The first term of the right-hand side (RHS) of equation (2.1) is the share of imported inputs used in producing one unit of a good. By multiplying this share by export value, we obtain the dollar value of import content of export. *VS* is zero if Country 3 does not export any goods that use imported intermediate inputs. Aggregate *VS* is obtained by summing *VS* for each sector. Since we are interested in the composition of *VS*, *VS* is normalized by the total export of Country 3.

$$VS \text{ share of total exports} = \frac{VS_R}{X_R} = \frac{\sum_i VS_{Ri}}{\sum_i X_{Ri}} \qquad (2.2)$$

where X denotes export, and R and i denote country and industrial sector, respectively. VS's share of total exports is rearranged as follows:

$$\frac{VS_R}{X_R} = \frac{\sum_i VS_{Ri}}{\sum_i X_{Ri}} = \frac{\sum_i (VS_{Ri}/X_{Ri})*X_{Ri}}{\sum_i X_{Ri}} = \sum_i \left[\left(\frac{X_{Ri}}{X_R}\right)\left(\frac{VS_{Ri}}{X_{Ri}}\right)\right] \quad (2.3)$$

The VS share of total exports is the export weighted average of the sector-wise VS export share. To implement this calculation using the input–output table, we use the following equation:

$$VS_R/X_R = (uA^MX)/X_R \qquad (2.4)$$

where u is a $1 \times n$ vector of 1s, A^M is an $n \times n$ import coefficient matrix, and X is an $n \times 1$ vector of Country R's exports.

The input–output table has a feature to capture direct and indirect usage of inputs by using the Leontief inverse matrix. We employ this feature in the VS calculation. We can thus capture the whole input amount required to produce a country's exports.

Equation (2.5) calculates the VS share of total exports.

$$VS_R/X_R = (uA^M[I - A^D]^{-1}X/X_R \qquad (2.5)$$

where I is an $n \times n$ identity matrix, A^D is an $n \times n$ domestic coefficient matrix, and $[I - A^D]^{-1}$ is a Leontief inverse matrix, respectively. The Leontief inverse matrix can be expanded as:

$$[I - A^D]^{-1} = I + A + A^2 + A^3 + \cdots \qquad (2.6)$$

Multiplying equation (2.6) by X, we can capture the ultimate amount of the goods induced by X:

$$\begin{aligned}[I - A^D]^{-1}X &= (I + A + A^2 + A^3 + \cdots)X \\ &= X + AX + A^2X + A^3X + \cdots\end{aligned} \qquad (2.7)$$

The first term of the RHS of equation (2.7) is the direct output requirement to produce export demand. The second term shows domestic input to meet direct output requirement. The third term shows input requirement to meet requirement of the second term. That is, to export automobiles, automobile output must rise (the first term). Producing more autos requires steel (the second term). Producing steel requires iron ore (the third term), and so on. The Leontief inverse simply iterates this procedure in order to calculate the total use of imported inputs in production and export.

Our data have matching bilateral trade flows and bilateral import matrices, thus the equation would be:

$$VS_R/X_R = \left(\sum_S u[A^{SR}[I - A^{RR}]^{-1}X_R] \right)/X_R \qquad (2.8)$$

where S is the import partner country for R.

Our data have nine countries, which correspond to S. A^{SR} is country R's import coefficient matrix from country S. A^{RR} is a domestic input coefficient. X_R is country R's export vector to each country. To calculate VS_i and VS_f, export vector X is divided into two, exports used as intermediate inputs in subsequent production and exports used as final goods.

These calculations assume that the input–output coefficients reported in the various IO tables are representative for all firms within each industrial sector. However, as Hummels et al. (2001) point out, this could result in either an overestimate or an underestimate of VS, depending on sector composition. For example, suppose an industry has two firms: one uses imported intermediates but does not export, while the other exports but uses no imported intermediates. The firm-level VS should be zero, but our industry-level measure will record positive values for VS. This sort of issue seems especially important if firms within an industry use very different types of inputs or face significantly different trade costs. Koopman et al. (2008) provide simple evidence of this compositional issue by separately calculating VS measures for export-oriented *vis-à-vis* domestically oriented Chinese firms. They find that if processing trade is considered, the share of foreign content of China's export is twice as high as the estimates that do not distinguish between processing exports and normal exports.

Similarly, we can capture Country 1's participation in the linkage as shown in Figure 2.2. $VS1$ measures the value of Country 1's intermediate exports embodied in export goods of all the countries within the region. The difference between VS and $VS1$ is that $VS1$ captures domestic value added in the export of foreign countries, while VS captures the foreign value added in the export of the home country. More intuitively, VS captures a country's role in internationally fragmented production process as an assembler, while $VS1$ captures that as a supplier of parts and components. Again, $VS1$ can be calculated only when bilateral exports of intermediate inputs are observed, as is the case with the Asian IO data. We also

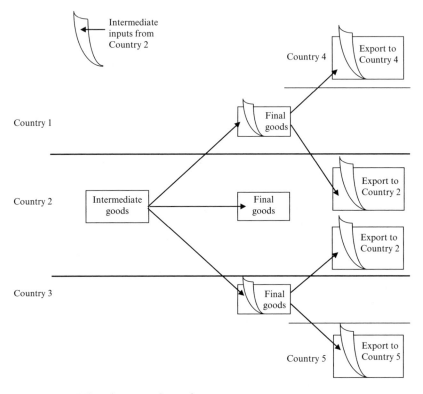

Figure 2.2   VS1 chain involving five countries

divide *VS*1 into two parts: *VS*1_*i* and *VS*1_*f* as well as *VS*. *VS*1_*i* measures Country 1's intermediate exports embodied in exports of intermediate goods, while *VS*1_*f* measures those in exports of final goods.

   *VS*1 can be calculated in a similar manner; it measures export intermediates that are embodied in another country's exports.

$$VS1_R = \sum_{s}^{n} (\text{inputs exported from Country } _R \text{ to Country } _S / \text{gross output } _S) \text{ *exports } _S \quad (2.9)$$

The formal input–output table calculation is

$$VS1_R = \boldsymbol{u} \sum_{S}^{n} [A^{RS}X_S]/X_R \quad (2.10)$$

where A^{RS} is an intermediate goods export matrix from Country *R* to Country *S*. To capture indirect and direct effects, we include the Leontief inverse matrix in equation (2.9).

$$VS1_R = \sum_{S}^{n} \boldsymbol{u}[A^{RS}[I - A^{SS}]^{-1}X_S]/X_R \qquad (2.11)$$

where A^{SS} is a domestic input coefficient matrix of Country S.

2.3.2 Level and Growth of Vertical Specialization

In this subsection we provide the results of the vertical specialization calculation by country. Figure 2.3 shows the aggregate values for VS, VS_i and VS_f in each year for all the Asian IO countries. Most of the countries except Singapore show an increase in their VS export share within the region over time. Japan and Korea have similar trends: around 1990, VS shares go down and then go up. The VS share of the USA and Japan are low over time, ranging between 0.01 and 0.05. VS shares for South East Asian countries such as Malaysia, the Philippines and Thailand are high, ranging from 0.2 to 0.37. On the other hand, China and Indonesia exhibit relatively low VS shares. This may reflect higher rates of protection in these countries, or the fact that in a large country a wider range of intermediate inputs can be produced.

This result is consistent with the result of Hummels et al. (2001). They point out that large countries tend to have lower VS shares and small countries tend to have higher VS shares. The magnitudes of VS shares in this chapter are smaller than those in Hummels et al. There are two possible explanations for this, related to the degree of disaggregation across industries and across regions. Our data include 30 sectors, of which 21 are manufacturing sectors, while Hummels et al. (2001) divide output into 35 sector, of which 22 are manufacturing sectors. In addition, we examine only imports and exports within one region covered explicitly by the AIO tables, while Hummels et al. treat imports and exports from all over the world. If we included imports from the rest of the world, we would expect the results to be higher than the result currently presented, mainly because East Asia has developed production linkages with the EU since 1985.

Since the total value of vertical specialization (VS) equals the sum of VS_i and VS_f, we can calculate the share of each component in the total. That is, we can see whether the imported inputs in question are used for final goods (VS_f) or are in the middle stage of production (VS_i). All countries in our data except China have larger VS_i shares than VS_f share in 2000. The average VS_i shares in total of nine countries in 2000 is 67.1 percent, while that of China is 41.5 percent. From 1990 to 2000, the share of VS_i in total VS is trending down for three countries (China, Indonesia and Malaysia), with an especially rapid fall for China at 22 percent. China's exceptional result suggests that it engages more in the final assembly stage

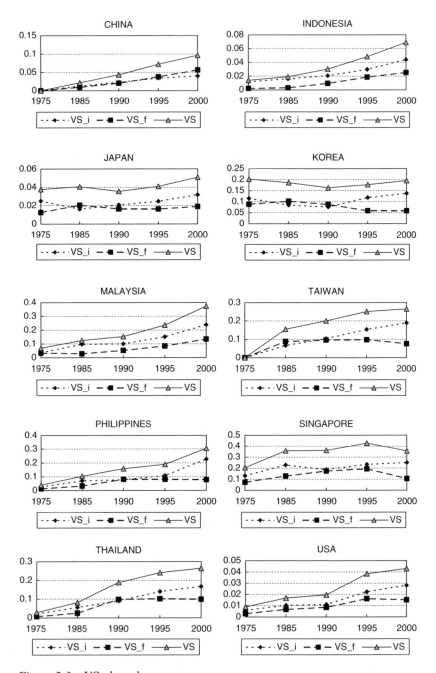

Figure 2.3   VS share by country

than in middle stage of the production. The Malaysian data exhibit an interesting feature. After the VS_i share reached its peak at 77.6 percent in 1985, the VS_f share grew rapidly. This may indicate a transition from being a 'middle' to a 'final' producer. In contrast, from 1990 to 2000, four countries (Korea, Taiwan, the Philippines and Thailand) experienced significant declines in the VS_f share and increases in the VS_i share. This may indicate participation in a more complicated production chain.

We next examine which industrial sectors contribute most to VS, and how this varies across countries and over time. In order to examine this question, we first calculate each sector's VS share in total export, and then estimate the percentage contribution of each sector's VS in total VS. We focus our attention on textiles, chemicals and electronics, as these sectors represent the most VS-intensive sectors in the data.

Figure 2.4 shows VS share of these sectors in total VS by country. Except for China and Indonesia, electronics contributes most to VS and textiles least. For China and Indonesia, chemicals have historically represented the largest contribution to VS, but the composition is changing sharply for China with the growth of electronics.

We now turn to calculations of $VS1$, which measures a country's exports of intermediate inputs rather than its imports. The results of the $VS1$ calculation appear in Figure 2.5. Overall we see the same trend as we saw in the results for VS, although the level of $VS1$ (average 0.15) is lower than that of VS (average 0.20). The interesting finding here is that the countries that have a low VS share tend to have a high $VS1$ share and vice versa. This would seem to reflect the position of each country within the international value chain. The USA and Japan uses few imported inputs, but they are large suppliers of exported inputs. Taiwan, which is a heavy user of imported inputs, supplies few exported inputs. Also of interest, the difference in exported input intensity ($VS1$) *across* countries is much smaller than the difference in imported input intensity (VS).

We next analyze which sectors contribute to the growth of the VS share and how this varies across countries and over time. In order to examine this question, we first calculate each sector's $VS1$ share in total exports, and then estimate the percentage contribution of each sector's $VS1$ in total $VS1$. We focus on three sectors that represent the largest $VS1$ shares: chemicals, non-ferrous metal and electronics products. (Textiles, while important users of imported inputs, are not an imported source of exported inputs, and therefore much less important for $VS1$ relative to VS.)

Figure 2.6 shows the $VS1$ share of these sectors in total $VS1$ by country. Again, electronic products are the most important. Ferrous and non-ferrous metals were said to be 'industry's rice' in that they were inputs used by many sectors in periods during which Japan experienced high economic

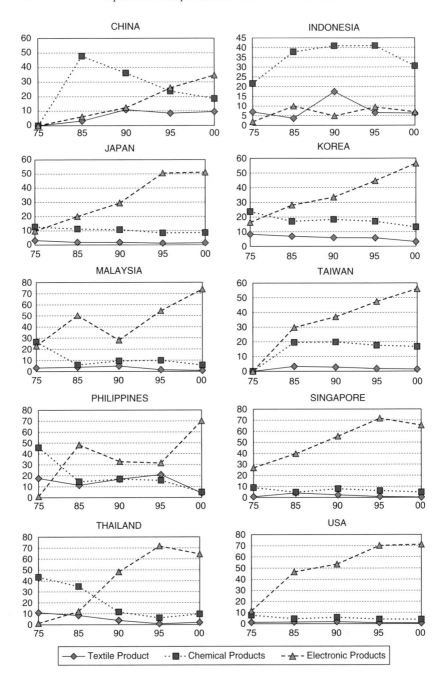

Figure 2.4   VS *share by sector in total* VS

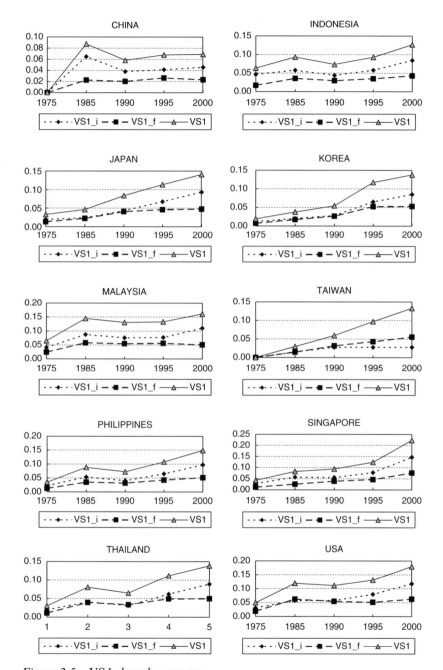

Figure 2.5   VS1 share by country

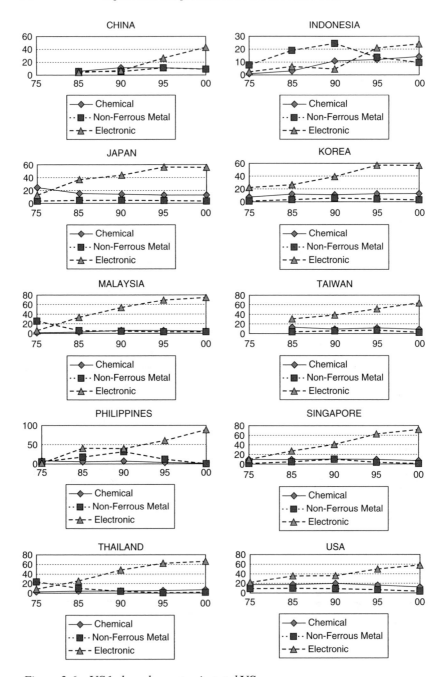

Figure 2.6   VS1 share by sector in total VS

growth. Figures 2.5 and 2.6 suggest that electronic products are 'industry's rice' for the Asian economies as a whole.

2.3.3 Growth of Vertical Specialization and Trade

We employ growth accounting in order to examine the role of *VS* in the trade growth. We decompose export growth into three parts, *VS_i* growth, *VS_f*, and other export growth.

$$
\Delta \frac{X_{R,t}}{GO_{R,t}} = \Delta \frac{VS\_i_{R,t}}{GO_{R,t}} + \Delta \frac{VS\_f_{R,t}}{GO_{R,t}} + \Delta \frac{(X_{R,t} - VS\_i_{R,t} - VS\_f_{R,t})}{GO_{R,t}}
\tag{2.12}
$$

where $\Delta Z_t = Z_t - Z_{t-1}$. Table 2.3 shows the result of the growth accounting calculation.[6] We chose the period from 1990 to 2000 because the year 1990 is crucial in that the relative importance of *VS_i* and *VS_f* in total has changed after that date.

From the calculation, we found that vertical specialization contributes to trade growth more than 20 percent for most of the countries except China, Indonesia, Japan and the USA, whose *VS* are low. If we compare the contribution ratio of *VS_i* and *VS_f*, we notice that *VS_i* contributes more than *VS_f* to trade growth in most of the countries. This implies that to simulate trade growth via vertical specialization, tariff reduction on intermediate goods, not on final goods is recommended.

2.3.4 Geographical Decomposition of Vertical Specialization

Is the flow of vertical specialization trade in East Asia a North–North or a North–South phenomenon, and how does this vary over time? Answers to these questions are important because they help us to understand why fragmentation occurs.

In order to capture the geographic orientation of vertical specialization in East Asia, we grouped ten countries into three categories: North, South and China. North includes Japan and the USA. South represents developing countries in 1975, and consists of seven countries, Korea, Taiwan, Indonesia, Malaysia, the Philippines, Singapore and Thailand. China is a new emerging market with interesting features, so we prepared an individual category for China. A geographic orientation calculation using the data in 1990 and 2000 is provided in Table 2.4.

Table 2.4 describes the origin and destination of vertically specialized trade for each country. To understand the table, examine the first row, corresponding to China's trade in 1990. For that country, 61.6 percent of imported inputs eventually used in exports came from the North. Of these

Table 2.3   Growth accounting, 1990–2000

Country	Change in export share of output	VS_i contribution	VS_f contribution	Other export cont.
China	0.07	0.06	0.10	0.83
Indonesia	0.18	0.08	0.06	0.86
Japan	0.09	0.06	0.03	0.91
Korea	0.17	0.22	0.00	0.78
Malaysia	0.42	0.40	0.25	0.35
Taiwan	0.26	0.64	0.03	0.32
Philippines	0.29	0.37	0.07	0.56
Singapore	0.42	−0.59	0.80	0.79
Thailand	0.25	0.24	0.09	0.67
USA	0.03	0.14	0.06	0.80

northern inputs that were subsequently exported, 84 percent went back to the North while 16 percent went to the South. The remaining imported inputs (38.4 percent) came from the South, with a very similar distribution of export destinations.

What can be learnt from this table? In 1990 there were large differences across countries both in the input origin and export destination of their trade. At the low end, less than half of Japan's imported inputs destined for export came from the North, while 84 percent of Korean and Taiwanese imported inputs originated in the North. Similarly, less than half of US *VS* exports went to the North, while over 80 percent of *VS* exports from China, Korea and the Philippines went to the North. The second thing we learn is that in a short ten-year window there has been a tremendous change in the source of imported inputs. The northern share has fallen dramatically, with increases in both southern and Chinese sources. This growth has also made the importing countries much more similar in their distribution of purchases.

2.4   FRAGMENTATION INDEX

From the result of the vertical specialization calculation, we know that most of the countries in the region have been involved in production link-ages since the 1990s. However, we do not know the nature of input sourc-ing, i.e. whether production relies on widely spread production networks or on simple international inputs from the index of vertical specialization.

Table 2.4 Distribution of VS (%)

	N-	(-N	-S	-CHN)	S-	(-N	-S	-CHN)	CHN-	(-N	-S	-CHN)
					Import origin group (export destination group)							
1990												
China	**61.6**	(84.0	16.0	-)	**38.4**	(83.5	16.5	-)	**0.0**	(-	-	-)
Indonesia	**50.9**	(65.8	29.7	4.6)	**43.0**	(71.0	24.5	4.5)	**6.1**	(64.3	31.2	4.5)
Japan	**46.3**	(52.3	43.3	4.5)	**45.5**	(51.1	44.0	4.9)	**8.2**	(45.2	48.3	6.5)
Korea	**83.6**	(82.0	15.9	2.1)	**16.4**	(84.3	14.0	1.7)	**0.0**	(-	-	-)
Malaysia	**53.5**	(58.4	38.8	2.8)	**43.5**	(59.5	37.7	2.8)	**3.1**	(53.1	42.0	4.9)
Taiwan	**84.0**	(75.4	19.3	5.3)	**16.0**	(76.7	18.5	4.8)	**0.0**	(-	-	-)
Philippines	**60.6**	(80.9	18.2	0.9)	**37.7**	(85.2	13.9	0.9)	**1.7**	(86.8	11.7	1.5)
Singapore	**59.8**	(63.7	34.7	1.6)	**34.3**	(58.4	38.4	3.2)	**5.9**	(41.4	52.8	5.8)
Thailand	**58.9**	(73.0	25.6	1.4)	**36.7**	(74.4	23.9	1.7)	**4.4**	(78.9	18.7	2.3)
USA	**51.4**	(44.8	49.9	5.3)	**43.6**	(46.1	49.1	4.8)	**5.0**	(48.4	45.9	5.7)
2000												
China	**40.6**	(80.7	19.3	-)	**59.4**	(81.4	18.6	-)	**0.0**	(-	-	-)
Indonesia	**46.9**	(48.3	44.6	7.1)	**41.8**	(54.2	38.6	7.2)	**11.3**	(53.5	39.4	7.1)
Japan	**32.2**	(46.3	42.5	11.2)	**55.0**	(45.0	43.1	11.9)	**12.9**	(43.3	43.4	13.3)
Korea	**64.5**	(58.2	22.8	19.0)	**25.5**	(58.1	23.0	19.0)	**10.0**	(56.4	20.6	23.0)
Malaysia	**46.0**	(57.2	35.9	6.9)	**49.7**	(57.4	35.6	7.0)	**4.3**	(56.6	36.0	7.4)
Taiwan	**59.3**	(58.7	18.5	22.8)	**34.7**	(61.1	18.8	20.1)	**5.9**	(57.0	18.2	24.8)
Philippines	**55.9**	(65.2	29.6	5.2)	**41.1**	(69.0	26.3	4.7)	**3.0**	(77.4	19.1	3.5)
Singapore	**50.8**	(45.8	46.7	7.4)	**42.0**	(44.7	47.7	7.6)	**7.3**	(43.2	49.0	7.8)
Thailand	**51.3**	(59.4	32.8	7.8)	**39.2**	(59.1	32.6	8.3)	**9.6**	(60.3	31.8	7.9)
USA	**33.9**	(33.1	55.6	11.3)	**55.3**	(32.3	56.6	11.1)	**10.8**	(34.8	53.9	11.4)

In order to examine this question, we construct a new measurement of fragmentation.

2.4.1   Fragmentation Index: The Concept

We first construct the production specialization index as follows:

$$I_i = \sum_c \min\left(\frac{Y_{ic}}{Y_i}, \frac{Y_c}{Y}\right) \tag{2.13}$$

where i, c and Y are industry, country and output respectively. Y_i is world output of i, Y_c is total output in Country c, so the second fraction is the share of Country c in world output. Suppose that every country produces a share of good i in proportion to its share of world production (i.e. if Japan has 10 percent of world output, it also has 10 percent of world output of cars). Then

$$\frac{Y_{ic}}{Y_i} = \frac{Y_c}{Y}, \text{ and } \sum_c \frac{Y_{ic}}{Y_i} = 1 = \sum_c \frac{Y_c}{Y}$$

In other words, the index takes a value of 1 at a maximum. Suppose instead that output of i is unevenly distributed across countries. Then for many countries it will be the case that

$$\frac{Y_{ic}}{Y_i} < \frac{Y_c}{Y}, \text{ so } \min\left(\frac{Y_{ic}}{Y_i}, \frac{Y_c}{Y}\right) = \frac{Y_{ic}}{Y_i}, \text{ and for others } \frac{Y_{ic}}{Y_i} > \frac{Y_c}{Y},$$

$$\text{so } \min\left(\frac{Y_{ic}}{Y_i}, \frac{Y_c}{Y}\right) = \frac{Y_c}{Y}$$

The more unevenly output of i is distributed, the smaller the index becomes. At the limit, suppose only one country j produces good i, then the value of the index is just Y_j/Y. The index is as small as possible when the smallest country in the world produces the entire world supply of good i.

Now we need to adapt equation (2.11) to refer to sourcing inputs. That is,

$$I_{mi} = \sum_j \sum_c \min\left(\frac{M_{jimc}}{GO_{mi}}, \frac{GO_{jc}}{GO}\right) \tag{2.14}$$

where j is input from country c and m is the market where goods i are produced.

From equation (2.14), we can examine whether a particular market's

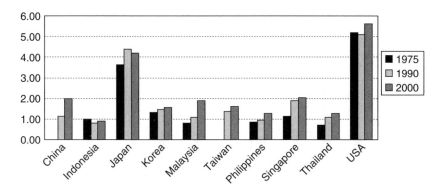

Figure 2.7   Total fragmentation index

purchases of inputs is in proportion to their provision in the world economy.

The index tends to be high if an industry imports evenly from various sources. Also, it tends to be high if a market imports inputs from an industry that has a high market share in the world. A high level of an industry's index reflects that the industry has attained a certain level of development.

2.4.2   Level of Fragmentation Index in East Asia

Figure 2.7 shows the total fragmentation index in the years 1975, 1990 and 2000; for most of the countries the fragmentation index is increasing over time. Japan and the USA have the highest levels of the index, which means that they engage in a complex form of fragmentation, compared to Indonesia, the Philippines and Thailand, which show a low level of fragmentation. It is interesting that China, Japan and the USA show this high level; the result is opposite to what we obtained from the *VS* calculation. The result indicates that these countries rely on widespread production networks, even though the *VS* index is low. We select three industries, chemical products, electronic products and precision machines, which attain a high level of the index, to examine the difference in the fragmentation index among sectors (see Figure 2.8). The fragmentation index of each sector has a similar trend to the total fragmentation index. Electronic products show a high index over time and over countries, indicating that it is a complex form of the production.

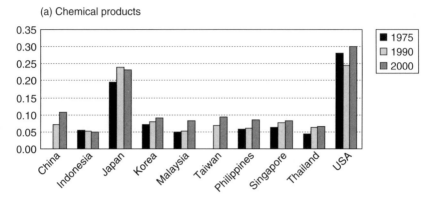

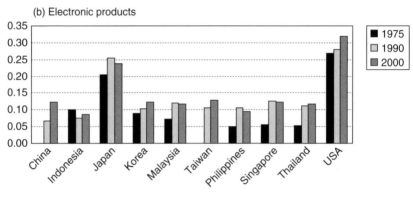

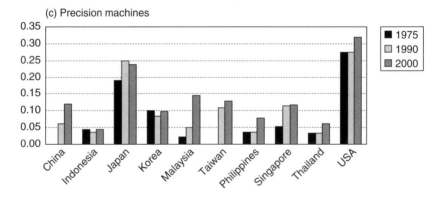

Figure 2.8   Fragmentation index among sectors

2.5 CONCLUDING REMARKS

In recent decades, the international fragmentation and resulting intermediate input has grown substantially. This chapter examines to what extent
international fragmentation of production has deepened in East Asia as
measured by vertical specialization and fragmentation indices calculated
from the AIO. Our main findings are as follows. Vertical specialization is greatest in small countries, but it is rising over time for almost all
our sample. Vertical specialization varies substantially across industries,
with electronic products being the most vertically specialized. Vertical
specialization accounts for more than 20 percent of trade growth in high-
VS countries, and a lower share in countries such as China, Indonesia,
Japan and the USA, which exhibit lower degress of vertical specialization. Geographically, vertical trade with northern countries has historically dominated, but South–South vertical specialization is increasing in
importance.

NOTES

1. Examples on this approach are given in Chapter 3, p. 42.
2. In this chapter, we use domestic (foreign) value added and domestic (foreign) content
   interchangeably.
3. These tables are published as IDE (1983, 1991, 1996, 2001, 2006a, 2006b), and are available by 56 sectors for the year 1975, 24 sectors for the year 1985, 78 sectors for the years
   1990 and 1995, and 76 sectors for the year 2000.
4. For the year 1975 table, China and Taiwan are not included.
5. For the methodology of compiling AIO table, see Inomata (1997), Oyamada et al. (2005)
   and IDE (2006a).
6. In Table 2.3, there is a negative percentage in the contribution of VS_i in Singapore. The
   reason is that the growth of the export share and that of the VS_f share to gross output
   are negative, while the growth of the VS_i share is positive. A negative percentage can
   occur when negative growth in a category total incorporates positive growth in a sub-
   category.

REFERENCES

Amiti, Mary and Jozef Konings (2007), 'Trade liberalization, intermediate inputs,
   and productivity: evidence from Indonesia', *American Economic Review*, **97** (5),
   1611–38.
Arndt, Sven W. and Henryk Kierzkowski (2001), *Fragmentation: New Production
   Patterns in the World Economy*, Oxford: Oxford University Press.
Blanchard, Olivier and Michael Kremer (1997), 'Disorganization', *Quarterly
   Journal of Economics*, **112** (4), 1091–126.
Campa, Jose and Linda S. Goldberg (1997), 'The evolving external orientation

of manufacturing: a profile of four countries', *Economic Policy Review*, **3** (2), 53–81.

Deardorff, Alan V. (2001), 'Fragmentation in simple trade model', *North American Journal of Economics and Finance*, **12**, 121–37.

Ethier, Wilfred J. (1982), 'National and international returns to scale in the modern theory of international trade', *American Economic Review*, **72** (3), 389–405.

Hummels, David, Jun Ishii and Kei-Mu Yi (2001), 'The nature and growth of vertical specialization in world trade', *Journal of International Economics*, **54**, 75–96.

Inomata, Satoshi (1997), 'On the adjustment of national I–O framework for the compilation of 1990 Asian Input–Output Table', in *Report on Compilation Work for 1990 International Input–Output Table (IV)*, *Asian International Input–Output Series no. 54*, Tokyo: Institute of Developing Economies.

Institute of Developing Economies (1983), *Asian International Input–Output Table 1975*, Tokyo: Institute of Developing Economies.

Institute of Developing Economies (1991), *Asian International Input–Output Table 1985*, Tokyo: Institute of Developing Economies.

Institute of Developing Economies (1996), *Asian International Input–Output Table 1990*, Tokyo: Institute of Developing Economies.

Institute of Developing Economies (2001), *Asian International Input–Output Table 1995*, Tokyo: Institute of Developing Economies.

Institute of Developing Economies (2006a), *Asian International Input–Output Table 2000 Volume 1: Explanatory Book*, Chiba: Institute of Developing Economies.

Institute of Developing Economies (2006b), *Asian International Input–Output Table 2000 Volume 2: Data*, Chiba: Institute of Developing Economies.

Jones, Ronald W. and Henryk Kierzkowski (1990), 'The role of services in production and international trade: a theoretical framework', in Ronald W. Jones and Anne O. Krueger (eds), *The Political Economy of International Trade: Essays in Honor of Robert E. Baldwin*, Cambridge, MA: Blackwell, pp. 131–48.

Jones, Ronald, Henryk Kierzkowski and Lurong Chen (2005), 'What does evidence tell us about fragmentation and outsourcing?', *International Review of Economics and Finance*, **14** (3), 305–16.

Koopman Robert, Zhi Wang and Shang-Jin Wei (2008), 'How much of Chinese exports is really made in China? Assessing domestic value-added when processing trade is pervasive', mimeo.

Ng, Francis and Alexander J. Yeats (1998), 'Good governance and trade policy: are they the keys to Africa's global integration and growth?', World Bank Policy Research Working Paper no. 2038.

Ng, Francis and Alexander J. Yeats (1999), 'Production sharing in East Asia: who does what for whom, and why?', World Bank Policy Research Working Paper no. 2197.

Ng, Francis and Alexander J. Yeats (2003), 'Major trade trends in East Asia: what are their implications for regional cooperation and growth?', World Bank Policy Research Working Paper no. 3084.

Oyamada, Kazuhiko, Shinya Arakawa, Satoshi Inomata, Hiroshi Kuwamori, Jun Nakamura, Nobuhiro Okamoto, Takao Sano, and Yoko Uchida (2005), 'Data estimation in Asian International input–output Table? Focusing on Indonesia, Malaysia, the Philippines, Singapore and Thailand', *GTAP 6 Data Package Documentation, III.11.F*, Center for Global Trade Analysis, Purdue University.

Sanyal, Kalyan K. and Ronald W. Jones (1982), 'The theory of trade in middle products', *American Economic Review*, **72** (1), 16–31.
Yi, Kei-Mu (2003), 'Can vertical specialization explain the growth of world trade?', *Journal of Political Economy*, **111** (1), 52–102.

APPENDIX

Table 2A.1   Share of VS_i and VS_f in total VS (%)

	1975		1985		1990		1995		2000	
	VS_i	*VS_f*	*VS_i*	*VS_f*	*VS_i*	*VS_f*	*VS_i*	*VS_f*	*VS_i*	*VS_f*
China	–	–	57.7	42.3	53.2	46.8	47.5	52.5	41.5	58.5
Indonesia	84.3	15.7	84.0	16.0	68.5	31.5	61.6	38.4	63.6	36.4
Japan	66.7	33.3	39.8	50.5	58.4	46.2	60.2	39.8	62.6	37.4
Korea	56.5	43.5	45.4	54.6	46.6	53.4	67.0	33.0	70.3	29.7
Malaysia	51.6	48.4	77.6	22.4	65.9	34.1	64.2	35.8	64.0	36.0
Taiwan	–	–	42.9	57.1	51.8	48.2	61.1	38.9	71.4	28.6
Philippines	68.0	32.0	68.3	31.7	49.0	51.0	57.4	42.6	74.3	25.7
Singapore	64.2	35.8	63.8	36.2	51.9	48.1	54.7	45.3	70.3	29.7
Thailand	75.9	24.1	68.9	31.1	48.0	52.0	58.0	42.0	62.8	37.2
USA	67.1	32.9	60.5	39.5	56.7	43.3	57.9	42.1	65.0	35.0

3. Some evidence on the nature and growth of input trade

David Hummels and Laura Puzzello

3.1 INTRODUCTION

Why do countries trade intermediate inputs? Recent studies have documented that trade in intermediate inputs is a large and growing fraction of overall trade.[1] With this documentation has come an increasing interest in explaining why this trade takes place and whether it is in important ways different from trade in final goods. For example, input trade may be driven by factor endowment differences (as in Arndt, 1997, 1998; Deardorff, 2001a, 2001b), by the balance of scale economies versus trade costs (as in Krugman and Venables, 1995, 1996; Venables, 1996), by multinational firms seeking to trade specialized inputs on an intra-firm basis (as in Helpman, 1984; Zhang and Markusen, 1999; Venables, 1999). Many of these motivations and explanations simply borrow theoretical determinants from the larger literature on trade in final consumer goods.

We extend a standard model of international trade with intermediate inputs. This model, originally due to Krugman and Venables (1995, 1996), is widely used in literatures on international trade and agglomeration economies. It assumes a strong form of symmetry between intermediate and final goods: the sensitivity of a good's demand to relative prices and trade costs is assumed to be independent of its 'end-use'. We derive an implication that, for a given industry, the input share of bilateral trade depends exclusively on the industrial absorption share of intermediates from that industry. That is, the intermediate input share of bilateral trade in an industry should not be explained by factor and trade costs once its industrial absorption share is controlled for. An empirical failure of the theory would instead imply that the effect of factor costs and trade barriers is not symmetric across final and intermediate international flows.

We empirically test this prediction using a unique data set, the Asian International Input–Output Tables. These tables allow us to examine country- and industry-level determinants of the sourcing of intermediate goods and the extent of vertical specialization.

This is not the first study to look at input trade and its determinants; however, existing papers have two important flaws: they require definitions of intermediate versus final goods that are problematic, and they lack information on where the input is used. In a typical approach researchers examine the definition of particular product codes with the SITC or HS nomenclatures and then determine whether the code in question is an intermediate or final good. Examples include the UN's BEC or 'Broad Economic Category' classification, and the US 'end-use' classifications. Several authors have also identified intermediates as those goods whose product code definitions include the words 'parts' or 'components'. Of course, any such division is arbitrary – including goods that are not intermediates and excluding goods that are intermediates. For example, many chemical compounds are inputs into production, in some sense 'parts', but are categorized by their appropriate molecular name.

Similarly, the same product can be both an input and a final good. Many food products such as wheat flour are both inputs (for restaurants and food processing firms) and final consumer goods. Automobile tires are purchased both by firms as an input into car production, and by final consumers installing tires on their cars. In both examples, tires and wheat flour are used in similar manners by firms and consumers, the primary differences being who is doing the assembly, whether the 'assembled' good is now tradable, and whether the assembler can change locations in response to cost pressures. For example, the firm that uses tires or wheat flour can assemble them into a tradable good, and that firm is itself internationally mobile, potentially relocating production to be close to input supplies. In contrast, the assembly by the household is for use by the household itself but not for trade, and the household is not internationally mobile.

This point suggests that when explaining the sourcing of intermediates and the extent of vertical specialization one would also like to know where inputs are used. One country may import ball-bearing while another imports machine tools – this may reflect differences in their comparative advantage in ball-bearing versus machine tools, or it may simply reflect differences in which industries use these inputs. This suggests a second problem with using an 'intermediates' definition with simple trade data – machine tools and ball-bearings are likely employed in many different industries. Even if one can convincingly define goods as intermediate trade flow data, this does not indicate in which sector particular intermediates are used. Without this information one is unable to explore the role played by the 'using' industry, and whether the 'using' industry is itself mobile in response to the availability of parts and components.

A consequence of this definitional problem is that many papers that separate 'intermediates' and 'final goods' in regressions find similar correlates

in each case. That is, these goods do not appear to look statistically different. This may be because intermediate and final goods are, in fact, similar.
Or it may be due to wholesale misclassification.

By using the Asian IO table data we solve both problems. First, intermediate inputs are defined by their use rather than by product code definition. Second, we can observe the share of each industry's output that is
absorbed by other industries and by final consumers. In these respects our
approach is similar to that employed by Hummels et al. (2001), who use
OECD input–output tables for related purposes. An important difference
is that we are able to observe from where, internationally, particular goods
are sourced. This enables us to examine a richer set of determinants related
to exporter characteristics.

Our approach is also related to a distinct literature that examines the
determinants of intra-firm sales, which are sales of intermediate inputs
between affiliates of the same multinational firm. This literature has three
problems. One, intra-firm sales data are quite limited in time series and
geographic coverage. Two, to the extent that intermediate inputs are also
traded on an arm's-length basis, intra-firm sales miss this trade. Three,
multinational firms may span multiple industries, making it difficult to
draw inferences about the role of the 'using' industry.

3.2   DATA DESCRIPTION

Our empirical analysis uses the Asian International Input–Output (AIO,
henceforth) tables for the reference years 1975, 1985, 1990, 1995 and 2000.
These tables contain information on ten national input–output tables:
China, Indonesia, Japan, Korea, Malaysia, the Philippines, Singapore,
Taiwan, Thailand and the USA.[2] Bilateral details are retrieved exploiting
trade data.

The special feature of the AIO tables is that transactions in intermediates
and final goods are distinguished on the basis of country-specific surveys.
The distribution structure of a certain imported good to domestic industries
is assumed to be the same, no matter from which country it is imported. All
import values of a certain good, irrespective of its domestic destination, are
assigned by the country of origin according to each country's share in the
total volume of import of that good. Accordingly, the amount of intermediate good g used for production of good h, where g is produced by country
j and h by country i, $M_{ji}(g, h)$, is imputed as follows:

$$M_{ji}(g, h) = \frac{Tot.\ \text{Imports}_{ij}(g)}{Tot.\ \text{Imports}_i(g)} * M_i^{-i}(g, h)$$

where $M_i^{-i}(g, h)$ is the amount of imported intermediate good g used to produce country i's good h. Importantly, these imputations are adjusted when possible for additional information on the source country of imported intermediate, and suggestions from local specialists. For additional information on the methodology of compiling AIO tables, see Inomata (1997), Oyamada et al. (2005) and IDE (2006).

These tables are available for 56 sectors in the year 1975, 38 sectors in 1985, 78 sectors in 1990 and 1995, and 76 sectors in 2000. Our analysis uses an aggregation of the AIO tables to 30 sectors[3] to make data comparable over time.

In Table 3.1 we report statistics on the importance of input trade for each country and each year. Panel A reports IT/GO – imported inputs as a share of gross output (= total input) in tradable sectors of the economy. In larger economies (the USA, Japan, China, Indonesia) the IT/GO ratio is quite small. This may reflect the greater availability and diversity of domestically produced inputs. For the remaining economies, imported inputs represent a significant fraction of gross output – as high as one quarter for Malaysia and Singapore. The final column of panel A shows that imported inputs as a fraction of gross output are growing very rapidly in all countries except Korea.

Table 3.1 panel B reports IT/TT – import of intermediate inputs as share of total import. This is the statistic that we shall primarily focus on in our empirical analysis of the determinants of input trade. Again, most of the larger and more developed economies import fewer inputs as a share of total trade, although the differences are less pronounced than was seen in panel A. In terms of growth rates, China, Malaysia, the Philippines and Thailand are the large positive outliers while Korea saw little growth and input trade as a share of total trade significantly shrank for Japan, Taiwan and the USA. There are three possibilities behind the shrinking share of input trade. First, these last three countries are shifting away from assembly operations and so purchase fewer inputs than they did previously. Second, they still purchase foreign inputs but are shifting away supply sources covered by the Asian IO tables (e.g. US sourcing from NAFTA countries would not be counted). Third, non-input imports are simply growing much faster than input imports in these countries. Of these explanations the last seems the most likely given the evidence in panel A showing that imported inputs as a share of gross output are small but growing for all three countries.

Finally, input trade is a two-way street. In panel C we reverse the perspective and examine the importance of exported inputs as a share of total exports for each country. Here we see growth in exported inputs for Japan, Korea, Taiwan and Singapore, but shrinkage for the remaining countries.

Table 3.1   Relative importance of inputs, traded goods

	1975	1985	1990	1995	2000	Total percent Change
(A) Unit input usages of imported intermediates (IT/GO, %)						
China	–	1.5	1.7	2.8	3.3	120.5
Indonesia	3.2	3.1	3.2	3.8	4.1	29.8
Japan	2.0	2.2	1.9	2.0	2.4	19.6
Korea	8.5	7.8	7.3	7.6	8.7	2.3
Malaysia	4.2	9.1	10.0	16.0	24.7	486.1
Taiwan	–	6.7	9.3	12.5	15.2	126.2
Philippines	4.0	4.6	6.4	8.0	16.0	303.1
Singapore	16.3	26.2	28.1	28.3	24.5	50.3
Thailand	3.1	5.1	10.9	12.0	13.7	339.3
USA	0.7	1.1	1.2	1.8	2.2	229.9
(B) Input share of trade (IT/TT, %)						
China	–	36.1	61.7	62.3	65.2	80.8
Indonesia	38.8	51.2	38.7	45.6	49.7	27.9
Japan	71.8	61.1	51.7	47.3	43.6	−39.3
Korea	67.2	69.7	67.4	64.0	71.1	5.8
Malaysia	36.9	46.0	36.2	45.3	71.4	93.4
Taiwan	–	69.1	64.6	63.1	63.3	−8.5
Philippines	41.5	66.6	47.4	46.2	63.1	52.1
Singapore	54.2	62.4	53.8	59.7	61.8	14.1
Thailand	45.3	45.7	53.6	56.7	67.9	49.9
USA	43.3	29.8	24.7	31.2	33.9	−21.6
(C) Exported inputs in total exports (%)						
China	–	64.9	52.1	44.6	36.7	−43.4
Indonesia	86.9	94.1	81.6	70.3	71.3	−18.0
Japan	53.5	36.8	42.5	51.1	55.0	2.8
Korea	47.2	41.6	39.8	61.6	64.7	37.0
Malaysia	69.6	86.7	73.4	63.0	62.1	−10.8
Taiwan	–	35.2	42.6	54.5	67.4	91.4
Philippines	83.6	64.0	48.7	55.6	66.0	−21.0
Singapore	49.2	52.2	48.0	50.7	66.9	35.9
Thailand	74.2	62.9	43.1	49.1	55.4	−25.4
USA	70.6	66.7	61.3	58.9	61.5	−12.8

The patterns revealed in panels B and C for Japan are especially interesting. They indicate a shift away from assembly and a shift toward provision of inputs for assembly elsewhere.

3.3   THE MODEL

In this section we extend a standard model of international trade with intermediate inputs. This model is originally due to Krugman and Venables (1995, 1996), and is also used in Hillberry and Hummels (2002) and Redding and Venables (2004). It assumes a strong form of symmetry between intermediate and final goods: the sensitivity of a good's demand to relative prices and trade costs is assumed to be independent of its 'end-use'. We derive an implication that, for a given industry, the input share of bilateral trade depends exclusively on the industrial absorption share of intermediates from that industry. That is, the intermediate input share of bilateral trade in an industry should not be explained by factor and trade costs once its industrial absorption share is controlled for.

We follow the model derivation and extension in Hillberry and Hummels (2002). In this model goods are both final goods and intermediate inputs. Demands in the first case are given by consumers and in the second case by using industries. In the case of a one-sector economy, total expenditures for a good depend on consumer income and on the extent of industry in a location. In a more general model with H industries, expenditures on goods produced by industry h in a location depend on consumer income and on the industrial structure in that location. For example, if h is auto parts, expenditures on auto parts rise if a location primarily produces automobiles and falls if a location primarily produces agriculture.

Consider a world with $i = 1, \ldots, R$ countries. Consumers have identical Cobb–Douglas preferences across commodities $h = 1, \ldots, H$ and Dixit–Stiglitz preferences over differentiated varieties:

$$U_i = \prod_h C_{i,h}^{\eta_h} \text{ with } C_{i,h} = \left(\sum_{m_h} (c_{i,m_h}^h)^{\frac{\sigma-1}{\sigma}} \right)^{\frac{\sigma}{\sigma-1}} \tag{3.1}$$

where η_h is the consumers' expenditure share in varieties of sector h, and σ is the elasticity of substitution betweens pairs of differentiated varieties. Let σ be the same for all sectors h.

Firms use two primary factors, capital (K) and labor (L), and intermediates for the production of a given variety. Both factors are perfectly mobile within a country but immobile across countries. Each variety/good is used for consumption and production. In order to produce a variety of good h, firms in country *i* use fixed and marginal quantities of a composite input Z, which consists of labor, capital and intermediates:

$$Z_i^h = (K_i^h)^{\mu_k^h}(L_i^h)^{\mu_L^h}\prod_g (M_i^{gh})^{\mu_g^h} \text{ with } \mu_k^h + \mu_L^h + \sum_g \mu_g^h = 1 \quad (3.2)$$

where μ_k^h, μ_L^h and μ_g^h are respectively the cost shares of capital, labor and intermediate input *g* in the production of good *h*. M_i^{gh} is the bundle of intermediates from sector *g* used in the production of good *h*.

$$M_i^{gh} = \left(\sum_{n_g} (m_{n_g}^{gh})^{\frac{\sigma-1}{\sigma}}\right)^{\frac{\sigma}{\sigma-1}} \quad (3.3)$$

where $m_{n_g}^{gh}$ is the quantity of a firm's output from sector *g* used in sector *h*. We assume the elasticity of substitution between varieties of intermediates is the same across sectors and equal to the elasticity of substitution in demand.[4]

Given the description of technology in (3.2), industry *h* spends a proportion μ_g^h of total costs/revenues in intermediates from sector *g*:

$$\overline{P_i^g}M_i^{gh} = \mu_g^h X_i^h \quad (3.4)$$

where $\overline{P_i^g}$ is the price index characterizing sector *g*, and X_i^h is the gross output of industry *h*. The shares μ_g^h correspond to the standard use coefficients in an input–output table.

We have assumed that utility has CES (constant elasticity of substitution) over distinct varieties of good *g*. This implies that final consumer demand for each variety of good *g* originating in exporter *j* can be written

$$c_{ji}^g = \frac{(p_j^g\tau_{ij})^{-\sigma}}{(\overline{P_i^g})^{1-\sigma}}*\eta^g Y_i \quad (3.5)$$

Industrial demands arising from sector *h* for good *g* are the same, except that we replace the share of consumer income spent on good *g*, $\eta^g Y_i$, with the input–output coefficient μ_g^h multiplied by output of sector *h*,

$$m_{ji}^{gh} = \frac{(p_j^g\tau_{ij})^{-\sigma}}{(\overline{P_i^g})^{1-\sigma}}*\mu_g^h X_i^h \quad (3.6)$$

Summing over all using industries, we arrive at country *i*'s total industrial use for good *g* sold by exporter *j*:

$$m_{ji}^g = \sum_h m_{ji}^{gh} = \frac{(p_j^g\tau_{ij})^{-\sigma}}{(\overline{P_i^g})^{1-\sigma}}*\sum_h \mu_g^h X_i^h \quad (3.7)$$

Adding together final consumer and industrial demands for a variety of good g produced in country j, we have

$$q_{ji}^g = c_{ji}^g + m_{ji}^g = \frac{(p_j^g \tau_{ij})^{-\sigma}}{(\overline{P}_i^g)^{1-\sigma}} * E_i^g \tag{3.8}$$

where total expenditure on good g by importer i is

$$E_i^g = \eta^g Y_i + \sum_h \mu_g^h X_i^h$$

Equations (3.7) and (3.8) give us the quantity consumed for a single variety. To translate that into total expenditures, we multiply by the number of distinct varieties produced by exporter j, N_j^g, and the price per variety, to yield

$$T_{ji}^g = N_j^g p_j^g q_{ji}^g = N_j^g \frac{(p_j^g)^{1-\sigma} \tau_{ij}^{-\sigma}}{(\overline{P}_i^g)^{1-\sigma}} * E_i^g \tag{3.9}$$

Industrial expenditures on good g produced by exporter j arising from using sector h in country i are then

$$M_{ji}^{gh} = N_j^g p_j^g m_{ji}^{gh} = N_j^g \frac{(p_j^g)^{1-\sigma} \tau_{ij}^{-\sigma}}{(\overline{P}_i^g)^{1-\sigma}} * \mu_g^h X_i^h \tag{3.10}$$

Equations (3.10) and (3.9) are complicated expressions involving many variables that are difficult to measure. But note that by taking a ratio of the two we eliminate all these variables except for the expenditures shares

$$\frac{M_{ji}^{gh}}{T_{ji}^g} = \frac{\mu_g^h X_i^h}{E_i^g} \tag{3.11}$$

We also find it useful to construct total expenditures on input g from country j by summing over all using sectors h. That yields

$$M_{ji}^g = N_j^g p_j^g m_{ji}^g = N_j^g \frac{(p_j^g)^{1-\sigma} \tau_{ij}^{-\sigma}}{(\overline{P}_i^g)^{1-\sigma}} * \sum_h \mu_g^h X_i^h \tag{3.12}$$

Taking the ratio of (3.12) and (3.9), we have input trade as a share of total trade:

$$\frac{M_{ji}^g}{T_{ji}^g} = \frac{\sum_h \mu_g^h X_i^h}{E_i^g} \tag{3.13}$$

This is the key prediction of the model. Input trade as a share of total trade depends exclusively on the industrial absorption share for industry g's products. This is completely independent of exporter characteristics. That is, exporter characteristics such as size (operating through N_j^g), product prices and trade costs affect the level of input trade and the level of final consumer trade. But because exporter characteristics affect both in precisely the same way, the characteristics cancel out in equation (3.13). It is not generally possible to test this conjecture as other data sets lack information either on the sourcing of inputs and/or on the end-use destination of those inputs. However, since the AIO tables contain both pieces of information, we can construct the elements in equations (3.11) and (3.13), and formally examine both hypotheses.

3.4   EMPIRICS

As a starting point we use AIO tables data to estimate fairly standard gravity-style regressions motivated by equations (3.9) and (3.10). We first relate sales of inputs g from exporter j to importer i to be used in industry h to the determinants of trade suggested by equation (3.10).

$$\log(M_{ji}^{gh}) = \alpha + \beta_1 \log(\mu_g^h X_i^h) + \beta_2 \log\left[\left|\left(\frac{K}{L}\right)_i - \left(\frac{K}{L}\right)_j\right|\right] + \beta_3 \log(1 + tar_{ji}^g)$$

$$+ \beta_4 \log(DIST_{ij}) + \beta_5 Contig_{ji} + \beta_6 Lang_{ji} + \beta_7 \log(GO_j^g) + u_{ji}^{gh} \quad (3.14)$$

where tar_{ji}^g is the tariff rate on country i's imports of good g produced by country j, $(K/L)_i - (K/L)_j$ is the difference in trade partners' relative factor endowments, $DIST$ is the geographical distance in km between trading partners; $Contig$ and $Lang$ are dummy variables which take the value one if the trading partners share a border or speak a common primary language,[5] respectively, and GO_j^g is gross output of good g in exporter j. We then estimate the same equation, but using total trade as the dependent variable and replacing industrial absorption with total absorption.

$$\log(T_{ji}^g) = \alpha + \beta_1 \log(E_i^g) + \beta_2 \log\left[\left|\left(\frac{K}{L}\right)_i - \left(\frac{K}{L}\right)_j\right|\right] + \beta_3 \log(1 + tar_{ji}^g)$$

$$+ \beta_4 \log(DIST_{ij}) + \beta_5 Contig_{ji} + \beta_6 Lang_{ji} + \beta_7 \log(GO_j^g) + u_{ji}^{gh} \quad (3.15)$$

Results are reported in the first two columns of Table 3.2.[6] The gross output and expenditure variables are highly significant in both regressions,

Table 3.2   *Regression results for year 2000, no domestic flows*

	OLS	OLS	OLS
	$\log(M_{ji}^{gh})$	$\log(T_{ji}^{g})$	$\log\left(\dfrac{M_{ji}^{gh}}{T_{ji}^{g}}\right)$
$\log(\mu_g^h X_i^h)$	0.7109***		
	(0.0152)		
$\log(E_i^g)$		0.5495***	
		(0.0305)	
$\log\left(\dfrac{\mu_g^h X_i^h}{E_i^g}\right)$			0.9823***
			(0.0059)
$\log\left(\left\|\Delta\left(\dfrac{K}{L}\right)\right\|\right)$	0.0033	0.1625***	−0.0756***
	(0.0558)	(0.0560)	(0.0275)
$\log(1+tar_{ji}^{g})$	0.0341	−0.0486	−0.0389*
	(0.0485)	(0.0533)	(0.0214)
$\log(DIST)$	−0.2533***	−0.2850***	0.0703*
	(0.0782)	(0.0843)	(0.0379)
Contig	1.2136***	1.2014***	0.1521**
	(0.2392)	(0.2644)	(0.0703)
Lang	0.4829***	0.3113**	0.1483**
	(0.1583)	(0.1409)	(0.0695)
$\log(GO_j^g)$	0.5480***	0.7152***	−0.0434***
	(0.0320)	(0.0289)	(0.0114)
Constant	−10.0221***	−8.7749***	−0.0996
	(0.8597)	(0.8732)	(0.3565)
R^2	0.5545	0.4721	0.7256
N	45436	2371	45436

Note: Standard errors clustered at country-pair level are in parentheses.

as are the three variables meant to measure trade costs: distance, contiguity and common language. Differences in factor endowments are highly significant for total trade (countries trade with partners with different endowments) but not for input trade.

The next step is to examine whether input trade and total trade depend on different determinants, or on the same determinants to a different degree. We use the AIO table data to calculate the left- and right-hand sides of equation (3.13) for each industry g that exporter j ships to importer i. In Figure 3.1 we display values for the USA as importer, buying 30 goods g from nine different exporters, for 270 observations. We plot the intermediate input share of total US imports of g from j, $(M_{j,us}^{g})/(T_{j,us}^{g})$, on the

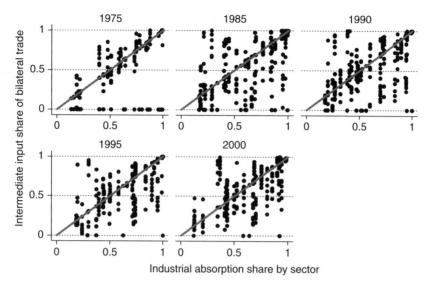

Figure 3.1 *Trade partner independence of US intermediate input share of bilateral trade*

vertical axis and US expenditures on g for industrial uses relative to total expenditures on g, $(\Sigma_h \mu_g^h X_{us}^h)/(E_{us}^g)$, on the horizontal axis. Note that there are only 30 distinct values for expenditures on the horizontal axis.[7] Were equation (3.13) to precisely and completely characterize trade, the intermediate input share of bilateral trade would be independent of the source country. Consequently, one unique observation should characterize each product g and fall exactly on the 45 degree line.

Figure 3.1 shows how this prediction performs empirically, looking at the USA separately for each year in the sample. In each year, for each sector's industrial absorption share we observe more than one value of the input share of bilateral trade, i.e. the intermediate inputs share of bilateral trade is not independent of the source country. Table 3.3 reports the correlation coefficients between the left- and right-hand sides of equation (3.13) for each of the Asian IO country importers in each year. We find positive correlations between the left- and right-hand sides of equation (3.13) for all countries and years, but these correlations are far from 1.

More formally, we examine whether the intermediate input share of trade at the industry level depends on expenditure data taken from the IO tables. Taking logs of equation (3.11), we estimate the following model:

$$\log\left(\frac{M_{ji}^{gh}}{T_{ji}^g}\right)_t = \alpha + \beta\log\left(\frac{\mu_g^h X_i^h}{E_i^g}\right)_t + \varepsilon_{jit}^{gh} \qquad (3.16)$$

Table 3.3   Input shares of bilateral trade and industrial absorption shares, correlations

	1975	1985	1990	1995	2000
China	–	0.54	0.45	0.46	0.56
Indonesia	0.71	0.52	0.55	0.70	0.62
Japan	0.54	0.51	0.57	0.63	0.63
Korea	0.47	0.37	0.41	0.53	0.64
Malaysia	0.54	0.40	0.54	0.47	0.61
Philippines	0.50	0.66	0.65	0.69	0.74
Singapore	0.63	0.62	0.65	0.71	0.66
Thailand	0.41	0.47	0.51	0.62	0.63
Taiwan	–	0.44	0.48	0.58	0.66
USA	0.42	0.59	0.60	0.61	0.64

where ε_{jit}^{gh} is a normally distributed random error. According to the theory, in each time period, the estimated coefficient for the constant should be zero and that of the slope equal to 1. We pool over all i–j–g–h variation, estimate separate samples for each year, and report results in Table 3.4.

Two things are notable in this table. First, the estimated coefficients are statistically different from the prediction of 1 but they are large and highly significant, and the simple model explains approximately 70 percent of the variation in the input to total trade ratio.[8] Second, the intercepts are negative rather than the predicted zero. This suggests that input trade relative to total trade is much lower than the model predicts.

What causes deviations of input trade from the baseline prediction in equations (3.11) and (3.13)? One particular deviation of the data from the model can be seen by noting that many of the input trade shares in Figure 3.1 line up at zero. These are cases where an importer's industrial absorption share for a given good is positive while its input share of bilateral trade is zero. This turns out to be a common pattern. In Table 3.5 we display the frequency of unpredicted zeros, i.e. cases where industrial input expenditures are positive but input trade from a particular source country is zero. The first row sums over all using industries h for a given i–j–g triplet, while the second row calculates the frequency for each i–j–g–h case. When summing over all using industries, unpredicted zeros occur between 11 and 22 percent of the time. When considering each using industry separately, the number rises substantially, to between 28 and 44 percent of cases. In both rows, the frequency of unpredicted zeros drops substantially over time.

What does this tell us? Simply that input demands are much more highly specialized than consumer demands. In the simple model above,

Table 3.4 *Baseline regression results, full sample*

OLS	Pooled $\log\left(\frac{M_{ji}^{gh}}{T_{ji}^{g}}\right)$	1975 $\log\left(\frac{M_{ji}^{gh}}{T_{ji}^{g}}\right)$	1985 $\log\left(\frac{M_{ji}^{gh}}{T_{ji}^{g}}\right)$	1990 $\log\left(\frac{M_{ji}^{gh}}{T_{ji}^{g}}\right)$	1995 $\log\left(\frac{M_{ji}^{gh}}{T_{ji}^{g}}\right)$	2000 $\log\left(\frac{M_{ji}^{gh}}{T_{ji}^{g}}\right)$
$\log\left(\frac{\mu_g^h X_i^h}{E_i^g}\right)$	0.9391***	0.9183***	0.8993***	0.9210***	0.9407***	0.9764***
	(0.0058)	(0.0110)	(0.0099)	(0.0091)	(0.0094)	(0.0066)
Constant	−0.6713***	−0.4333***	−0.7533***	−0.8568***	−0.7930***	−0.5116***
	(0.0334)	(0.0523)	(0.0493)	(0.0517)	(0.0470)	(0.0366)
R^2	0.7042	0.7880	0.6636	0.6541	0.6781	0.7655
N	195311	21505	36278	39459	45360	52709

Notes: * Standard errors clustered at country-pair level are in parentheses. Tests on the slope being equal to 1 are rejected in all regressions with a *p*-value of 0.000.

Table 3.5   Frequencies of unpredicted zeros (%)

	1975	1985	1990	1995	2000
% of sample with $\dfrac{\sum_h \mu_g^h X_i^h}{E_i^g} > 0 \ \& \ \dfrac{M_{ji}^g}{T_{ji}^g} = 0$	22	17	15	12	11
% of sample with $\dfrac{\mu_g^h X_i^h}{E_i^g} > 0 \ \& \ \dfrac{M_{ji}^{gh}}{T_{ji}^g} = 0$	40	44	43	38	28

both consumers and producers have love of variety in their utility/cost functions, which causes them to buy goods from all available sources. That is manifestly not the case with input trade – producers buy from a much narrower set of suppliers. That is precisely what one would expect if the inputs themselves were specifically adapted to particular end products.

We now examine whether, once expenditures are controlled for, the intermediate input shares depend on other arguments in equation (3.10), such as trade costs and the factor abundance (working through product prices). If so, we can reject the symmetry assumption used throughout the literature on intermediate input trade in favor of a hypothesis that this trade is fundamentally different.

The first specification we estimate adds bilateral trade cost controls to the baseline regression, as follows:

$$\log\left(\frac{M_{ji}^{gh}}{T_{ji}^g}\right) = \alpha + \beta_1 \log\left(\frac{\mu_g^h X_i^h}{E_i^g}\right) + \beta_2 \log(DIST_{ij}) + \beta_3 Contig_{ji}$$
$$+ \ \beta_4 Lang_{ji} + \beta_5 HOME + \varepsilon_{jit}^{gh} \qquad (3.17)$$

where *HOME* is an indicator variable that takes the value 1 if the input share of bilateral trade is actually the input share of domestic intermediates in total consumption of domestic varieties. We estimate equation (3.17) separately for each year and report results in Table 3.6.

Several things are notable about the results. Expenditures shares are again large and positive and close to 1. Bilateral distance has no effect on the input share of trade but the other trade cost measures do. Contiguous countries have a larger than predicted share of input trade, as do countries sharing a common language. But the largest effect is the *HOME* dummy. In all years except for 1975, the ratio of input to total trade is far greater for domestic than for foreign suppliers. Recall, if trade costs are symmetric for inputs and final goods, their effect should wash out when we take the

Table 3.6 Regression results with bilateral controls

OLS	Pooled $\log\!\left(\dfrac{M_{ji}^{gh}}{T_{ji}^{g}}\right)$	1975 $\log\!\left(\dfrac{M_{ji}^{gh}}{T_{ji}^{g}}\right)$	1985 $\log\!\left(\dfrac{M_{ji}^{gh}}{T_{ji}^{g}}\right)$	1990 $\log\!\left(\dfrac{M_{ji}^{gh}}{T_{ji}^{g}}\right)$	1995 $\log\!\left(\dfrac{M_{ji}^{gh}}{T_{ji}^{g}}\right)$	2000 $\log\!\left(\dfrac{M_{ji}^{gh}}{T_{ji}^{g}}\right)$
$\log\!\left(\dfrac{\mu_g^h X_i^h}{E_i^g}\right)$	0.9517***	0.9150***	0.9072***	0.9453***	0.9550***	0.9852***
	(0.0059)	(0.0117)	(0.0115)	(0.0084)	(0.0092)	(0.0057)
$\log(DIST)$	0.0229	−0.0016	0.0080	0.0214	0.0376	0.0085
	(0.0230)	(0.0281)	(0.0320)	(0.0340)	(0.0334)	(0.0279)
Contig	0.2152***	0.1470	0.1253	0.2171**	0.2924***	0.1136
	(0.0647)	(0.1097)	(0.1115)	(0.1082)	(0.0992)	(0.0780)
Lang	0.1735***	−0.0204	0.1490*	0.1854*	0.2382***	0.2181***
	(0.0491)	(0.1059)	(0.0794)	(0.0941)	(0.0629)	(0.0572)
HOME	0.5583***	−0.0629	0.2678**	0.7353***	0.7789***	0.5868***
	(0.0745)	(0.0967)	(0.1065)	(0.0991)	(0.0940)	(0.1022)
Constant	−0.9247***	−0.4323*	−0.8598***	−1.0839***	−1.1960***	−0.6607***
	(0.1947)	(0.2336)	(0.2694)	(0.2836)	(0.2831)	(0.2434)
R^2	0.7096	0.7884	0.6654	0.6641	0.6869	0.7712
N	195311	21505	36278	39459	45360	52709

Notes: * Standard errors clustered at country-pair level are in parentheses. Tests on the slope being equal to 1 are rejected in all regressions with a *p*-value of 0.000.

ratio in equation (3.11). This result then suggests that intermediate inputs are more sensitive to trade costs than final goods.

The only year for which results are surprising is 1975. Indeed, once expenditures are controlled for, none of the bilateral-specific variables are significant. This does not appear to be due to country coverage, which is more sparse in 1975 (excluding China and Taiwan). Restricting country coverage in subsequent years to those observations that appear in the 1975 data, we find similar results.

Next, we eliminate domestic shipments from our sample and focus only on international trade. We also include variables intended to capture factor endowment differences. To explain, our model predicts that bilateral trade flows for a given variety depend on its price relative to the average domestic price for similar varieties. As prices depend on factor costs and the domestic price index for each good is mostly determined by domestic varieties, factor abundance differences affect the level of bilateral trade flows. However, under the null hypothesis in equation (3.11), the input share of bilateral trade is not responsive to factor abundance differences across trade partners.

We use two specifications. In the first we exploit the strong positive correlation between a country's per capita GDP and its capital–labor endowment to proxy factor abundances in each year to estimate:

$$\log\left(\frac{M_{ji}^{gh}}{T_{ji}^{g}}\right)_{t} = \alpha + \beta_{1}\log\left(\frac{\mu_{g}^{h}X_{i}^{h}}{E_{i}^{g}}\right)_{t} + \beta_{2}\log\left[\left|\left(\frac{gdp_{i}}{Pop_{i}}\right)_{t} - \left(\frac{gdp_{j}}{Pop_{j}}\right)_{t}\right|\right]$$

$$+ \beta_{3}\log(DIST_{ji}) + \beta_{4}Contig_{ji} + \beta_{5}Lang_{ji} + \varepsilon_{jit}^{gh} \qquad (3.18)$$

where the absolute difference in GDP per capita of trading partners proxies for their difference in relative factor endowments. The results in Table 3.7 show that per capita income differences do affect input shares of bilateral trade even after controlling for expenditures. In particular, an increase of 1 percent in the gap of countries' GDP per capita reduces the input share of bilateral trade, on average and *ceteris paribus* by 0.07 percent.[9] This effect is precisely estimated in each year with the exception of 1990. It then appears that factor cost differentials affects trade in intermediates and final goods asymmetrically.

Finally, we use explicit measures of capital/labor ratios along with tariffs for the year 2000 only[10] and estimate:

$$\log\left(\frac{M_{ji}^{gh}}{T_{ji}^{g}}\right) = \alpha + \beta_{1}\log\left(\frac{\mu_{g}^{h}X_{i}^{h}}{E_{i}^{g}}\right) + \beta_{2}\log\left[\left|\left(\frac{K}{L}\right)_{i} - \left(\frac{K}{L}\right)_{j}\right|\right]$$

$$+ \beta_{3}\log(1 + tar_{ji}^{g}) + \beta_{4}\log(DIST_{ij}) + \beta_{5}Contig_{ji}$$
$$+ \beta_{6}Lang_{ji} + \beta_{7}\log(GO_{j}^{g}) + u_{ji}^{gh} \qquad (3.19)$$

Table 3.7 Regression results with bilateral controls, no domestic flows

OLS	Pooled $\log\left(\frac{M^{gh}_{ji}}{T^g_{ji}}\right)$	1975 $\log\left(\frac{M^{gh}_{ji}}{T^g_{ji}}\right)$	1985 $\log\left(\frac{M^{gh}_{ji}}{T^g_{ji}}\right)$	1990 $\log\left(\frac{M^{gh}_{ji}}{T^g_{ji}}\right)$	1995 $\log\left(\frac{M^{gh}_{ji}}{T^g_{ji}}\right)$	2000 $\log\left(\frac{M^{gh}_{ji}}{T^g_{ji}}\right)$
$\log\left(\frac{\mu^h_g X^h_i}{E^g_i}\right)$	0.9452***	0.8787***	0.8789***	0.9417***	0.9510***	0.9890***
	(0.0074)	(0.0131)	(0.0126)	(0.0107)	(0.0112)	(0.0066)
$\log\left(\left|\Delta\left(\frac{gdp}{Pop}\right)\right|\right)$	−0.0661***	−0.0736***	−0.0698***	−0.0459	−0.0636***	−0.0760***
	(0.0176)	(0.0215)	(0.0225)	(0.0359)	(0.0223)	(0.0219)
log(DIST)	0.0574	0.0025	0.0327	0.0658	0.0770*	0.0307
	(0.0359)	(0.0393)	(0.0516)	(0.0499)	(0.0453)	(0.0426)
Contig	0.2196***	0.0515	0.1255	0.2499**	0.3045***	0.0963
	(0.0745)	(0.1257)	(0.1232)	(0.1235)	(0.1006)	(0.0778)
Lang	0.1935***	0.0406	0.1693**	0.1951**	0.2422***	0.2502***
	(0.0479)	(0.1053)	(0.0764)	(0.0914)	(0.0618)	(0.0598)
Constant	−1.1000***	−0.4461	−1.0953**	−1.3716***	−1.3845***	−0.6592*
	(0.2964)	(0.3189)	(0.4208)	(0.4202)	(0.3929)	(0.3418)
R²	0.6550	0.7007	0.5872	0.5936	0.6392	0.7407
N	159532	16244	28934	31738	37617	44999

Notes: *Standard errors clustered at country-pair level are in parentheses. Tests on the slope being equal to 1 are rejected in all regressions with a p-value of 0.000, except for the year 2000, which is characterized by a p-value of 0.1008.

The third column of Table 3.2 reports our findings. Input shares of bilateral trade are lower the higher is the tariff imposed on the imported intermediate and the larger is the gap in countries relative factor endowments. Results are in line with our previous estimates.

3.5   GROWTH REGRESSIONS

An additional implication of the theoretical model outlined in section 3.3 is that the growth rate of intermediate input shares of bilateral trade equals the growth rate of industrial absorption shares. This becomes immediately apparent taking logs of equation (3.11) and the difference between two time periods:

$$\log\left(\frac{M_{ji}^{gh}}{T_{ji}^{g}}\right)_{t} - \log\left(\frac{M_{ji}^{gh}}{T_{ji}^{g}}\right)_{t-1} = \log\left(\frac{\mu_{g}^{h}X_{i}^{h}}{E_{i}^{g}}\right)_{t} - \log\left(\frac{\mu_{g}^{h}X_{i}^{h}}{E_{i}^{g}}\right)_{t-1} \quad (3.20)$$

We relate changes in the input share of trade to changes in the industrial absorption share, along with additional trade cost controls using the following specification:

$$\Delta\log\left(\frac{M_{ji}^{gh}}{T_{ji}^{g}}\right)_{t} = \alpha + \beta_{1}\Delta\log\left(\frac{\mu_{g}^{h}X_{i}^{h}}{E_{i}^{g}}\right)_{t} + \beta_{2}\log(DIST_{ji}) + \beta_{3}Contig_{ji}$$
$$+ \beta_{4}Lang_{ji} + \beta_{5}HOME + v_{jit}^{gh} \quad (3.21)$$

We estimate changes between each of the five-year data windows, as well as pooling all the changes into a single regression. The estimates in Table 3.8 provide three interesting insights. First, growth in the input share of trade is positively related to growth in the industrial share of expenditures. Second, between 1975 and 1990 the *HOME* dummy is large and significantly positive, but it becomes large and negative between 1995 and 2000. In other words, in the first 15 years of the sample, reliance on domestic sources for inputs relative to total trade grew substantially. However, in the last five-year period, domestic sourcing fell dramatically. Similarly, the contiguity variable has little effect on the growth of inputs/total trade until the last period. Between 1995 and 2000, the sourcing of inputs/total trade from contiguous countries fell dramatically. Put together, this suggests significant increases in the use of foreign inputs relative to domestic inputs and increases in the use of inputs sourced from far-off foreign sources relative to nearby foreign sources. These patterns seem consistent with the growing importance of global production networks after the 1980s.

Table 3.8   Growth regressions results with bilateral controls

OLS	Pooled	1975–85	1985–90	1990–95	1995–2000
	$\Delta\log\!\left(\dfrac{M_{ji}^{gh}}{T_{ji}^{g}}\right)$	$\Delta\log\!\left(\dfrac{M_{ji}^{gh}}{T_{ji}^{g}}\right)$	$\Delta\log\!\left(\dfrac{M_{ji}^{gh}}{T_{ji}^{g}}\right)$	$\Delta\log\!\left(\dfrac{M_{ji}^{gh}}{T_{ji}^{g}}\right)$	$\Delta\log\!\left(\dfrac{M_{ji}^{gh}}{T_{ji}^{g}}\right)$
$\Delta\log\!\left(\dfrac{\mu_{g}^{h}X_{i}^{h}}{E_{i}^{g}}\right)$	0.8594***	0.9118***	0.8623***	0.7309***	0.8521***
	(0.0129)	(0.0131)	(0.0164)	(0.0274)	(0.0187)
$\log(DIST)$	−0.0162	−0.0024	−0.0154	0.0204*	−0.0455
	(0.0111)	(0.0239)	(0.0287)	(0.0116)	(0.0330)
Contig	−0.1007***	−0.0320	−0.0806	0.0824*	−0.2265**
	(0.0315)	(0.1369)	(0.0851)	(0.0418)	(0.0863)
Lang	0.0195	0.2572	−0.0380	−0.0621**	0.0414
	(0.0296)	(0.1706)	(0.0712)	(0.0275)	(0.0737)
HOME	−0.0202	0.3107***	0.1885*	0.0025	−0.2824***
	(0.0387)	(0.1015)	(0.1000)	(0.0426)	(0.1041)
Constant	0.1133	−0.3181	−0.0270	−0.1500	0.5233*
	(0.0972)	(0.2187)	(0.2519)	(0.0999)	(0.2822)
R^2	0.3218	0.5328	0.2935	0.1580	0.3142
N	125524	16438	30519	36894	41673

Notes: *Standard errors clustered at country-pair level are in parentheses. Tests on the slope being equal to 1 are rejected in all regressions with a *p*-value of 0.000.

3.6   CONCLUSIONS

In this chapter we examine the determinants of input trade. We employ an extension of a widely used model of intermediate input trade in which inputs and final goods are considered symmetric up to differences in expenditure shares. This provides a null hypothesis that inputs and final goods are determined by the same factors.

Our estimates provide the following insights. First, the extent of industrial absorption relative to final consumption as measured by input–output tables does help explain the input share of trade. Second, contrary to the maintained assumption of symmetry from our null hypothesis, this is not the only determinant of input trade. Input trade is more likely to be characterized by zeros, less sensitive to factor endowment differences than final goods trade, and more sensitive to trade costs as measured by home bias, contiguity and common language. However, the role of home bias and contiguity is eliminated by the year 2000, consistent with the popular view of the internationalization of input trade.

NOTES

1. Borga and Zeile (2004); Campa and Goldberg (1997); Feenstra (1998); Feenstra and Hanson (1999); Hanson et al. (2001, 2005); Hummels et al. (1998, 2001); Yeats (2001).
2. For the year 1975 table, China and Taiwan are not included.
3. The aggregation produces three primary sectors, 21 secondary sectors and six service sectors.
4. The implication we focus on in this chapter holds as long as the elasticity of substitution between varieties of a given good is independent of its 'end-use'.
5. Data for geographical factors are taken from the CEPII data set.
6. See note 10 for a description of the sample.
7. The year 1975 is an exception, as we have data on 29 distinct goods.
8. These results are robust to the following changes: inclusion of year and/or source–destination sector fixed effects, and exclusion from the sample observations on the input shares of domestic intermediates.
9. These results are robust to the inclusion of year and/or source–destination sector fixed effects.
10. The sample coverage is slightly different from the one used in most of our empirical analysis as data on *ad valorem* tariff rates are taken from the GTAP database version 6, with reference year 2001. Establishing the concordance between the original AIO tables and the GTAP database allows us to focus on 34 sectors instead of 30 sectors. Data on countries factor endowments for the year 2000 are constructed as documented in Puzzello (2008).

REFERENCES

Arndt, S. (1997), 'Globalization and open economy', *North American Journal of Economics and Finance*, **8** (1), 71–9.

Arndt, S. (1998), 'Super-specialization and the gains from trade', *Contemporary Economic Policy*, **16** (4), 480–85.

Borga, M. and W. Zeile (2004), 'International fragmentation of production and the intra-firm trade of U.S. multinational companies', US Bureau of Economic Analysis Working Paper WP2004-02.

Campa J. and L. Goldberg (1997), 'The evolving external orientation of manufacturing industries: evidence from four countries', *Economic Policy Review*, **3** (2), 53–81.

Deardorff, A. (2001a), 'Fragmentation in simple trade models', *North American Journal of Economics and Finance*, **12** (2), 121–37.

Deardorff, A. (2001b), 'Fragmentation across cones.' in S. Arndt and H. Kierzkowski (eds), *Fragmentation: New Production Patterns in the World Economy*, Oxford: Oxford University Press, pp. 35–51.

Feenstra, R. (1998), 'Integration of trade and disintegration of production in the global economy', *Journal of Economic Perspectives*, **12** (4), 31–50.

Feenstra, R. and G. Hanson (1999), 'The impact of outsourcing and high-technology capital on wages: estimates for the United States, 1979–1990', *Quarterly Journal of Economics*, **114** (3), 907–40

Hanson, G.H., R.J. Mataloni and M.J. Slaughter (2001), 'Expansion strategies of U.S. multinational firms', in D. Rodrik and S. Collins (eds), *Brookings Trade Forum, 2001*, pp. 245–94.

Hanson, G., R. Mataloni and M. Slaughter (2005), 'Vertical production networks in multinational firms', *Review of Economics and Statistics*, **87** (4), 664–78.

Helpman, E. (1984), 'A simple theory of international trade with multinational corporations', *Journal of Political Economy*, **94** (3), 451–71.

Hillberry, R. and D. Hummels (2002), 'Explaining home bias in consumption: the role of intermediate input trade', NBER Working Paper no. 9020.

Hummels, D., D. Rapoport and K.-M. Yi (1998), 'Vertical specialization and the changing nature of world trade', *Federal Reserve Bank of New York Economic Policy Review*, June, 79–99.

Hummels, D., J. Ishii and K. Yi (2001), 'The nature and growth of vertical specialization in world trade', *Journal of International Economics*, **54**, 75–96.

Inomata, S (1997), 'On the adjustment of national I–O framework for the compilation of 1990 Asian Input–Output Table', *Report on Compilation Work for 1990 International Input–Output Table (IV)*, Asian International Input–Output Series, No. 54, Tokyo: Institute of Developing Economies.

Institute of Developing Economies (2006), *Asian International Input–Output Table 2000 Volume 1: Explanatory Book*, Chiba: Institute of Developing Economies.

Krugman, P. and A.J. Venables (1995), 'Globalization and the inequality of nations', *Quarterly Journal of Economics*, **110** (4), 857–80.

Krugman, P. and A.J. Venables (1996), 'Integration, specialization and adjustment', *European Economic Review*, **40**, 959–67.

Oyamada, K., S. Arakawa, S. Inomata, H. Kuwamori, J. Nakamura, N. Okamoto, T. Sano and Y. Uchida (2005), 'Data estimation in Asian International Input–Output Table? Focusing on Indonesia, Malaysia, the Philippines, Singapore and Thailand', *GTAP 6 Data Package Documentation*, III.11.F, Center for Global Trade Analysis, Purdue University.

Puzzello, L. (2008), 'A symmetry hypothesis and measurement biases in the factor content of trade', mimeo.

Redding, S. and A. Venables (2004), 'Economic geography and international inequality', *Journal of International Economics*, **62**, 53–82.

Venables, A. (1996), 'Equilibrium location of vertically linked industries', *International Economic Review*, **37** (2), 341–59.

Venables, A. (1999), 'Fragmentation and multinational production', *European Economic Review*, **43**, 935–45.

Yeats, A. (2001), 'Just how big is global production sharing?', in Sven W. Arndt and Henryk Kierzkowski (eds), *Fragmentation: New Production Patterns in the World Economy*, Oxford: Oxford University Press, pp. 108–43.

Zhang, K. and J. Markusen (1999), 'Vertical multinational and host-country characteristics', *Journal of Development Economics*, **59**, 233–52.

4. Characteristics and determinants of East Asia's trade patterns

Daisuke Hiratsuka

4.1 INTRODUCTION[1]

East Asia has a growing influence on the global economy. By product, in 2005, East Asia, composed of the ten ASEAN countries plus the six countries of China, India, Japan, Republic of Korea, New Zealand and Australia, produced 24.66 million automobiles, accounting for 37.1 percent of the world total automobile production in that year.[2] This figure surpassed that of the EU-25 (27.3 percent) and NAFTA (24.6 percent). East Asia is the world's largest manufacturer of many products, with a 67.3 percent share in synthetic fiber production, 80.8 percent in cell phones, 96.8 percent in computers, 100 percent in hard-disk drives and digital cameras in 2006 (METI, 2007). East Asia has become the world's factory for many manufactured products.

In the background of East Asia's world factory, two separate types of production operation are undertaken by multinationals in the region. One is a horizontal production operation, defined by Markusen (1984) to mean that the products and services produced in foreign countries are roughly similar to those the firm produces for its home market. The other is vertical production operation, defined by Helpman (1984) to mean that the production process is geographically fragmented by stages of production. In reality, production operation, if including services, may lie in between the two: multinationals locate their R&D, design centers, production plants and training centers in different countries depending on factor prices, skill and technology levels, market size and policies, and have production plants in multiple countries.

East Asia's factory, thus, has both characteristics of horizontal production operation, where similar skill-level countries produce similar products; and vertical production operation, where skilled-labor-abundant countries produce skilled-labor-intensive products and unskilled-labor-abundant countries produce unskilled-labor-intensive products. On the basis, the 'factory' exports goods to the world. So, a question arises: what features do multinationals' international production operations have? One way of responding to this question is to analyze multinationals' activities in East Asia regarding procurements by origin and shipments by destination. However, such complete information is not available.

So, instead, this chapter investigates the determinants of East Asia's trade patterns, specifically the relationship of market sizes, geographical distances and differences in skill and technology levels (captured by differences in nominal per capita GDP in terms of US dollars) to those trade patterns. In particular, the effects of skill differences with trade partners between Asia and other countries are highlighted, since skill differences seem to affect vertical production operation. Answers to these questions can provide some insights into the role and perspective of East Asia's factory in the global economy.

The next section looks at the trade patterns of East Asia by distinguishing intermediate goods and final goods. Section 4.3 looks at procurement in the hard-disk-drive and automobile industries, confirming that affiliates operating in East Asia have the characteristics of both horizontal and vertical multinationals. Section 4.4 discusses the econometric model specification that meets the perspectives of international trade and multinational affiliates. Sections 4.5 and 4.6 investigate the determinants of trade patterns of East Asia by using gravity models incorporating the skill differences. The empirical results verify that the skill-level differences affect the behaviors of multinationals and, thereby, determine East Asia's trade patterns of either intermediate goods or final goods for intraregional trade, but not for interregional trade. These contrasting results can be interpreted as showing that multinationals operate vertical productions intensively in East Asia by using different skill and technology levels within the region. At the same time, they have interregional production bases such as East Asia, Europe and North America. Section 4.7 concludes that East Asia will increase intraregional trade through vertical production operation, which takes advantage of skill differences across countries.

4.2 CHARACTERISTICS OF TRADE PATTERNS OF EAST ASIA

What trade patterns and trends are observed for East Asia's trade? In the context of production networks, intermediate goods and final goods must be distinguished. The UN COMTRADE provides broad economic categories (BEC), which groups commodities according to their main end-use. Trade data by end-use are convenient for examining trade patterns. However, BEC trade data are available only after 1998 for most of the countries. In order to see the changes in trade patterns over time, this section uses the RIETI (2007) trade database, which classifies all trade commodities according to five production stages of primary goods, processed goods, parts and components, capital goods, and consumer goods. The RIETI has released five sets of production-stage trade data between 1980 and 2006, compiled from the UN COMTRADE SITC series: the SITC series is converted into the BEC series by using the conversion code lists between the SITC and the BEC, and then the BEC series is reconverted into five production stages.

Figure 4.1 shows the world export share of the ASEAN+6 (East Asia) by production stage. In 1980, the world export shares of ASEAN+6 were 20 percent for consumer goods, 16 percent for capital goods, 14 percent

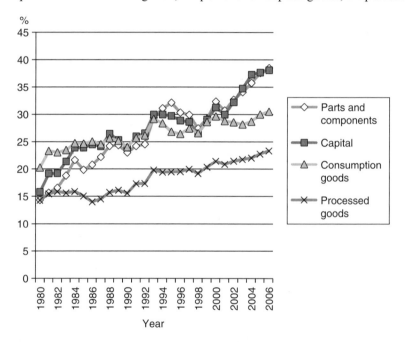

Notes: RIETI (2007) is based on BEC-basis data, which are recalculated from the SITC basis for the long term (1980–2006). The trade goods by production stage include the following items. primary goods: items under BEC code 111, 21 31; processed goods: BEC code 121, 22, 32; parts and components: BEC code 42, 53; capital goods: BEC code 41, 521; consumption goods: BEC code 112, 122, 51, 522, 61, 62, 63.

Source: Compiled using RIETI (2007).

Figure 4.1   World export share of the ASEAN+6 (East Asia) by production stage (%)

for parts and components, and 14 percent for processed goods. In 2006, ASEAN+6 accounted for 38 percent of world exports of parts and components, and an equal percentage for capital goods, which includes personal computers. Corresponding figures for consumer goods and processed goods are 31 percent and 23 percent, respectively. These figures show that East Asia is the world's factory.

Equally important, intraregional trade in East Asia is increasing. Figure 4.2 shows the trend of the share of intra-ASEAN+6 trade (exports and imports) by production stage. For primary goods, the share is about 70 percent of total trade, indicating that most primary goods are traded between geographically close countries. For processed goods, the share increased from 45 percent in 1980 to 52 percent in 1988, and has since remained at about 52–54 percent. For parts and components, the share

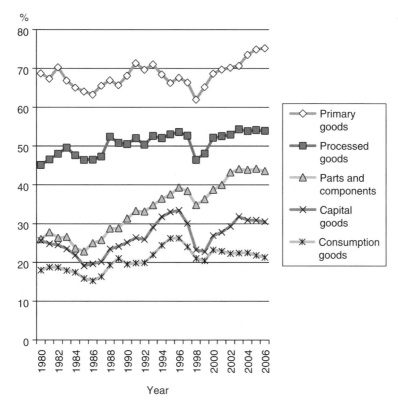

Notes and source: As for Figure 4.1.

Figure 4.2   Intra-ASEAN+6 trade ratio by production category

increased from 26 percent in 1980 to 44 percent in 2006. Thus many primary and intermediate products are traded within the ASEAN+6 region.

However, in relation to consumer goods, the intra-ASEAN+6 trade share remained at 20 percent throughout the period; most consumer goods are traded with partner countries outside the region. There are two possible reasons for the low intraregional trade of consumer goods. One is that trade costs for consumer goods are still high because of high tariffs within the region, and the other is that trade between East Asian countries is small since most of the individual economies are relatively small.

Looking at the intra-ASEAN+6 trade share by production stage, trade patterns within East Asia have changed drastically. The share of parts and components in intra-ASEAN+6 total trade (exports and imports) increased from 6.2 percent in 1980 to 27.4 percent in 2006, while that of primary goods decreased from 36.0 percent to 10.5 percent. On the other hand, the share of processed goods remained at 30–35 percent throughout the period (Figure 4.3). The trade share of intermediate goods, which is the total of processed goods and parts and components, increased gradually, from 41.2 percent in 1980 to 59.7 percent in 2006. This indicates that East Asia has increased intermediate trade within the region.

4.3   ACTIVITIES OF MULTINATIONALS IN EAST ASIA

Multinationals actively participate in East Asia and contribute strongly to the observed trade patterns. To understand the characteristics of operations by multinationals, this section uses case studies to examine parts procurement at the firm level in the electronics and automobile industries.

4.3.1   The Electronics Industry

Electronics is a typical industry, with characteristics of both horizontal and vertical production operation. Production operation style varies according to the type of products. Microprocessor producers have production plants overseas similar to those in their home country. The hard-disk-drive (HDD) industry is an extreme case in that East Asia produces 100 percent of the world's HDD; that is, design and silicon wafer materials are developed in the home countries, and final assembly takes place in multiple sites in East Asia. Currently, Seagate, Maxtor, Western Digital, Hitachi, Toshiba and Fujitsu are the major producers. Each has multiple assembly plants operating in ASEAN and China; for example, Hitachi has

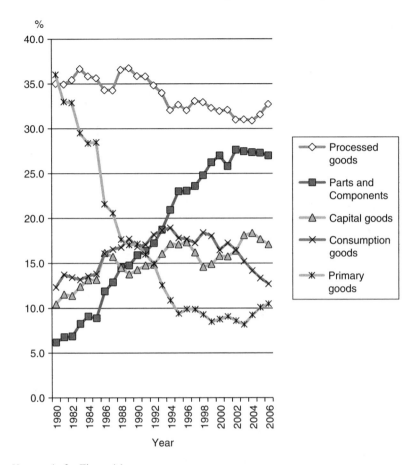

Notes: As for Figure 4.1.

Source: RIETI (2007).

Figure 4.3 Trade pattern inside ASEAN+6 by production category (%)

assembly plants in Singapore, Thailand (two plants), the Philippines and China. These plants produce almost similar products, and some produce exactly the same products. Hence each HDD producer has the characteristic of horizontal operation by a multinational. Their main markets are within the region, with the parent countries being the USA and Japan, for example.

Figure 4.4 shows the procurement of an HDD assembly plant in China, which is a typical case for the electronics industry in East Asia. The

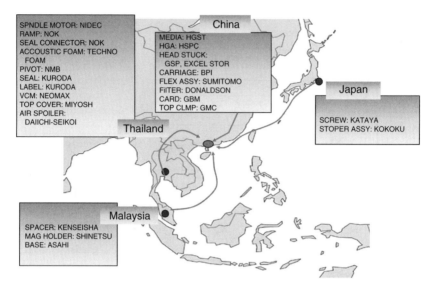

Source: Hiratsuka (2006).

*Figure 4.4   International procurement: an example of a hard-disk-drive
              assembler in China*

electronics industry procures parts and components from multiple sources
located in different countries, and thus has many domestic and foreign
suppliers, but mainly from East Asia. For instance, the HDD factories
in China use suppliers of spindle motors, seal connectors, pivots, seals,
labels, voice coil motors (vcms), top covers and air spoilers from Thailand,
spacers, mag holders, and bases from Malaysia, and screw and stopper
assemblies from Japan.

Procurement by HDD assemblers is evidence of a vertical production
network. Furthermore, the production network has a tree structure.
Figure 4.4 shows the final assembly of HDDs. The suppliers in Figure
4.4 produce materials and parts. For example, the disk (media), which
is a component to store data, is produced by several suppliers located in
Singapore (Hoya), Malaysia (Komag) and Japan (Hoya). Those disk suppliers procure substrates from Japan and Malaysia. The major materials
for the blank substrates are procured from two suppliers in Japan (see
Figure 4.5). Therefore disks are made in a sequential process, starting
from the blank, moving to the substrate, and then finally to the disk. Other
parts and components have similar characteristics as disks.

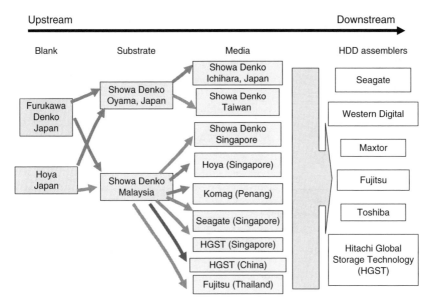

Source: Compiled by the author.

Figure 4.5   Supply chain of media (components of hard-disk drives)

4.3.2   The Automobile Industry

The automobile industry demonstrates another typical horizontal multinational pattern. It produces the same final product in multiple locations, substituting international production for trade (Markusen, 1984). For example, Toyota has multiple automobile production plants in East Asia: seven automobile and parts production plants in China, four plants in Thailand, two plants in India, and one plant in each of Indonesia, Malaysia and the Philippines. Major multinationals have multiple plants in East Asia. Automobile affiliate assemblers operating in ASEAN and China used to procure most of their parts and components from domestic suppliers in host countries, but key parts such as engines and transmissions from the parent countries. This structure is now changing: affiliate automobile assemblers tend to procure key parts from affiliate plants in other countries. Figure 4.6 shows the component complementary operation of a Japanese automobile maker operating in ASEAN.

Japanese automobile assemblers Toyota and Honda have multiple plants in Indonesia, Malaysia, the Philippines and Thailand, and procure most of the parts and components, except key parts, from domestic

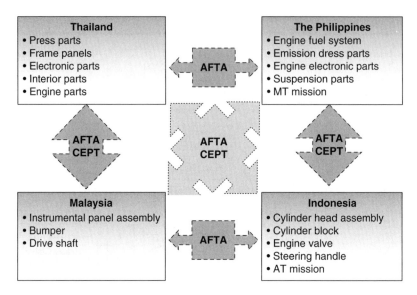

Source: Compiled by the author.

*Figure 4.6   Complementary parts supply system by an automobile
             assembler in ASEAN*

suppliers. At present, taking advantage of the ASEAN Free Trade Area
(AFTA), under which the tariffs on manufactured goods were reduced to
less than 5 percent in 2003, Japanese automobile assemblers procure key
parts from the first-tier suppliers located in the four ASEAN countries. As
shown in Figure 4.6, affiliate assemblers operating in the four countries
import cylinder-head assemblies, cylinder blocks, engine valves, steering
handles and AT transmissions from Indonesia; instrumental panel assemblies, bumpers and drive shafts from Malaysia; engine-fuel systems, emis-
sion parts, engine electronic parts, suspension parts and MT transmissions
from the Philippines; and press parts, frame panels, electronic parts, inte-
rior parts and engine parts from Thailand. In summary, the automobile
industry has both horizontal and vertical characteristics.

4.4   ECONOMETRIC MODEL SPECIFICATION

In East Asia, electronics and automobile multinationals have both horizontal and vertical characteristics, forming the trade patterns of the region.
What model can be used to explain these patterns? Markusen et al. (1996)

and Markusen (1997, 2002) presented a model to discuss two extreme horizontal and vertical operations in a unified theoretical treatment. The key assumptions of the unified treatment known as the knowledge–capital (KK) model, are as follows:

1. The location of knowledge-based activities, such as R&D, management, marketing, financing and other headquarters activities are geographically separated from production, and are easily supplied to geographically separated production facilities.
2. Those knowledge-based activities are skilled-labor-intensive relative to other production activities.
3. The services of knowledge-based activities are joint inputs to geographically separated production facilities.

The first two assumptions give rise to vertical multinationals in which skilled-labor-intensive operations are located in a skilled-labor-abundant country and unskilled-labor-intensive operations are located in an unskilled-labor-abundant country. The third assumption gives rise to horizontal multinationals that have plants in multiple countries. In the KK model, both horizontal and vertical multinationals can arise, depending on a country's characteristics such as its own economic size, the size differences with other countries, factor endowment differences, trade costs and investment costs (Markusen and Maskus, 2001). A key distinction between the pure horizontal model and the KK model is that the former assumes that headquarter activities use factors in the same proportions, whereas the KK model assumes the headquarter services use skilled labor more intensively than all other activities.

The original KK model consists of 41 non-linear equations. Carr, Markusen and Maskus (CMM, 2001) derived a reduced-form equation from the equations that makes it possible to evaluate the efficacy of the KK model of multinational activity.[3] The CMM model specification has been the basis of empirical studies on the KK model. Such studies estimated the KK model by using data on the sales of foreign affiliates of US parent firms and the sales of US affiliates of foreign parents. They obtained the empirical result that affiliate sales are strongly sensitive to bilateral aggregate economic activity (positive), squared differences in GDP (negative), differences in skilled-labor endowments (positive), and the interaction between economic size and endowment differences (negative). These results, in particular, show that the skill-level-difference term is significantly positive, lending support to the KK model hypothesis that skilled-labor-abundant countries produce skilled-labor-intensive products and unskilled-labor-abundant countries produce unskilled-labor-intensive products.

Blonigen, Davies and Head (BDH, 2003) corrected a misspecification of the skill-difference terms in the CMM model, employing absolute terms for skill difference. They obtained negative coefficients of absolute differences in skilled-labor endowments, as opposed to the CMM results.

CMM (2001) and BDH (2003) investigated multinational activities, focusing on US multinational affiliates operating overseas and foreign affiliates operating in the USA. However, using survey data may be problematic in that the home country is one of the two countries in every country-pair observation in their sample. In addition, complete information sets of international procurements and shipments of multinationals operating in East Asia are not available from the survey. For these reasons, a similar specification of BDH (2003) is applied to bilateral trade data. The estimated model specification is as follows:

$$TRADE = \beta_0 + \beta_1 \,(GDPSUM) + \beta_2 \,(GDPDIFSQ) + \beta_3 \,(AB\_SKDIFF) + \beta_4 \,(DIST) + \beta_5 \,(CONTIG) + \beta_6 \,(COMLANGUAGE) + \beta_7 \,(COLONY) \qquad (4.1)$$

where the variable $TRADE$ is the total trade consisting of exports and imports between trade partners. The first independent variable ($GDPSUM$) is joint market size, captured by the combined nominal GDP of importing and exporting countries, which is a proxy for total market size, and should positively affect trade. Its coefficient is expected to have a positive sign, and the elasticity of $TRADE$ with respect to this combined GDP is greater than 1. The second independent variable ($GDPDIFSQ$) is the square of the difference in country size between importing and exporting countries. Its coefficient is expected to be negative because $TRADE$ has an inverted-U-shaped relationship to differences in country size, with a maximum at zero difference.

The third independent variable (AB_SKDIFF) is the absolute gap of skill-level difference between importing and exporting countries, which can be represented by differences in nominal per capita GDP in terms of the US dollar. AB_SKDIFF is expected to show a positive relation with $TRADE$; that is, bilateral trade increases as skill levels diverge. This suggested that vertical production operation (international fragmentation) exceeds horizontal production operation (similar productions are operated in multiple countries). On the contrary, if AB_SKDIFF shows a negative sign that bilateral trade decreases as skill levels converge, it suggests that similar productions are operated in multiple countries.

CMM (2001) and BDH (2003) use an intersection term between the absolute gap of GDP size and absolute gap of skill-level difference. This intersection term, which should have a negative sign, is omitted in the

Table 4.1 Correlation coefficient matrix of independent variables

	SUMGDP	GDPDIFSQ	AB_SKDIFF	[AB_GDPDIFF] *[AB_SKDIFF]
GDPSUM	1			
GDPDIFSQ	−0.3208	1		
AB_SKDIFF	−0.0022	0.154	1	
[AB_GDPDIFF] *[AB_SKDIFF]	−0.1891	0.704	0.6759	1

Source: Compiled by the author.

estimated model because it has high correlations with *GDPDIFSQ* and *AB_SKDIFF* of 0.70 and 0.68, respectively (see Table 4.1).

The fourth independent variable, geographical distance (*DIST*), is expected to have a negative relationship with bilateral trade as it is a proxy for transportation costs. Other control variables are *CONTIG* (dummy variable indicating whether the two countries are contiguous), *COMLANGUAGE* (dummy variable indicating whether the two countries share a common official language) and *COLONY* (dummy variable indicating whether the two countries have had a colonial relationship). These control variables are expected to have positive relationship with bilateral trade.

TRADE, which is a dependent variable, is the total trade of exports and imports of the reported countries, obtained from bilateral trade data of the UN COMTRADE database by broad economic categories (BEC). GDP and population are obtained from the World Development Indicator, the World Bank, and control variables such as geographical distance and other dummy variables from the CEPII database. The reported countries number 14 (ASEAN+6 minus 2), namely: Australia, Brunei, Cambodia, China, India, Indonesia, Japan, Korea, Malaysia, the Philippines, Singapore, Thailand, Vietnam and New Zealand. Myanmar and Laos are excluded due to lack of data. The period for the estimation is 1998 to 2006 because BEC category data are available after 1998 for most countries, as summarized in Table 4.2.

4.5 DETERMINANTS OF EAST ASIA'S BILATERAL TRADE WITH WORLD PARTNERS

The model estimates bilateral trade (*TRADE*), which combines exports and imports, by the BEC group. The estimated results are summarized in Table 4.3. The coefficients on *GDPSUM* satisfy the hypothesis, for all

Table 4.2   Availability of BEC UN COMTRADE

	1995	1996	1997	1998	1999	2000	2001	2002	2003	2004	2005	2006
Australia	O		O	O	O	O	O	O	O	O	O	O
Brunei			O	O			O	O	O			O
Cambodia						O	O	O	O	O		
China	O			O	O	O	O	O	O	O	O	O
India	O		O	O	O	O	O	O	O	O	O	O
Indonesia	O		O	O	O	O	O	O	O	O	O	O
Japan	O			O	O	O	O	O	O	O	O	O
Korea				O	O	O	O	O	O	O	O	O
Malaysia	O	O		O	O	O	O	O	O	O	O	O
New Zealand	O			O	O	O	O	O	O	O	O	O
The Philippines		O	O	O	O	O	O	O	O	O	O	O
Singapore	O	O		O	O	O	O	O	O	O	O	O
Thailand	O	O	O	O	O	O	O	O	O	O	O	O
Vietnam			O	O	O	O	O	O	O	O	O	O

Source: Compiled by the author.

the goods, either intermediate or finished, that the elasticity of this sum is greater than 1, and is statistically significant at the 1 percent level. The results show that bilateral trade is sensitive to economic size between bilateral trade partners.

The coefficients on *GDPDIFSQ* show negative signs and are statistically significant at the 1 percent level for goods, as theoretically expected, of all the goods except transport equipment passenger cars (BE-51) and other transport equipment (BE-52). The negative sign shows that bilateral trade has an inverted-U-shaped relationship to differences in country economic size: when difference in economic size becomes large, bilateral trade between the countries increases. But when difference in economic size becomes too large, bilateral trade between the countries decreases.

The coefficients of *AB_SKILLDIF* (absolute per capita GDP gap in absolute terms between importing and exporting countries), which is a proxy for skill-level difference, show negative signs for all the goods, and are statistically significant at the 1 percent significance level except for semi-durable goods. That is, bilateral trade in the case of East Asia for interregional, that is, intraregional plus interregional trade, decreases as skill-level differences diverge. This suggests that similar forms of production are operated in multiple regions for intra- plus interregional trade for East Asia countries. Perhaps multinationals have established

Table 4.3   Estimated results of bilateral trade of 14 East Asian countries between 1998 and 2006

	Total goods	Industrial supplies nes processed	Capital goods	Parts and accessories for capital goods	Transport equipment passenger motor cars	Transport equipment other	Parts and accessories for transport equipment	Consumption goods nes, durable	Consumption goods nes, semi-durable	Consumption goods nes, non-durable
	BE-TOTAL	BE-22	BE-41	BE-42	BE-51	BE-52	BE-53	BE-61	BE-62	BE-63
ln $(GDPSUM)$	1.73***	1.72***	1.67***	1.69***	1.48***	1.29***	1.71***	1.65***	1.71***	1.59***
	(144.88)	(128.82)	(95.73)	(99.27)	(45.14)	(41.03)	(79.59)	(84.79)	(101.27)	(87.21)
ln $(GDPDIFSQ)$	−0.02***	−0.05***	−0.05***	−0.05***	0.01	0.00	−0.06***	−0.05***	−0.03***	0.05***
	(−11.32)	(−22.35)	(−17.54)	(−18.57)	(0.56)	(0.36)	(−12.13)	(−14.30)	(−9.21)	(7.74)
ln (AB_SKDIFF)	−0.18***	−0.16***	−0.13***	−0.14***	−0.59***	−0.20***	−0.22***	−0.26***	−0.08***	−0.88***
	(−8.66)	(−6.54)	(−4.03)	(−4.65)	(−9.96)	(−3.74)	(−5.45)	(−7.65)	(−2.55)	(−15.58)
ln $(DIST)$	−2.49***	−2.44***	−2.26***	−2.37***	−1.92***	−1.81***	−2.61***	−2.57***	−2.64***	−2.47***
	(−45.49)	(−43.41)	(−32.22)	(−33.06)	(−15.67)	(−17.21)	(−33.75)	(−32.93)	(−38.05)	(−36.02)
CONTIG	1.17***	1.48***	0.11	0.06	−1.63***	−0.33	−0.75***	−0.21	0.86***	0.22
	(5.11)	(6.08)	(0.34)	(0.17)	(−3.10)	(−0.87)	(−2.27)	(−0.72)	(2.93)	(0.69)
COMLANGUAGE	0.89***	1.29***	1.58***	1.83***	0.69***	1.74***	1.97***	1.69***	1.57***	1.15***
	(11.55)	(14.55)	(14.33)	(16.70)	(3.66)	(10.16)	(14.46)	(14.20)	(13.91)	(9.45)

Table 4.3 (continued)

	Total goods	Industrial supplies nes processed	Capital goods	Parts and accessories for capital goods	Transport equipment passenger motor cars	Transport equipment other	Parts and accessories for transport equipment	Consumption goods nes, durable	Consumption goods nes, semi-durable	Consumption goods nes, non-durable
	BE-TOTAL	BE-22	BE-41	BE-42	BE-51	BE-52	BE-53	BE-61	BE-62	BE-63
COLONY	2.58***	2.23***	3.13***	3.00***	1.62***	1.85***	2.32***	1.43***	2.12***	3.51***
	(8.25)	(6.55)	(9.27)	(8.25)	(4.06)	(4.84)	(6.79)	(4.70)	(6.85)	(10.73)
COST	−34.16***	−35.54***	−36.45***	−36.77***	−31.08***	−22.07***	−36.60***	−33.90***	−36.42***	−30.63***
	(−43.15)	(−42.43)	(−33.90)	(−34.15)	(−16.46)	(−12.64)	(−29.20)	(−27.66)	(−33.17)	(−27.76)
R^2·	0.5724	0.5908	0.5531	0.5503	0.408	0.3545	0.537	0.5388	0.5512	0.5312
Obs.	21372	16465	11416	12201	3094	4637	7531	8191	10898	10175

Notes:
Figures in parentheses are t-statistics; ***, ** and * show significance at the 1%, 5% and 10% levels, respectively.
nes = not elsewhere specified.

Source: UN COMTRADE, CEPII. GDP, and population are obtained from WDI-online database.

manufacturing and service activity bases in several strategic regions around the world, such as East Asia, the USA and Europe.

4.6 DETERMINANTS OF BILATERAL TRADE WITHIN EAST ASIA ASSOCIATED WITH SKILL DIFFERENCE

The model in the previous section showed the relationship between bilateral trade and skill-level difference with regard to both intra- and interregional cases in the whole world. The East Asia factory is characterized by vertical production operation (international fragmentation) within the region. So in order to see the relation between bilateral trade and skill-level difference for the case of intra-East Asia, the previous model needs to be modified as follows:

$$TRADE = \beta_0 + \beta_1 (GDPSUM) + \beta_2 (GDPDIFSQ) + \beta_3 (AB\_SKDIFF) + \beta_4 [(AB\_SKDIFF) \times (ASIA)] + \beta_5 (DIST) + \beta_6 (CONTIG) + \beta_7 (COMLANGUAGE) \beta_8 (COLONY) \quad (4.2)$$

where *ASIA* is an intra-East Asia dummy that is assigned the value of 1 for the 14 East Asian countries and 0 for other countries, and the term $(AB\_SKILLDIF) \times (ASIA)$ is the intersection term of absolute skill difference between importing and exporting countries and the East Asia dummy. The expected sign of the term AB_SKDIFF and the intersection term $(AB\_SKILLDIF) \times (ASIA)$ are negative and positive, respectively. This model specification makes it possible to identify the effect of skill-level difference on intra-East Asia trade.

Table 4.4 summarizes the estimated results of the model, which incorporates the intersection term of the East Asia dummy (*ASIA*) on skill difference. The coefficients on the third independent variable, $AB\_SKILLDIF$ (or absolute per capita GDP gap between importing and exporting countries), which is a proxy for skill-level difference, showed significantly negative signs. On the other hand, the coefficients of intersection terms of absolute skill difference and the East Asia dummy, the fourth independent variable of $(AB\_SKILLDIF) \times (ASIA)$, showed significantly positive signs for all goods, either intermediate or final, as shown in Table 4.4. Also, the absolute values of the positive coefficients on $(AB\_SKILLDIF) \times (ASIA)$ are all larger than those of the negative coefficients on $(AB\_SKILLDIF)$. For example, the coefficient on $(AB\_SKILLDIF) \times (ASIA)$ for total goods, 0.90, is larger than that on $(AB\_SKILLDIF)$, –0.24. Hence the net value of $(AB\_SKILLDIF)$ is 0.66 for total goods. The net value on absolute skill

Table 4.4   Estimated results of bilateral trade of 14 East Asian countries between 1998 and 2006

	BE-TOTAL	BE-22	BE-41	BE-42	BE-51	BE-52	BE-53	BE-61	BE-62	BE-63
	Total goods	Industrial supplies nes processed	Capital goods (except transport equipment)	Parts and accessories for capital goods (except transport equipment)	Transport equipment passenger motor cars	Transport equipment other	Parts and accessories for transport equipment	Consumption goods nes, durable	Consumption goods nes, semi-durable	Consumption goods nes, non-durable
ln (GDPSUM)	1.70***	1.70***	1.65***	1.67***	1.46***	1.28***	1.70***	1.63***	1.68***	1.59***
	(142.21)	(126.80)	(94.34)	(98.47)	(44.00)	(40.57)	(79.17)	(84.43)	(100.43)	(88.80)
ln (GDPDIFSQ)	−0.02***	−0.05***	−0.05***	−0.05***	0.00	0.00	−0.06***	−0.05***	−0.02***	−0.05***
	(−10.15)	(−21.17)	(−16.64)	(−17.62)	(0.45)	(0.68)	(−11.48)	(−13.29)	(−7.77)	(−16.46)
ln (AB_SKDIFF)	−0.24***	−0.23***	−0.23***	−0.25***	−0.73***	−0.32***	−0.33***	−0.40***	−0.19***	−0.06*
	(−11.22)	(−9.19)	(−7.25)	(−8.17)	(−12.11)	(−5.90)	(−8.22)	(−11.51)	(−6.28)	(−1.91)
ln (AB_SKDIF_ASLA)	0.90***	0.79***	1.11***	1.11***	0.88***	0.77***	0.82***	1.11***	1.12***	0.92***
	(17.02)	(13.51)	(16.99)	(17.03)	(9.63)	(10.13)	(12.49)	(17.09)	(18.30)	(15.21)
ln (DIST)	−2.17***	−2.14***	−1.75***	−1.84***	−1.34***	−1.33***	−2.20***	−2.00***	−2.10***	−2.02***
	(−37.41)	(−36.30)	(−23.82)	(−24.13)	(−9.97)	(−11.75)	(−26.16)	(−23.79)	(−28.31)	(−27.02)
CONTIG	1.36***	1.66***	0.48	0.48	−1.01*	0.11	−0.46***	0.22	1.27***	0.58
	(6.07)	(6.90)	(1.61)	(1.38)	(−1.95)	(0.29)	(−1.42)	(0.77)	(4.40)	(1.85)

COMLANGUAGE	0.88***	1.28***	1.57***	1.84***	0.68***	1.75***	1.97***	1.71***	1.58***	1.13***
	(11.33)	(14.48)	(14.36)	(17.15)	(3.63)	(10.23)	(14.67)	(14.52)	(14.15)	(9.20)
COLONY	2.78***	2.40***	3.40***	3.25***	1.93***	2.12***	2.57***	1.72***	2.43***	3.51***
	(8.66)	(6.91)	(10.09)	(9.09)	(5.02)	(5.59)	(7.55)	(5.72)	(7.82)	(11.35)
COnST	-36.03***	-37.47***	-39.84***	-40.68***	-35.03***	-25.86***	-39.49***	-38.05***	-40.16***	-35.85***
	(-45.23)	(-44.36)	(-36.98)	(-37.16)	(-17.91)	(-14.73)	(-30.93)	(-30.49)	(-36.23)	(-32.82)
R^2	0.5778	0.5961	0.5648	0.5614	0.4243	0.3679	0.5466	0.5575	0.5663	0.542
Obs.	21372	16465	11416	12201	3094	4637	7531	8191	10898	10175

Notes: As for Table 4.3.

Source: As for Table 4.3.

difference is positive for each item such as processed industrial supplies, parts and accessories for capital goods, parts and accessories for transport goods and consumption goods. These net positive values show that bilateral trade increases as skill-level differences diverge for intra-East Asia trade, and suggest that vertical production in terms of skill-level difference is prevalent in East Asia. The opposite signs on skill-level difference between intraregion and interregion provide some insights into the characteristics of East Asia as the world's factory. Skilled-labor-abundant countries produce skill-labor-intensive products and unskilled-labor-abundant countries produce unskilled-labor-intensive products in the case of intraregional trade for East Asia, while similar forms of production are operated in the case of intraregional trade for East Asia.

As for other independent variables, the first independent variable (*GDPSUM*) shows the expected positive sign, and to be greater than 1. Also, the second independent variable (*GDPDIFSQ*) is the square of the difference in country economic size between importing and exporting countries, showing the expected negative signs. This suggests that East Asia's bilateral trade has an inverted-U-shaped relationship to differences in country economic size. East Asia tends to increase bilateral trade with large economic size partners. But too much difference in economic size between bilateral trade partners leads to small bilateral trade.

The fifth independent variable, geographical distance (*DIST*), is expected to have a negative relationship with bilateral trade. The coefficients on *DIST* are negative and significant at the 1 percent level for all the goods. The coefficient on *DIST* is −2.17 for total goods. High coefficients on geographical distance mean that East Asia's bilateral trade is rather sensitive to geographical distance or transport costs, and tends to stay within the region. By good, high coefficients are observed for parts and accessories for transport equipment (−2.20) and processed industrial supplies (−2.14), and low coefficients are observed for other transport equipment (−1.33) and passenger transport equipment (−1.34).

The sixth independent variable, *CONTIG* (the two countries are contiguous), is positive and significant for total goods. By good, only processed industrial goods and semi-durable consumption goods are significant at the 1 percent level, while capital goods, part and accessories for capital goods, other transport goods, and durable consumption goods are not significant. The results don't prove that having a common border determines bilateral trade.

The seventh independent variable, *COMLANGUAGE* (the two countries share a common official language), and the eight-independent variable, *COLONY* (dummy variable indicating whether the two countries have had a colonial relationship), determine East Asia's bilateral trade for all the goods.

4.7 CONCLUSIONS

This chapter investigated the characteristics and determinants of trade patterns in East Asia. First, it was shown that East Asia is becoming the world's factory: East Asia's exports account for about 40 percent of world trade for parts and components, and for capital goods, and 30 percent for consumer goods. One of the prominent features of East Asia's trade is that intraregional trade ratios are increasing, to more than 50 percent for processed goods, and to 40 percent for parts and components, while the ratio remains at 20 percent for consumer goods. Looking at production operations, East Asia's factory has both characteristics of horizontal production operation (similar productions are operated in multiple countries), where similar skill-level countries produce similar product in terms of skill level, and vertical production operation (international fragmentation), where skilled-labor-abundant countries produce skilled-labor-intensive products and unskilled-labor-abundant countries produce unskilled-labor-intensive products.

The hypothesis that skilled-labor-abundant countries produce skilled-labor-intensive products and unskilled-labor-abundant countries produce unskilled-labor-intensive products was tested by using trade data to distinguish intermediate and final goods for East Asia's trade.

Surprisingly, the estimated parameters of skill-level difference (absolute gap of per capita GDP between importing and exporting countries) were significantly negative for intermediate goods and final goods in the case of intra- plus interregional trade for East Asia bilateral trade. This result suggests that similar skill-level countries produce similar skilled-labor-intensive products in the case of intra- plus interregional bilateral trade. On the other hand, the intersection term between skill-level difference and the East Asia dummy was significantly positive for all the goods in the case of intraregional trade for East Asia's bilateral trade. Its absolute values of positive coefficients for intraregional trade are larger than those of negative ones for intra- plus interregional trade, and thus the net effect of skill-level difference on trade is positive for all the goods in the case of intraregional trade for East Asia. This suggests that in the case of intra-East Asia, skilled-labor-abundant countries produce skilled-labor-intensive products and unskilled-labor-abundant countries produce unskilled-labor-intensive products.

The opposite signs on skill-level differences between intraregional trade and interregional trade for East Asia can be interpreted to mean that in East Asia vertical productions are operated within region and, thereby, East Asia works just as a factory. On the other hand, similar production regions are located in the world such as East Asia, Europe and the USA.

Geographical distance has a negative effect on East Asia's bilateral trade. Also, common language positively affects East Asia's bilateral trade.

Considering the above factors, East Asia may increase intraregional trade, in particular, through vertical production operation, which takes advatanges of skill differences across countries.

NOTES

1. I thank Kazunobu Hayakawa, a colleague at IDE, for assistance with data compilation and helpful comments on the econometric analysis.
2. East Asia here is the so-called ASEAN+6, which includes India, Australia and New Zealand, addition to ASEAN, China, Japan and the Republic Korea. The process to create the ASEAN+6 started in 2005, and its regional cooperation is increasing in importance. Furthermore, the three countries are enhancing economic relations with ASEAN, such as ASEAN–India FTA and ASEAN–CER (Australia and New Zealand) FTA. In addition, trade is greatly expanding with other parts of East Asia: India is increasing trade in particular for parts and components with other East Asia countries, and Australia and New Zealand are increasing exporting primary goods to other East Asia countries and importing finished goods from them.
3. They used Thomas F. Rutherford's (1999) solver Mathematical Programming System for General Equilibrium (MPS/GE) and a subsystem of the program General Algebraic Modeling System (GAMS).

REFERENCES

Blonigen, Bruce A., Ronald B. Davies and Keith Head (2003), 'Estimating the knowledge–capital model of the multinational enterprise: comment', *The American Economic Review*, **93** (3), 980–94.

Carr, David L., James R. Markusen and Keith E. Maskus (2001), 'Estimating the knowledge–capital model of the multinational enterprise', *American Economic Review*, **91** (3), 693–708.

Helpman, Elhanan (1984), 'A simple theory of trade with multinational corporations', *Journal of Political Economy*, **92**, 451–71.

Hiratsuka, Daisuke (2006), 'Vertical intra-regional production networks in East Asia: case of the hard disk drive Industry in East Asia', in D. Hiratsuka (ed.), *East Asia's De Facto Economic Integration*, London: Palgrave Macmillan, ch. 6.

Markusen, James R. (1984), 'Multinationals, multi-plant economies, and the gains from trade', *Journal of International Economics*, **16**, 205–26.

Markusen, James R. (1997), 'Trade versus investment liberalization', NBER Working Paper No. 6231.

Markusen, James R. (2002), *Multinational Firms and the Theory of International Trade*, Cambridge, MA: MIT Press.

Markusen, James R. and Keith E. Maskus (2001), 'Multinational firms: reconciling theory and evidence', in Magnus Blomstrom and Linda S. Goldberg (eds), *Topics in Empirical International Economics: A Festschrift in Honor of Robert E. Lipsey*, Chicago, IL: University of Chicago Press for National Bureau of Economic Research, pp. 71–98.

Markusen, James R., Anthony J. Venables, Denise Eby-Konan and Kevin Honglin Zhang (1996), 'A unified treatment of horizontal direct investment, vertical direct investment, and the pattern of trade in goods and services', NBER Working Paper no. 5696.

Ministry of Economy, Trade and Industry, Japan (METI) (2007), *White Paper on International Economy and Trade 2007*, Japan: METI.

Research Institute of Economy, Trade and Industry (RIETI) (2007), RIETI International Trade Database (RIETI-TID) (http://rieti.imari.co.jp/), accessed 23 September 2009.

Rutherford, Thomas F. (1999), 'Applied general equilibrium modeling with MPSGE as a GAMS subsystem: an overview of the modeling framework and syntax', *Computational Economics*, **14** (1–2), 1–46.

5. Japan's parts and components exports and complementarity with foreign investment

Kazuhiko Yokota

5.1 INTRODUCTION

The rapid growth in the volume of world manufacturing trade over the past few decades has long been a source of bafflement among economists because declines in tariffs and transportation costs have been too modest to explain global trade expansion. We seem, however, to be approaching a consensus on the factors that have led to the expansion of world manufacturing trade.

Krugman (1995) argues that since World War II, there has been a general trend toward free trade, and he emphasizes the role of unilateral action toward free trade by the developing countries as a source of trade expansion. Feenstra (1998) emphasizes the importance of an increased convergence in economic size, vertical specialization and outsourcing.

Some empirical studies, meanwhile, have emphasized trade in parts and components as a cause of growth in world trade. Baier and Bergstrand (2001), for example, indicate that the major elements of trade expansion may come from increased vertical specialization and the outsourcing of intermediate production.[1] Taking a more direct approach, Hummels et al. (2001) show the importance of vertical specialization in accounting for the increase in trade. They note that vertical specialization accounted for 21 percent of the exports of ten selected OECD and four selected emerging countries during the latter half of the 1990s.

Theoretical contributions such as those by Bergoeing et al. (2004) and Yi (2003) also suggest vertical specialization as a (partial) solution to the puzzle posed by the increase in world trade. Bergoeing et al. (2004) note that trade data are double-counted because there is back-and-forth trade involving intermediate and final goods, while Yi (2003) shows that lower trade barriers propagate trade via vertical specialization.

Vertical specialization can be viewed as trade that is related to the operations of multinational enterprises (MNEs).[2] MNEs have exploited the relative skill- or capital-intensiveness of home and host countries by breaking the production process into many steps in the production of many goods, retaining the final assembly for their affiliates in the host country.[3]

Among the world's major regions, however, East Asia has displayed by far the fastest rate of growth in trade volume over the last 20 years. While world trade in final goods increased more than eight-fold from 1980 to 2005, the trade in final goods within the East Asian region grew more than 20-fold during the same period. More surprisingly, while trade in parts and components increased more than 13-fold worldwide from 1980 to 2005, the East Asian regional trade in parts and component grew more than 77-fold during the same 25 years. Parts and components trade accounts for the lion's share of the increase in total trade in East Asia, and Japan is the largest exporter of parts and components within the region, followed by China, Korea, and Taiwan.[4]

This, more than anything else, indicates the importance of MNE-related or foreign direct investment (FDI)-related trade, which often takes the form of vertical linkages between downstream affiliates and upstream exporters. In theoretical terms, there exist two kinds of relationship between exports and FDI: substitution and complementarity. Theoretically, there can be a substitutive relationship between exports and FDI in trade in final or consumption goods because of the horizontal nature of MNEs, while there can be a complementary relationship between exports and FDI in parts and components, indicating a vertical production network, or fragmentation.[5] Empirical studies such as those by Lipsey and Weiss (1981, 1984), Swenson (1997), Head and Ries (2001), and Pantulu and Poon (2003) identify a complementary relationship between exports and FDI, while Blonigen (2001) and Belderbos and Sleuwaegen (1998) identify a substitutive relationship between the two.

Lipsey and Weiss (1981, 1984) and Pantulu and Poon (2003) use aggregate trade data and the substitutive relationship is also found in product-level data (Blonigen, 2001; Belderbos and Sleuwaegen, 1998). The complementary nature of the results of the existing studies should be interpreted carefully, because in arriving at estimations, they use aggregate trade data that include both parts and components, and final goods in the samples. In such cases, it is difficult to reconcile the results with the idea of vertical specialization.

On the other hand, Head and Ries (2004) note that 'the success of the latter two studies in detecting substitution may arise from their focus on narrow product lines and because exports were restricted by government policy during the sample period'.[6] As evidence for the substitutive relationship between exports and FDI, Blonigen (2001) uses parts and components associated with the automobile industry and Belderbos and Sleuwaegen (1998) use parts and components related to the electronics industry. However, parts and components may be traded vertically according to the ideas of vertical specialization, or fragmentation. This consideration, again, makes it difficult to reconcile the results with the idea of vertical specialization.

The main purpose of this chapter is, hence, to test the relationship between exports and FDI, using a data set classified by production stages. Trade data are broken down into parts and components, and final (consumption) goods by production stages, and the data are directly applied to test the relationship between exports and FDI by industry. Needless to say, trade data for parts and components classified by production stage are more appropriate for testing the relationship between exports and FDI in reconciling the results with the idea of vertical specialization.

Apart from the academic interest inherent in the FDI–trade relationship, the question of complementarity or substitution leads to a genuine economic concern, namely, the hollowing-out problem. Most observers believe that FDI and trade are alternative modes in the exchange of goods and services, and that the hollowing-out problem in the manufacturing sector is worsening as more firms cut costs by moving their manufacturing facilities overseas. However, the situation depends solely on the relationship between exports and FDI. This, in substance, is an empirical problem.

This chapter is organized as follows: section 5.2 provides an overview of the trends in world parts and components trade and Japanese parts and components exports to the rest of East Asia. Section 5.3 describes the estimation strategy for analyzing the relationship between Japanese exports and FDI. Section 5.4 then discusses the data. Section 5.5 presents the estimated results and discusses them. The final section draws together some overall conclusions.

5.2   PARTS AND COMPONENTS TRADE IN EAST ASIA

As has been pointed out in the introduction, world trade in parts and components has grown rapidly. Figure 5.1 shows the trend in the parts and components trade in the world market from 1980 to 2005. For purposes of comparison, the figure shows trade in final goods as well as in parts and components. Final goods are represented by consumption goods.[7] The figure shows an upward trend in both types of goods over the 26-year

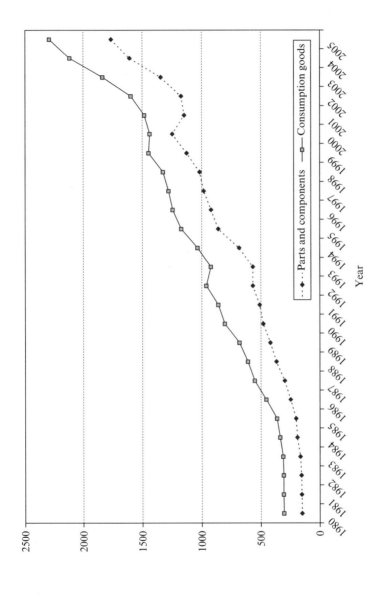

Source: RIETI database (http://rieti.imari.co.jp/).

Figure 5.1 World exports of parts and components, and of consumption goods, 1980–2005 (US$ billion)

period, and especially after the decline in 2000, which was caused by the reduction in demand for information technology (IT) related goods as well as the decline of oil prices. After 2000, trade in both consumption goods and in parts and components increased at an even faster pace than before. Notable findings are that the consumption goods have been larger than the parts and components trade over the observed period, although both have almost same upward trends. It is not possible to see clearly the different trends between consumption goods and parts and components trades. The figure simply shows that both types of goods have increased in the world market as globalization proceeds.

On the other hand, Figure 5.2 depicts the exports of parts and components and consumption goods from Japan to Asian countries. In this chapter, Asian countries include China, Hong Kong, India, Indonesia, Malaysia, the Philippines, Korea, Singapore, Taiwan, Thailand, Brunei, Cambodia and Vietnam. The figure clearly shows that although the parts and components exports from Japan fluctuate over the observed period, they surpass the consumption goods exports from Japan after 1981. The reason for fluctuations in parts and components exports are mainly a slowdown of world demand in the mid 1990s, the Asian crisis in 1997, the reduction in demand for IT-related products in 2001 and so on. Exports of Japanese parts and components to Asian countries were US$3.8 billion, while those of consumption goods totaled US$4.0 billion in 1980. However, exports of Japanese parts and components exceeded those of consumption goods in 1981 and the gap between the two increased.

It should be noted that although consumption goods exports grow at a relatively slow pace, they continue to increase the volume of consumption goods exports, with some declines in 1998 and 2001. Total exports of Japanese parts and components, and consumption goods, therefore, have basically an upward trend from 1980 to 2005.

5.3   ESTIMATION STRATEGY

As indicated in the introduction, there are two types of relationship between exports and foreign production: substitution and complementarity. Theoretically, there are three possible cases in which a home country can provide final goods to a foreign country: by exports, by substitutive (horizontal) FDI, and by complementary (vertical) FDI. Figure 5.3 shows diagrammatically the four configurations in which an upstream firm produces parts and components for a downstream firm that produces final goods for the market.

The top-left section of Figure 5.3 shows the case where an upstream firm

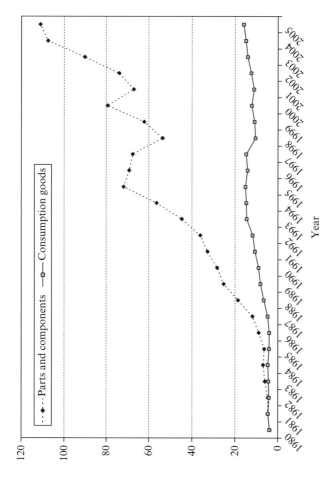

Note: Asia includes China, Hong Kong, India, Indonesia, Malaysia, the Philippines, Korea, Singapore, Taiwan, Thailand, Brunei, Cambodia and Vietnam.

Source: As for Figure 5.1.

Figure 5.2   Parts and components, and consumption goods exports from Japan to the rest of Asia, 1980–2005 (US$ billion)

I. Substitution effect

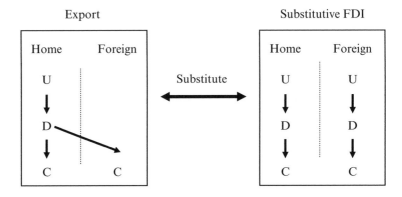

II. Complementarity effect

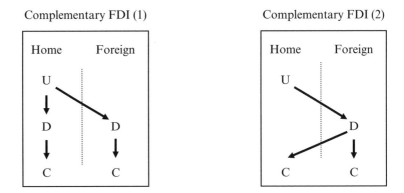

Note: U, D and C indicate upstream firm, downstream firm and consumers, respectively.

Source: Author's representation, modified from Head and Ries (2004), Table 7.

Figure 5.3   Typology of the relationship between exports and FDI

in the home country provides parts and components goods to the down-stream firm and the downstream firm provides final goods to the home market and exports to foreign markets. On the other hand, the top-right section of Figure 5.3 represents the case of FDI where a firm invests in a foreign country and builds both upstream and downstream production facilities. In this case, there is no trade between the home and foreign countries. In other words, it represents a case of substitution between exports and FDI. In this substitute configuration, goods exported from the home to foreign countries seem to be mainly final goods. There is no vertical production relationship for final (consumption) goods production.

The bottom-left and bottom-right configurations in Figure 5.3 show complementary cases between exports and FDI. While the bottom-left section shows a case in which a firm invests in and builds a downstream factory in a foreign country, the bottom-right section shows one in which a firm moves the downstream process into a foreign country completely and a downstream firm provides the final goods both to the home and foreign markets. These two cases represent the complementary configuration between exports and FDI.[8] In this complementary configuration, goods exported from the home to foreign countries are mainly parts and components in the form of vertical linkages or fragmentation.

I analyze two possible relationships between exports and FDI, according to the above configurations. In the substitute case, it is plausible to assume that the majority of traded goods are final goods. However, final goods basically include consumption and capital goods. Capital goods can be exported for further production processing, which is similar to the parts and components goods trade. In this following analysis, I use consumption goods as a major component of final goods.

Following Lipsey and Weiss (1981, 1984) and Blonigen (2001), I include the market size of a host country as a determinant of exports from the home country. Following Amiti and Wakelin (2003), I also include trade costs in the right-hand side of the estimated equation. Hence the estimated equation in this chapter is as follows:

$$X_{jt} = \beta_0 GDP_{jt}{}^{\beta_1} \, Distance_{ij}{}^{\beta_2} \, FDI_{jt}{}^{\beta_3} \qquad (5.1)$$

where X_{jt} is Japanese exports to country j in year t. Japanese consumption exports and parts and components exports to country j are used for estimation. GDP_{jt} is the real GDP of country j in year t, which is a proxy for the market size of country j. $Distance_{ij}$ is the distance in kilometers between Japan and country j, which is a proxy for trade cost. FDI_{jt} is the number of Japanese affiliates in country j in year t, which is a proxy for cumulative FDI in that region. The number of Japanese affiliates in country j is the sum of existing firms and new entrants in year t. Instead of the number of Japanese affiliates, I also use the Japanese firms' employment figures for the proxy of cumulative FDI in country j in year t. However, these two versions of FDI variables are highly correlated (the correlation coefficient is 0.984) and both have almost the same results. Therefore I report only the results of the former case.

The estimated equation is a special version of the gravity equation that is widely used for accounting for the determinants of bilateral trade flows.

Equation (5.1) includes the GDP of country j and the distance between countries i and j as a proxy for trade costs that preserve the gravity equation's characteristics. The only difference between equation (5.1) and the gravity equation is that equation (5.1) incorporates only one exporting country, Japan, while the gravity equation usually includes multiple exporting countries.[9]

Therefore the same problems exist for estimating equation (5.1) as in the gravity equation. Anderson and van Wincoop (2003) raise this: they claim that two important problems are due to the lack of a theoretical foundation for empirical gravity equations. First, estimation results are biased due to omitted variables. Second, comparative statics exercises are not correct. They develop a general equilibrium gravity model that includes a 'multilateral resistance term'.

Feenstra (2004, pp. 152–63) summarizes the treatment of these problems econometrically as follows: the first approach suggests introducing a price effect in the gravity equation (Baier and Bergstrand, 2001), and the second approach addresses using the estimated multilateral resistance term (Anderson and van Wincoop, 2003). The last approach, which I use in this chapter, is to use a fixed effect to account for unobserved heterogeneity among countries. This, needless to say, requires panel data.

On the other hand, the omitted variable is one of the sources of endogeneity problems. Endogeneity bias has been a problem in estimating cross-country gravity equations. Endogeneity bias occurs when any independent variables are correlated with an error term, which is usually assumed to be iid (independent and identically distributed). In this case, the ordinary least squares (OLS) method yields biased and inconsistent coefficients estimates. As Baier and Bergstrand (2007) suggest, in the course of a discussion of gravity estimation, the most important sources of endogeneity bias are the omission of variables and selection biases.

I estimate equation (5.1) in several ways: First is the basic estimation that includes market size, trade cost, and FDI variables as well as a year dummy to explain unobserved common time variations. Taking the logarithmic formulation of equation (5.1), I estimate the following equation with the year dummy:

$$\ln X_{jt} = \beta_0 + \beta_t + \beta_1 \ln GDP_{jt} + \beta_2 \ln Distance_{ij} + \beta_3 \ln FDI_{jt} + \varepsilon_{jt} \tag{5.2}$$

where β_t is the time effect for explaining unobserved time variations. ε_{jt} is assumed to be a log-normally distributed error term.

Equation (5.2), however, does not include destination-specific fixed effects and therefore the coefficients reflect both within- and between-destination variations. Second is the equation with importer dummy variables in order to avoid the endogeneity problem (possibly caused by an omitted variable and selection biases). If the estimation does not include destination-specific fixed effects, the coefficients reflect both within- and between-destination variations. Hence omitted characteristics of destinations can generate positive bias (Head and Ries, 2004). I use a destination-specific fixed-effect model with the time dummy.[10] Hence equation (5.2) is rewritten as follows:

$$\ln X_{jt} = \beta_0 + \beta_t + \beta_1 \ln GDP_{jt} + \beta_2 \ln FDI_{jt} + \gamma \delta_j + \varepsilon_{jt} \qquad (5.3)$$

where δ_j is the fixed effect to explain a country's heterogeneity. δ_j is an indicator variable that takes unity if country j is an importer, otherwise zero. It should be noted that trade cost on the right-hand side is dropped from equation (5.3) because the country dummy fully explains trade cost (distance, in this study) variation.

As noted by Baier and Bergstrand (2007), a simultaneity problem can also be a source of the endogeneity problem. Hence a third approach is to consider the possible treatment of simultaneity. Although the instrumental variable (IV) method is a better way of handling the simultaneity problem, as noted by Blonigen (2001), it is difficult to obtain an appropriate IV for FDI. Therefore, instead of using IV, the third estimation uses lagged independent variables in equation (5.3).

5.4 DATA

Trade flow data are available from the Research Institute of Economy, Trade and Industry (RIETI) database (http://rieti.imari.co.jp/). RIETI data cover 50 countries/regions, 13 industries, five production stages, and 26 years (1980–2005). The five production stages are: primary goods, processed goods, parts and components, capital goods and consumption goods. This study uses 14 Asian countries and analyzes 12 industries and two stages (parts and components, and consumption goods).

The 14 countries are China, Hong Kong, India, Indonesia, Japan, Malaysia, the Philippines, Korea, Singapore, Taiwan, Thailand, Brunei, Cambodia and Vietnam. The 12 industries are Foods; Textiles; Pulp, paper and wood; Chemicals; Oil and coal; Stone, clay, glass and concrete products; Iron and steel, nonferrous metals; General machinery; Electrical machinery;[11] Transportation equipment; Precision machinery; and Toys and miscellaneous goods.

RIETI data by production stages are obtained as follows: first, trade data are classified into 12 industries according to (2-digit) SITC revision 3. Then they are further classified into five production stages according to the UN's broad economic categories (BEC). Correspondence of each production stage to BEC is as follows:

Primary goods: 111, 21, 31
Processed goods: 121, 22, 32
Parts and components: 42, 53
Capital goods: 41, 521
Consumption goods: 112, 122, 51, 522, 61, 62, 63

These nominal export data are deflated by an exporter's GDP deflator. The number of foreign affiliates and the number of employees in foreign affiliates in East Asia are obtained from Toyo Keizai Inc. (2006). The GDP, GDP deflators and population for each country for each year are from the International Monetary Fund (various dates). Distance data come from Mayer and Zignago (2006).

5.5   RESULTS AND DISCUSSION

Tables 5.1 and 5.2 list the results of the estimation of equation (5.1). Table 5.1 summarizes the results of the case of consumption goods exports from Japan to country *j*. According to the upper panel in Figure 5.3, it is expected that the coefficient for FDI will be negative. In other words, the substitute relationship between exports and FDI is theoretically expected.

Looking at the coefficients for the log of GDP, coefficients are positive for eight industries,[12] although three of them are statistically significant, indicating that importer's market size matters for exports from Japan. The coefficients for the log of distance between Japan and country *j* are negative and statistically significant for all industries except for transportation machinery. Negative coefficients for distance are consistent with the theoretical prediction.

The coefficients for the log of FDI show a strong positive relationship between Japanese FDI and Japanese exports to country *j* in which nine of the ten industries have significant *t*-statistics at a 95 percent confidence level. This shows that there is a strong complementary relationship between exports and FDI in the sample of consumption goods.

However, judging from the low adjusted R^2 values in all estimations, there is a possibility that variable biases have been omitted. As Blonigen (2001) has suggested, endogeneity is likely to bias the estimates towards finding complementarity rather than substitution.

Table 5.1 Estimation results for consumption goods exports

	(1) Foods	(2) Textiles	(3) Pulp, paper, wood	(4) Chemicals	(5) Stone, glass and concrete products	(6) Iron and steel	(7) General machinery	(8) Trans. machinery	(9) Precision	(10) Toys and others
ln GDP_{jt}	−0.095	0.165	0.521	0.398	0.082	0.164	0.055	−0.144	0.191	0.144
	(0.120)	(0.103)	(0.073)***	(0.077)***	(0.110)	(0.087)*	(0.058)	(0.103)	(0.129)	(0.092)
ln $Distance_{ij}$	−2.018	−2.133	−0.482	−0.617	−1.368	−0.886	−0.504	0.196	−0.950	−1.272
	(0.227)***	(0.200)***	(0.111)***	(0.149)***	(0.157)***	(0.140)***	(0.131)***	(0.267)	(0.190)***	(0.160)***
ln FDI_{jt}	0.295	0.263	0.126	0.401	0.098	0.272	0.113	0.051	0.151	0.188
	(0.052)***	(0.054)***	(0.034)***	(0.053)***	(0.041)**	(0.047)***	(0.047)**	(0.060)	(0.060)**	(0.039)***
Constant	33.417	31.636	14.801	16.801	24.965	20.665	19.859	19.02	21.184	25.795
	(2.772)***	(2.376)***	(1.501)***	(1.851)***	(2.131)***	(1.832)***	(1.447)***	(2.973)***	(2.580)***	(2.003)***
Observations	294	269	277	267	289	272	267	263	266	303
Adj. R^2	0.249	0.352	0.348	0.488	0.189	0.229	0.109	−0.02	0.067	0.198

Notes:
The dependent variable is the natural log of the real consumption exports from Japan to country *j*.
Robust standard errors are in parentheses. * Significant at 10%; ** significant at 5%; *** significant at 1%.

Source: Based on Head and Ries (2004).

Table 5.2 Estimation results for parts and components trade

	(1)	(2)	(3)	(4)	(5)	(6)	(7)	(8)
	Textiles	Pulp, paper, wood	Iron and steel	General machinery	Electrical machinery	Trans. machinery	Precision	Toys and others
ln GDP_{jt}	0.759	0.295	0.680	0.617	0.442	0.701	0.903	0.298
	(0.122)***	(0.061)***	(0.089)***	(0.076)***	(0.091)***	(0.073)***	(0.100)***	(0.123)**
ln $Distance_{ij}$	−0.519	−0.226	−0.128	−0.133	−1.065	−0.033	−0.972	−0.683
	(0.146)***	(0.145)	(0.141)	(0.117)	(0.164)***	(0.121)	(0.136)***	(0.181)***
ln FDI_{jt}	0.100	0.051	0.311	0.272	0.427	0.169	0.087	0.271
	(0.041)**	(0.029)*	(0.043)***	(0.043)***	(0.068)***	(0.040)***	(0.042)**	(0.046)***
Constant	9.980	15.033	9.105	13.079	22.727	10.822	13.603	15.002
	(2.257)***	(1.665)***	(1.793)***	(1.610)***	(2.029)***	(1.559)***	(1.895)***	(2.538)***
Observations	266	284	284	267	272	269	272	265
Adj. R^2	0.461	0.217	0.488	0.536	0.448	0.501	0.601	0.280

Notes:
The dependent variable is the natural log of the real parts and components exports from Japan to country j.
Robust standard errors are in parentheses. * Significant at 10%; ** significant at 5%; *** significant at 1%.

Source: As for Table 5.1.

Next, as regards the results of the parts and components exports model, Table 5.2 reports estimation results on parts and components exports in eight industries. By the definition of the production process for the BEC code, some industries have no parts and components trade, such as foods, chemicals, and stone, glass and concrete products. As expected, the coefficients for the log of GDP are all positive and highly statistically significant. The estimated coefficients for the log of distance are all negative, which supports the idea that transport cost reduces trade, although the coefficients in some industries are not statistically significant.

All coefficients for the log of FDI are positive and statistically significant at at least the 90 percent confidence level. This supports the complementarity between exports and FDI, indicating the vertical specialization in parts and components trade shown in the Figure 5.3.

However, as in Table 5.1, there is the possibility of omitted variable biases, judging from the low adjusted R^2 values in all equations. Therefore I examined the relationship between exports and FDI, using a destination-specific fixed-effect model so as to mitigate the endogeneity problem.

Tables 5.3 and 5.4 show the estimation results of equation (5.2) on consumption, and parts and components exports using destination-specific fixed effects. Note that since destination-specific fixed effects explain the characteristics of distance between Japan and country j, the estimation excludes distance in equation (5.3).

Table 5.3 shows the estimation results of consumption goods exports. Judging from the high adjusted R^2 compared with the results in Table 5.1, omitted variable biases are considerably mitigated. Market size expressed by the destination's GDP shows a positive relationship, and is statistically significant on consumption goods exports, at a 95 percent confidence level at least, in eight of the ten industries.

The coefficients for the log of FDI are positive and significant in seven out of the ten industries. The number of industries with positive and significant estimates decreases from nine in Table 5.1 to seven in Table 5.3. A notable finding is that the size of the estimate is smaller for almost all of the industries in Table 5.3 than it is for those in Table 5.1. This finding indicates that although the relationship between consumption exports and FDI is complementary in some industries, such as chemicals, stone, glass, and concrete products, and toys and others, the magnitude of the positive relationship between exports and FDI is smaller than that in equation (5.1).

Table 5.4 summarizes the estimated relationship between exports and FDI for parts and components exports based on equation (5.2). Except for the pulp, paper, and wood industry, all estimated coefficients for the log of FDI are positive and highly statistically significant, indicating the

Table 5.3   Estimation results for consumption goods exports with country fixed dummy

	(1)	(2)	(3)	(4)	(5)	(6)	(7)	(8)	(9)	(10)
	Foods	Textiles	Pulp, paper, wood	Chemicals	Stone, glass and concrete products	Iron and steel	General machinery	Trans. machinery	Precision	Toys and others
ln GDP_{jt}	0.716	0.479	0.182	0.546	0.091	0.331	0.086	0.751	0.233	0.489
	(0.115)***	(0.125)***	(0.086)**	(0.089)***	(0.109)	(0.084)***	(0.097)	(0.149)***	(0.087)***	(0.065)***
ln FDI_{jt}	0.056	0.038	0.055	0.122	0.079	0.025	-0.002	0.061	0.060	0.055
	(0.024)**	(0.035)	(0.024)**	(0.025)***	(0.025)***	(0.021)	(0.028)	(0.030)**	(0.023)**	(0.016)***
Constant	8.016	12.465	15.302	10.771	13.533	11.482	16.046	9.139	12.298	11.415
	(1.640)***	(1.775)***	(1.192)***	(1.250)***	(1.486)***	(1.184)***	(1.349)***	(2.081)***	(1.296)***	(0.940)***
Observations	294	269	277	267	289	272	267	263	266	303
Adj. R^2	0.884	0.888	0.823	0.929	0.848	0.865	0.780	0.739	0.930	0.927

Notes:
The dependent variable is the natural log of the real consumption exports from Japan to country *j*.
All estimations include importer country fixed and time effects. However, coefficients on time/fixed effects are not reported. Robust standard errors are in parentheses. * Significant at 10%; ** significant at 5%; *** significant at 1%.

Source: As for Table 5.1.

Table 5.4 Estimation results for parts and components exports with country fixed dummy

	(1)	(2)	(3)	(4)	(5)	(6)	(7)	(8)
	Textiles	Pulp, paper, wood	Iron and steel	General machinery	Electrical machinery	Trans. machinery	Precision	Toys and others
ln GDP_{jt}	0.465	0.282	0.590	0.336	0.681	0.149	0.433	−0.246
	(0.085)***	(0.086)***	(0.090)***	(0.095)***	(0.115)***	(0.096)	(0.090)***	(0.199)
ln FDI_{jt}	0.066	0.023	0.080	0.079	0.109	0.080	0.077	0.151
	(0.022)***	(0.017)	(0.021)***	(0.022)***	(0.026)***	(0.023)***	(0.023)***	(0.048)***
Constant	8.823	13.056	8.559	15.872	11.445	17.445	11.516	17.511
	(1.180)***	(1.222)***	(1.255)***	(1.292)***	(1.598)***	(1.321)***	(1.277)***	(2.804)***
Observations	266	284	284	267	272	269	272	265
Adj. R^2	0.901	0.847	0.921	0.899	0.915	0.883	0.922	0.593

Notes:
The dependent variable is the natural log of the real parts and components exports from Japan to country j.
All estimations include importer country fixed and time effects. However, coefficients on time/fixed effects are not reported. Robust standard errors are in parentheses. * Significant at 10%; ** significant at 5%; *** significant at 1%.

Source: As for Table 5.1.

existence of a vertical production relationship. The adjusted R^2 is very high for every industry except for toys and others, suggesting that omitted variable biases are reduced compared with the results of Table 5.2. Correcting these unobserved importer's characteristics variations, I obtain smaller coefficients for the log of FDI than those in Table 5.2. For example, a 1 percent increase in the number of Japanese affiliates in country j raises exports from Japan to country j by 0.1 percent in electrical machinery, while it raises exports from Japan to country j by 0.07 percent in the textile industry. Even after the correction of the importing country's heterogeneity, there is still strong support for complementary effects between exports and FDI in the parts and components trade, which again suggests the vertical production linkages or fragmentation.

Tables 5.5 and 5.6 summarize the estimation results of the exercises where independent variables are taken as a one-year lag. As has been pointed out, although using the IV method is a good way to reduce the simultaneity problem, an appropriate IV method is very difficult to find (Head and Ries, 2004). Hence I use lagged independent variables on the right-hand side of equation (5.3) instead. Estimation includes time and destination fixed effects, as in the equation (5.2).

The estimation results of consumption goods exports with lagged independent variables are summarized in Table 5.5. In general, the number of significant estimates declines from Table 5.3, for both GDP and FDI. Estimated coefficients for the log of FDI are positive and significant for the textiles, chemicals, transportation machinery, and toy industries. In four out of the ten industries, coefficients for the log of FDI are positive and significant, a decline from the seven industries in Table 5.3. Again, there is no support for the existence of substitute effects between consumption goods exports and FDI. However, if endogeneity problems are treated carefully, spurious estimates with a statistical significance may disappear. Although, of course, this does not support substitution effects between consumption goods exports and FDI, it suggests that complementary effects between consumption exports and FDI in some industries might be spurious.

On the other hand, Table 5.6 shows the estimation results of parts and component exports in which a complementary relationship between exports and FDI is expected, as discussed in section 5.3. Among the coefficients for the log of FDI, six out of eight are positive and significant, indicating a complementarity relationship between parts and components exports and FDI. Among eight industries, electrical machinery and iron and steel have relatively large coefficients compared with other industries. For example, a 1 percent increase in the number of Japanese affiliates in electrical machinery raises parts and components exports from Japan

Table 5.5 Estimation results for consumption goods exports with lagged independent variables

	(1)	(2)	(3)	(4)	(5)	(6)	(7)	(8)	(9)	(10)
	Foods	Textiles	Pulp, paper, wood	Chemicals	Stone, glass and concrete products	Iron and steel	General machinery	Trans. machinery	Precision	Toys and others
ln GDP_{jt-1}	0.471	0.053	0.05	0.407	-0.081	0.024	-0.017	0.585	0.05	0.032
	(0.133)***	(0.037)	(0.025)**	(0.093)***	(0.025)***	(0.093)**	(0.029)	(0.035)	(0.024)**	(0.019)*
ln FDI_{jt-1}	0.018	0.426	0.117	0.073	0.072	0.190	0.027	0.003	0.092	0.372
	(0.023)	(0.129)***	(0.096)	(0.022)***	(0.117)	(0.020)	(0.106)	(0.177)***	(0.088)	(0.079)***
Constant	12.149	12.863	16.55	13.36	16.202	13.597	17.159	11.877	14.667	13.272
	(1.893)***	(1.872)***	(1.360)***	(1.294)***	(1.624)***	(1.297)***	(1.510)***	(2.513)***	(1.259)***	(1.123)***
Observations	249	251	251	251	245	249	248	248	248	249
Adj. R^2	0.879	0.888	0.821	0.928	0.842	0.904	0.765	0.736	0.934	0.938

Notes:
The dependent variable is the natural log of the real consumption exports from Japan to country j.
All estimations include importer country fixed and time effects. However, coefficients on time/fixed effects are not reported. Robust standard errors are in parentheses. * Significant at 10%; ** significant at 5%; *** significant at 1%.

Source: As for Table 5.1.

Table 5.6　Estimation results for parts and components exports with lagged independent variables

	(1)	(2)	(3)	(4)	(5)	(6)	(7)	(8)
	Textiles	Pulp, paper, wood	Iron and steel	General machinery	Electrical machinery	Trans. machinery	Precision	Toys and others
ln $GDP_{jt\text{-}1}$	0.368	−0.012	0.05	0.068	0.067	0.045	0.075	−0.118
	(0.084)***	(0.016)	(0.084)***	(0.084)***	(0.105)***	(0.020)**	(0.081)***	(0.194)
ln $FDI_{jt\text{-}1}$	0.030	0.182	0.471	0.237	0.573	0.096	0.343	0.151
	(0.022)	(0.078)**	(0.020)**	(0.023)***	(0.022)***	(0.096)	(0.022)***	(0.044)***
Constant	10.765	15.061	11.004	18.026	14.086	18.914	13.453	16.487
	(1.172)***	(1.084)***	(1.147)***	(1.178)***	(1.459)***	(1.370)***	(1.148)***	(2.671)***
Observations	244	251	248	251	251	251	248	240
Adj. R^2	0.902	0.854	0.924	0.906	0.926	0.883	0.926	0.592

Notes:
The dependent variable is the natural log of the real parts and components exports from Japan to country j.
All estimations include importer country fixed and time effects. However, coefficients on time/fixed effects are not reported. Robust standard errors are in parentheses. * Significant at 10%; ** significant at 5%; *** significant at 1%.

Source:　As for Table 5.1.

to country *j* by 0.57 percent, while a 1 percent increase in the number of Japanese affiliates in the textile industry raises parts and components exports from Japan to country *j* by only 0.03 percent. Next to electrical machinery, the iron and steel industry and precision industry have relatively large estimated coefficients for FDI, which are 0.471 and 0.343 respectively. These results seem to support, in general, the existence of a complementary relationship between parts and components exports and FDI, even after controlling for endogeneity problems in terms of both omitted variables and simultaneous biases.

5.6   CONCLUSION

In this chapter, I have estimated the complementary effects between Japanese parts and components exports and Japanese FDI in Asian countries by applying panel data methods. The main purpose of the study was to identify the relationship between Japanese FDI and the parts and components trade in this area. After controlling for country size, distance and endogeneity problems, the results show that the complementarity effect of FDI on parts and components exports is largest in the electrical machinery industry and that the size of the impact on electrical machinery is larger by 16-fold than that on the textile industry. This result was anticipated because the parts and components trade in electrical machinery in the world has grown more rapidly than that of final consumption goods, which has never happened in other industries. It implies the existence of vertical linkages between Japan's exports and Japan's FDI in Asian countries.

This chapter has also questioned the existence of substitution effects between consumption goods exports and FDI. The results of the analysis showed that the complementarity effect is more important than the substitution effect in four out of the ten selected industries, and that there is no clear evidence that exports and FDI are either substitute or complement related in six out of the ten industries. This finding suggests that FDI-unrelated final goods exports are so large compared with FDI-related final goods exports that the substitution effect cannot predominate over the complementarity effect.[13]

For many years, Japanese FDI has been playing an important role in promoting both parts and components manufacture and final goods production in many industries and in many regions, especially in East Asia and the USA. Many observers of this trend have argued that the hollowing-out problem in the manufacturing sector is worsening as more companies cut costs by moving their manufacturing facilities overseas. However, as my statistical analysis suggests, the data do not support the existence of a hollowing-out situation in the period between 1980 and 2005 in parts and components, or in cases of final goods exports. Japanese outward FDI may actually promote domestic production of parts and components for export, and this may result from a vertical linkage structure or fragmentation activities in Japanese firms. Furthermore, even in the relationship between consumption goods exports and FDI, the substitution effect cannot be detected in all of the industries covered in this analysis.

NOTES

1. Baier and Bergstrand (2001) conclude that more than two-thirds of world trade can be explained by real GDP growth, one-quarter by tariff rate reductions and preferential trade agreements, less than 10 percent by transport cost reduction, and none by GDP convergence.
2. See Markusen (2002), and Barba Navaretti and Venables (2004) for related literature on multinational enterprises and international trade.
3. This view is closely related to the concept of vertical multinationals. See Markusen (2002) and Barba Navaretti and Venables (2004) for more details.
4. Hayakawa (2007) explains that trade in intermediate goods in East Asia accounts for a large part of the increase in machinery parts and components trade in this area.
5. Empirical studies on fragmentation focusing on Asian trade structures are found in, for example, Kimura et al. (2007, 2008) and Ando and Kimura (2003).
6. Head and Ries (2004), p. 421.
7. Capital goods are usually classified into final goods too. However, capital goods can be used for further processing of goods. In this sense, capital goods can be viewed as processed goods. In this chapter, since I analyze the substitutive or complementary relationship between exports and FDI, the inclusion of capital goods in final goods may be biased toward a complementary relationship between FDI and exports. Hence I exclude capital goods from final goods and use only consumption goods to define final goods.
8. An upstream firm can move into a foreign country and provide parts and components to the home country. However, this case indicates complementarity between imports and FDI, which is excluded from my analysis.
9. The gravity equation often includes common language and border contiguous dummies on the right-hand side. However, because Japan is the only exportering country, both common language and border contiguous dummies all take zeros. Hence these dummy variables are not used when estimating equation (5.1).
10. For references on country fixed effects to remove endogeneity bias, see, for example, Eaton and Kortum (2002) and Melitz (2008).
11. Regarding electrical machinery industry, while RIETI trade data decompose the electrical machinery industry into electrical machinery and household electric appliances, Toyo Keizai Inc. (2006) provides FDI data in one category, that is, electrical machinery. Therefore I combined two electrical industries in the RIETI data into one electrical machinery industry so as to match two different datasets.
12. Electrical machinery has no consumption goods according to the BEC classification. Its final product is all classified as capital goods.
13. Head and Ries (2004) argue that complementary effects between consumption goods exports and FDI may be a statistical phenomenon in which unobserved variation in the determinants of consumption goods exports can lead to a positive correlation between exports and FDI.

REFERENCES

Amiti, Mary and Katharine Wakelin (2003), 'Investment liberalization and international trade', *Journal of International Economics*, **61**, 101–26.

Anderson, James E. and Eric van Wincoop (2003), 'Gravity with gravitas: a solution to the border puzzle', *American Economic Review*, **93**, 170–92.

Ando, Mitsuyo and Fukunari Kimura (2003), 'The formation of international production and distribution networks in East Asia', NBER Working Paper no. 10167.

Baier, Scott L. and Jeffrey H. Bergstrand (2001), 'The growth of world trade: tariffs, transport costs, and income similarity', *Journal of International Economics*, **53**, 1–27.

Baier, Scott L. and Jeffrey H. Bergstrand (2007), 'Do free trade agreements actually increase members' international trade?', *Journal of International Economics*, **71**, 72–95.

Barba Navaretti, Giorgio and Anthony J. Venables (2004), *Multinational Firms in the World Economy*, Princeton, NJ: Princeton University Press.

Belderbos, Rene and Leo Sleuwaegen (1998), 'Tariff jumping DFI and export substitution: Japanese electronics firms in Europe', *International Journal of Industrial Organization*, **16**, 601–38.

Bergoeing, Raphael, Timothy J. Kehoe, Vanessa Strauss-Khan and Kei-Mu Yi (2004), 'Why is manufacturing trade rising even as manufacturing output is falling', *American Economic Review*, **94** (2), 134–38.

Blonigen, Bruce A. (2001), 'In search of substitution between foreign production and exports', *Journal of International Economics*, **53**, 51–104.

Eaton, Jonathan and Samuel Kortum (2002), 'Technology, geography, and trade', *Econometrica*, **70**, 1741–80.

Feenstra, Robert C. (1998), 'Integration of trade and disintegration of production in the global economy', *Journal of Economic Perspectives*, **12** (4), 31–50.

Feenstra, Robert C. (2004), *Advanced International Trade: Theory and Evidence*, Princeton, NJ: Princeton University Press.

Hayakawa, Kazunobu (2007), 'Growth of intermediate goods trade in East Asia', *Pacific Economic Review*, **12** (4), 511–23.

Head, Keith and John Ries (2001), 'Overseas investment and firm exports', *Review of International Economics*, **9** (1), 108–22.

Head, Keith and John Ries (2004), 'Exporting and FDI as alternative strategies', *Oxford Review of Economic Policy*, **20** (3), 409–23.

Hummels, David, Jun Ishii and Kei-Mu Yi (2001), 'The nature and growth of vertical specialization in world trade', *Journal of International Economics*, **53**, 1–27.

International Monetary Fund (various dates), *International Financial Statistics*.

Kimura, Fukunari, Yuya Takahashi and Kazunobu Hayakawa (2007), 'Fragmentation and parts and components trade: comparison between East Asia and Europe', *North American Journal of Economics and Finance*, **18**, 23–40.

Kimura, Fukunari, Kazunobu Hayakawa and Zheng Ji (2008), 'Does international fragmentation occur in sectors other than machinery?' *Asian Economic Journal*, **22** (4), 343–58.

Krugman, Paul (1995), 'Growing world trade: causes and consequences', *Brookings Papers on Economic Activity*, no. 1, 327–77.

Lipsey, Robert E. and Merle Weiss (1981), 'Foreign production and exports in manufacturing industries', *The Review of Economics and Statistics*, **63** (4), 488–94.

Lipsey, Robert E. and Merle Weiss (1984), 'Foreign production and exports of individual firms', *The Review of Economics and Statistics*, **66** (2), 304–8.

Markusen, James R. (2002), *Multinational Firms and the Theory of International Trade*, Cambridge, MA: MIT Press.

Mayer, Thierry and Soledad Zignago (2006), 'Notes on CEPII's distance measures', http://www.cepii.fr/anglaisgraph/bdd/distances.htm.

Melitz, Jacques (2008), 'Language and foreign trade', *European Economic Review*, **52** (4), 667–99.

Pantulu, Jyothi and Jessie P.H. Poon (2003), 'Foreign direct investment and international trade: evidence from the US and Japan', *Journal of Economic Geography*, **3**, 241–59.

Swenson, D.L (1997), 'Explaining domestic content: evidence from Japanese and US automobile production in the United States', in Robert C. Feenstra (ed.), *Effects of US Trade Protection and Promotion Policies*. Chicago, IL: University of Chicago Press, pp. 33–53.

Toyo Keizai Inc. (2006), *Overseas Japanese Company Data*, CD-ROM.

Yi, Kei-Mu (2003), 'Can vertical specialization explain the growth of world trade?', *Journal of Political Economy*, **111**(1), 52–102.

6. Complex FDI in Japanese multinationals[1]

Kazunobu Hayakawa and Toshiyuki Matsuura

6.1 INTRODUCTION

Due to massive foreign direct investment (FDI) in East Asian countries since the Plaza Accord, Japanese multinational enterprises (MNEs) have set up multiple plants and affiliates in the region. In Asia,[2] Japanese MNEs in the information and communication devices industry have more than three manufacturing affiliates on average,[3] and the average number of such affiliates in Asia is rising. In particular, among large MNEs, the average number of affiliates increased from 3.87 to 4.17 between 1995 and 2001. Another remarkable fact is that this upward trend can be found only in Asia. What are the causes and consequences of setting up overseas affiliates?

In the FDI literature, many types of FDI classification have been proposed. Market-seeking, resource-seeking and efficiency-seeking FDIs are the traditional classification of FDI, which is based on the differences in MNEs' motives for FDI. Market-seeking FDI aims at securing and developing existing foreign markets and at gaining access to new markets. The aim of resource-seeking FDI is to secure access to raw materials required for production, while that of efficiency-seeking FDI is to exploit cheap primary factors, e.g. low wages, of the host country. Horizontal and vertical FDIs are other well-known classifications,[4] which focus on the MNEs' production structure. The former type of FDI (HFDI) duplicates a subset of their overall activities, and the latter type of FDI (VFDI) puts all of their production of a particular component part in a separate foreign plant. In addition, more specific types of FDI are also proposed. For example, export-platform FDI aims at serving 'third' markets with exports of final goods from the affiliate in the host country (Ekholm et al., 2007).[5]

The aim of this chapter is to classify the FDI types of each Japanese MNE and to discuss their motivation for investing and their impacts on performance at home. Specifically, we classify all Japanese MNEs according to their sales and procurement destinations, and match such classification with FDI types by MNEs' motive and production structure. The correspondence to classification according to motives enables us to clarify the causes of Japanese foreign investing, while their consequences are provided by matching with the classification according to production structures, as argued later. In classifying FDI types according to certain criteria, this chapter is related to studies by Feinberg and Keane (2006) and Matsuura and Hayakawa (2008). By using Bureau of Economic Analysis data on US MNEs, Feinberg and Keane (2006) find that 12 percent and 19 percent of the MNEs are pure HFDI and pure VFDI, respectively, and the rest of them adopt more complex integration strategies. Since we consider many more types of FDI, our chapter is an extension of such previous studies.

The rest of this chapter is organized as follows. In section 6.2, we provide the theoretical framework underlying the empirical analysis of this chapter. Explaining our empirical approach to differentiating statistically each FDI type, we report several results in section 6.3. In section 6.4, we draw some conclusions.

6.2   FOREIGN DIRECT INVESTMENT

We classify MNEs according to their main sales and procurement destinations. Three destinations are considered: local (host country), home (mother country), and third (countries other than host and mother countries). As shown in Table 6.1, according to the combination of the main sales destination and the main procurement destination, we have nine types of FDIs in total. In this section, we first provide the conditions for MNEs to conduct each type of FDI and then discuss the relationship of each type of FDI to existing FDI types in the literature. The impacts of each FDI type on performance at home are then discussed.

Before proceeding, several assumptions about MNEs are made. We assume increasing-return-to-scale technology and trade costs for shipping products between countries. If production processes can be fragmented,

Table 6.1   Patterns of sales and procurement destinations

Procure-ment	Sales		
	Local	Home	Third
Local	(I)	(IV)	(VII)
Home	(II)	(V)	(VIII)
Third	(III)	(VI)	(IX)

each process (e.g. downstream and upstream processes) also follows increasing-returns-to-scale production. For simplicity, we assume that the only primary factors are skilled and unskilled workers, and that the upstream process intensively uses skilled workers while the downstream process is unskilled worker intensive. The home country is assumed to have a comparative advantage in producing products that make more intensive use of skilled workers, i.e. upstream products.

6.2.1 Conditions for FDI Types

In this subsection, we discuss the determinants of each FDI type. In order to simplify the discussion, we consider separately the choice of the main sales destination and that of the main procurement destination. The choice between FDI and exporting is also considered.

In general, the MNEs procure upstream products with lower prices. Their (c.i.f. – cost, insurance, freight) prices are a function of primary factor prices such as skilled workers' wages and trade costs between the host country and a procurement destination (relatively negligible in the case of local procurement). Thus the MNEs' main procurement destination is determined by the benefits accruing from vertical division of labor. For instance, local procurement is preferable to offshore procurement (i.e. home or third) if such benefits between host and home/third countries are trivial. That is, a smaller gap in factor prices and larger trade costs between them make firms choose local procurement. In sum, the crucial elements for the choice of the main procurement destination are each country's factor prices and its trade costs with the host country (intranational transport costs in the case of local procurement).

The main sales destination depends on market size adjusted by trade costs with the host country. The larger the trade costs between the host country and a sales destination, the smaller the sales from supplying firms' products to the destination. Thus firms choose a country with the largest trade-costs-adjusted market size as their main sales destination. For example, the third country is likely to be chosen if trade costs between the host country and the third country are low enough and the third country's market is large enough. In sum, the crucial elements for the choice of the main sales destination are each country's market size and its trade costs with the host country.

Although firms choose the best combination of the sales and procurement destinations once they decide to invest abroad (and given the location of other plants with the same parents), they have another choice. That is, firms might supply their products from the home country through exporting rather than from abroad by setting up overseas plants. Exporting saves the fixed costs of setting up production plants abroad, while FDI might save shipping costs to the main sales destination. Therefore they perform FDI if such fixed costs are low enough and the shipping costs between the home country and the main destination are high enough. In addition, since the large economies of scale are able to cover the fixed costs of setting up a new plant, firms are more likely to choose FDI if the host country's market potential is larger.

Consequently, firms choose their operation type with the highest gross profit among FDIs and exports, which depends crucially on their inputs' prices (procurement destination) and their supply (sales destination). As a result, key factors in the selection of the operation type are the gap in factor prices among countries including the home country, the trade costs among them, and their market sizes. The combination of these elements determines the pattern of firms' sales and procurement and thus their FDI type.

6.2.2   Correspondence with Existing FDI Types

As mentioned in section 6.1, many kinds of FDI classification have been proposed in the FDI literature. In this subsection, we match such FDI types with the FDI patterns shown in Table 6.1.

First of all, the FDI classification according to motives for investing is matched as follows. The FDI types of which a main sales destination is home, i.e. (I), (II) and (III), are obviously the market-seeking motive, i.e. market-seeking FDI. Host countries of such FDI types should have a large market. On the other hand, the other FDI types, i.e. (IV)–(IX), should provide cheap factor prices instead of large demand and thus demonstrate the efficiency-seeking motive, i.e. efficiency-seeking FDI. In addition, types (I), (IV) and (VII) might be aiming to exploit the host country's natural resources, so they are categorized as having a resource-seeking motive, i.e. resource-seeking FDI, which is not considered henceforth in this chapter.

Second, matching with the classification according to MNEs' production structures is relatively complicated. In FDI types (IV), (V) and (VI), overseas plants' exports to the home country imply that their production processes are completely relocated from home. Thus those FDI types are categorized into VFDI, though not a part of production processes, but all their parts might be relocated in the case of types (IV) and (VI) since overseas plants do not procure their components from the home country. In addition, types (II) and (VIII) are also primarily the vertical type of FDI. Overseas plants in these types import their components from home, and sell their products according to market sizes adjusted by trade costs with the host country. On the other hand, the FDI types primarily fall into

HFDI if foreign plants are not related to home in terms of both sales and procurement. That is, the MNEs with the sales and procurement patterns of (I), (III), (VII) and (IX) are basically categorized into HFDI.

Last, it is worth noting that these matchings are not perfect. First, the correspondence with the classification according to motives should be taken as matching with the *main* motive for investing. Although the main aim of types (I), (II) and (III) is to get access to the local market, the MNEs categorized into such types might also intend to exploit simultaneously low-priced production factors in the host country. For example, since China has both plenty of cheap unskilled workers and a vast market, some Japanese FDIs to China may have not only market-seeking but also efficiency-seeking motives. Second, type (IX) should be categorized into VFDI rather than HFDI if overseas plants of type (IX) engage in vertical division of labor among more than two countries. That is, they may import their components from other countries' VFDI plants with the same parents. This type of VFDI has been recently been called 'complex VFDI'.

6.2.3 Impacts on Performance at Home

In this subsection, we discuss the impacts of each FDI type on performance at home, focusing on the impacts on productivity, employment and production. In particular, such impacts are examined in the case that a firm changes its status from a non-investor to an investor of each FDI type. That is, this chapter does not investigate changes in status from one FDI type to another. In discussing such impacts according to our FDI types, it is useful to examine the impacts of HFDI and VFDI on performance at home. Thus we first explore the impacts of HFDI and VFDI separately.

HFDI changes the home plant's average cost. The quantity of production in the home plant unambiguously decreases because it stops producing goods designed for the host country.[6] This decrease obviously raises its average cost, so the home plant's productivity definitely decreases. However, there may be knowledge/technology spillover from the overseas plant to the home plant as pointed out in previous studies, e.g. Navaretti et al. (2006). If such spillover effects exist and the home plant enjoys a sufficient decrease in marginal cost, the average cost may decline. In sum, the impact of HFDI on the home plant's productivity depends on the existence and magnitude of knowledge/technology spillover from host countries. If such spillover works strongly, the home plant's productivity rises, although its production and employment decrease.

The impacts of VFDI are relatively complicated. VFDI affects the home upstream plant's average cost through two kinds of change in its production quantity. The first is a decrease in quantity because firms must pay for transporting upstream products from the home country to the host country. The other is an increase in the production quantity of upstream products because the reduction in total cost for primary production factors in the firm reduces the price of downstream products. This in turn increases their production quantity and thus also the production quantity of upstream products. Because firms perform VFDI if shipping costs are low enough and the saving in total cost for primary production factors is large enough, the net impact of the production quantity of upstream products becomes positive. As a result, the average cost of the home upstream plant decreases, and thus its productivity rises. If the upstream process is much more skilled worker intensive than the downstream process, the domestic employment of skilled workers will also experience a remarkable increase. Consequently, in the comparison of performance only in domestic-remaining production processes between pre-investing and post-investing, all performance measures rise.

These results of the impacts of FDI according to production structures can be directly applied to those of FDI based on our classification, by employing the correspondence between these two classifications. That is, FDI types (II), (IV), (V), (VI) and (VII) have similar kinds of impacts as VFDI, while the similar impacts of HFDI appear in FDI types (I), (III), (VII) and (IX). But there are two noteworthy points. First, FDI types (IV) and (VI) will not yield positive impacts on home production if all the production activities are relocated from home. Then, since the vertical division of labor is conducted between overseas production activities and home non-production activities, positive impacts at home appear in the non-production activities. Second, if type (IX) is categorized into the complex VFDI, its impacts are similar to those of VFDI.

6.3   EMPIRICAL ANALYSIS

This section examines each FDI type in terms of its empirical significance. Our data source is the longitudinal data set of 'Basic Survey of Overseas Business and Activities', which is a firm-level survey by the Ministry of Economy, Trade and Industry. The aim of this survey is to obtain basic information on the activities of overseas affiliates of Japanese firms.[7] The survey covers all Japanese firms that had affiliates abroad. The survey includes two versions. One is the Basic Survey, which includes more detailed questions and is conducted every three years. The other is the Trend Survey, which is an abbreviated version and is carried out between the Basic Surveys. Major information provided by this survey includes the year of establishment of affiliates, the breakdown of sales and purchases, employment, costs, and R&D and so forth. For this chapter, the most important items in the survey are from which country the affiliate purchases its inputs and to which country the affiliate sells its products. In the survey, 'local' (Local), 'Japan' (Home) and 'others' (Third) are available as destinations. We employ mainly the Basic Survey of 2001.

The FDI types to be explored in this section are based on the discussion in the previous one. The results of section 6.2 can be summarized as follows. From the motive and production structure points of view, we can group our nine FDI types: types (I) and (III) are market-seeking HFDI, type (II) is market-seeking VFDI, types (IV), (V), (VI) and (VIII) are efficiency-seeking VFDI, and types (VII) and (IX) are efficiency-seeking HFDI. We further modify this classification in terms of three points. First, based on the recent significance of complex VFDI in Japanese MNEs (Matsuura and Hayakawa, 2008), we categorize (IX) into VFDI rather than HFDI, so type (IX) is grouped into the efficiency-seeking VFDI. Second, in order to highlight the empirical significance of the traditional HFDI setting (local procurement and local sales), we identify two types of market-seeking HFDI, i.e. (I) and (III), separately. Third, type (IV), which is one form of efficiency-seeking VFDI, is independently identified because this type is qualitatively slightly different from the other types of efficiency-seeking VFDI. That is, while both sales and procurement destinations in the other types are not a host country, type (IV) procures locally.

Consequently, we identify the following six groups empirically: LLFDI (I), HLFDI (II), TLFDI (III), LHFDI (IV), LTFDI (VII) and EVFDI (V, VI, VIII, IX). EVFDI means efficiency-seeking VFDI. The term 'regime' in the other FDI types denotes the main procurement and sales destinations (Local, Home, or Third). Regimes are denoted by a two-letter code, with the first letter referring to the capital letter of the main procurement destination, and the second letter referring to the capital letter of the main sales destination. Our classification procedure is as follows:

1. Is the host country the largest sales destination of the affiliate? Go to (2) if yes, and go to (3) otherwise.
2. Which is the largest procurement region, the host country, Japan, or others? The affiliate is categorized into LLFDI in the case of the host country, HLFDI in the case of Japan, and TLFDI in the case of others.
3. Is the host country the largest procurement region? Go to (4) if yes, and the affiliate is categorized into EVFDI otherwise.

Table 6.2   Number of affiliates by region and sector in 2001

	N. America	Asia	Europe	Others
Textiles	6	195	9	14
Chemicals	88	303	77	17
Primary metals	52	188	8	9
Metals	19	87	7	7
General mach.	75	236	61	8
Electrical mach.	41	227	35	11
IT mach.	87	470	73	25
Transport equip.	174	340	77	41
Precision mach.	32	81	33	6
Others	130	402	59	37
Total	704	2529	439	175

4. Which is the largest sales destination, Japan or others? The affiliate is
    categorized into LHFDI in the case of Japan and LTFDI in the case
    of others.

Table 6.2 reports the number of affiliates by region and sector in 2001.
The regional definition is presented in the Appendix. The large number in
Asian affiliates is outstanding: most of the Japanese MNEs invest in Asian
countries rather than OECD countries. In particular, the IT machinery
sector has a relatively large number. In North America and Europe, on
the other hand, there are relatively many affiliates in the transport equipment sector.

Table 6.3 shows the share of each FDI type by sector in the world. There
are three key points. First, around half of the Japanese FDIs are categorized into market-seeking HFDI (35 percent + 6 percent = 41 percent), i.e.
types (I) and (III). Thus outward FDIs may have had negative impacts
on the Japanese economy unless the MNEs enjoy strong spillover benefits. Particularly in the transport equipment sector, half of them are categorized into LLFDI. That is, they enter a country with a large market,
produce their products completely within the host country, and sell to
the host country. Second, in the textile sector, not only LLFDI but also
LHFDI and EVFDI have relatively large shares. This suggests that there
are a large number of efficiency-seeking MNEs in that sector and at least
domestic-remaining activities enjoy some positive impacts from investing.
Third, in the precision machinery sector, HLFDI and EVFDI, both of
which are VFDI, have relatively large shares. Thus, upstream production
at home in that sector may also have received positive impacts.

Table 6.3   FDI type by sector in 2001: world (%)

	LLFDI	HLFDI	TLFDI	LHFDI	LTFDI	EVFDI
Textile	23	7	11	20	7	31
Chemicals	44	24	8	5	7	11
Primary metal	39	28	9	8	4	11
Metals	37	25	6	7	5	19
General mach.	34	35	5	7	5	14
Electrical mach.	31	26	6	5	8	23
IT mach.	20	27	7	7	7	31
Transport equip.	50	30	3	3	3	11
Precision mach.	17	33	8	10	7	25
Others	42	14	5	18	7	14
Total	35	24	6	9	6	19

Notes: EVFDI means efficiency-seeking VFDI. In the other FDI types, the first capital letter of their abbreviation indicates the capital letter of the main procurement destination (Local, Home, or Third), and the second capital letter stands for the main sales destination.

Table 6.4   FDI Type by sector in 2001: North America (%)

	LLFDI	HLFDI	TLFDI	LHFDI	LTFDI	EVFDI
Textile	83	17	0	0	0	0
Chemicals	61	28	1	0	7	2
Primary metal	65	17	2	4	4	8
Metals	53	37	5	0	0	5
General mach.	33	52	1	3	3	8
Electrical mach.	27	59	7	5	0	2
IT Mach.	30	46	13	3	3	3
Transport equip.	71	20	1	2	1	5
Precision mach.	28	47	13	6	6	0
Others	55	22	8	11	2	2
Total	53	32	5	4	3	4

Notes: As for Table 6.3.

Tables 6.4–6.8 report the share of each FDI type by sector and region. The shares in North America are reported in Table 6.4. The share of market-seeking FDI is again high. This is consistent with the fact that North America is the largest market in the world. The large share of market-seeking FDI is detected not only in the transport equipment sector but also in the other sectors. Particularly in the general, electrical, IT and precision machinery sectors, most of the affiliates are categorized into HLFDI. That is, the North American affiliates in those sectors purchase highly specialized machinery parts and components from Japan, assemble them into finished machinery products, and sell them to the host country. Thus upstream machinery activities at home will receive positive impacts from investing. In the other sectors, the shares of LLFDI are high, so FDI to North America may be harmful to the Japanese economy without receiving strong spillover benefits.

Table 6.5 shows the case of Europe. Due to the rise of the shares of EVFDI, those of market-seeking FDI have slightly declined, compared with the case of North America. That is, there exist a relatively large number of efficiency-seeking Japanese affiliates in Europe. But in the electrical, IT and precision machinery sectors, most of the market-seeking affiliates are categorized into HLFDI, as in North America. That is, by importing highly specialized machinery parts and components from Japan, European affiliates supply their products to host countries. Thus the MNEs' overseas activities in developed countries (Europe and North America) improve home performance at least in upstream machinery sectors. The source of the rise of EVFDI shares in Europe is its large share in the textile sector: more than half of the textile affiliates are categorized into EVFDI, which indicates that vertical division of labor has developed in the textile sector. Indeed, since our European sample includes not only Western but also East European countries, we

Table 6.5   FDI type by sector in 2001: Europe (%)

	LLFDI	HLFDI	TLFDI	LHFDI	LTFDI	EVFDI
Textile	11	11	22	0	0	56
Chemicals	26	16	16	1	17	25
Primary metal	13	25	13	0	25	25
Metals	14	29	29	0	14	14
General mach.	31	23	13	0	8	25
Electrical mach.	17	37	6	3	11	26
IT mach.	18	34	10	6	8	25
Transport equip.	40	21	3	1	12	23
Precision mach.	9	52	18	0	9	12
Others	31	20	9	9	17	15
Total	26	26	11	3	12	23

Notes: As for Table 6.3.

would expect to see the benefits of the vertical division of labor with East European countries.

Table 6.6 shows the results for ASEAN countries. Three points are worth noting. First, contrary to the previous tables, the share of market-seeking FDI is not so high. This is consistent with the fact that ASEAN countries have cheaper labor and thus act as production countries rather than market countries. Second, the shares of LHFDI and LTFDI are relatively high in the textile and precision machinery sectors. This indicates that ASEAN countries serve as export bases (assembling local inputs and then exporting) in those sectors for Japanese efficiency-seeking MNEs. Third, the shares of EVFDI are high in the electrical, IT and precision machinery sectors. This result is consistent with the well-known fact that Japanese MNEs have formed extensive international production networks in those sectors. As a result, a large number of VFDI firms imply some positive impacts on home performance in upstream machinery sectors.

The above third point will be an important finding for the recent new FDI theory. As mentioned in the introduction, Ekholm et al. (2007) propose three kinds of export-platform FDI: third-country export-platform, global export-platform, and home export-platform. Third-country export-platform FDI refers to production solely for export to third countries, global export-platform FDI for balanced exports to both parent and third countries, and home-country export-platform FDI for exports only back to the parent. Since their model *assumes* that overseas affiliates always import components from the home country, these kinds

Table 6.6   FDI type by sector in 2001: ASEAN (%)

	LLFDI	HLFDI	TLFDI	LHFDI	LTFDI	EVFDI
Textile	14	0	12	22	20	29
Chemicals	44	17	13	8	9	9
Primary metal	33	32	12	6	4	11
Metals	28	30	8	8	5	23
General mach.	37	19	3	16	4	21
Electrical mach.	27	17	4	5	10	36
IT mach.	21	8	3	9	11	49
Transport equip.	36	31	2	7	5	19
Precision mach.	0	15	8	23	23	31
Others	35	9	4	21	9	22
Total	31	17	6	11	9	26

Notes: As for Table 6.3.

Table 6.7   FDI type by sector in 2001: NIEs (%)

	LLFDI	HLFDI	TLFDI	LHFDI	LTFDI	EVFDI
Textile	44	4	12	16	8	16
Chemicals	34	31	5	4	13	13
Primary metal	26	32	10	3	7	23
Metals	28	44	4	4	8	12
General mach.	35	27	2	13	4	19
Electrical mach.	33	23	2	3	12	26
IT mach.	17	25	10	8	10	30
Transport equip.	62	19	5	5	6	5
Precision mach.	16	42	0	16	2	23
Others	44	19	7	7	7	16
Total	33	26	6	7	8	19

Notes: As for Table 6.3.

Table 6.8   FDI type by sector in 2001: China (%)

	LLFDI	HLFDI	TLFDI	LHFDI	LTFDI	EVFDI
Textile	14	2	1	41	2	41
Chemicals	38	21	3	14	7	17
Primary metal	35	38	4	16	6	2
Metals	35	0	0	15	5	45
General mach.	41	27	0	7	3	22
Electrical mach.	38	22	3	9	6	23
IT mach.	12	20	5	8	5	51
Transport equip.	53	21	0	10	2	15
Precision mach.	17	26	0	17	0	39
Others	50	8	3	26	3	9
Total	33	17	2	18	4	26

Notes: As for Table 6.3.

of export-platform FDI correspond to either or both (V) and (VIII), i.e. a subset of EVFDI. Therefore the above third finding might indicate that active export-platform FDI is observed in such Japanese machinery FDI in ASEAN countries.

Tables 6.7 and 6.8 show the share of each FDI type in other East Asian countries. Table 6.7 is the case of NIEs (newly industrializing economies),

Table 6.9   *The combination of FDI type in fewer than three affiliates in 2001: world (%)*

	No	LLFDI	HLFDI	TLFDI	LHFDI	LTFDI	EVFDI
LLFDI	20	7					
HLFDI	12	4	2				
TLFDI	2	0	0	0			
LHFDI	12	1	1	0	2		
LTFDI	5	1	0	0	1	0	
EVFDI	16	2	3	0	1	2	2

Notes: The column 'No' indicates MNEs with only one affiliate. See also the notes to Table 6.3.

which is similar to that of Europe. On the other hand, Table 6.8 is the case of China; the results are qualitatively similar to those in ASEAN. However, it is worth noting that the share of LHFDI is high in China, compared even with that in ASEAN. In particular, its share in the textile sector is outstanding. This result indicates that China serves as an export base to Japan for Japanese textile MNEs, though this kind of efficiency-seeking FDI may not yield positive impacts on the performance of production activities at home.

Next, Table 6.9 reports the combination of FDI types in MNEs with fewer than three affiliates in the world in 2001. There are three points to note. First, most of them have only one affiliate. In particular, they are likely to have a single affiliate in either LLFDI or EVFDI. Second, the MNEs with just two affiliates usually have two LLFDI affiliates. They might set up an affiliate one by one in two large market regions, e.g. North America and Europe. Third, another combination with relatively large shares is that of EVFDI and HLFDI. An example of its possible pattern is shown in Figure 6.1. In this combination, Japan might be the export base of upstream products. MNEs locate their affiliate in Country A close to Japan and engage in vertical division of labor, and such an affiliate exports its products around Country A. At the same time, it locates another affiliate in Country B away from both Japan and Country A. The affiliate assembles the upstream products imported from Japan, and supplies its products to Country B.

Finally, we examine the changes of FDI types from 1995 to 2001. The results are reported in Tables 6.10–6.12. There are four noteworthy points. First, most of the affiliates do not experience changes of FDI type. Second, in North America, the changes from LTFDI/EVFDI to LLFDI have relatively high shares. Overall, this means that in North America, sales and procurement destinations tend to become local over time. Third, in

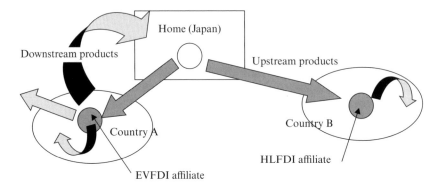

Figure 6.1   The combination of EVFDI and HLFDI

Table 6.10   Transition matrix of FDI type from 1995 to 2001: North America (%)

		2001						
		LLFDI	HLFDI	TLFDI	LHFDI	LTFDI	EVFDI	Total
	LLFDI	75	11	4	2	4	3	100
	HLFDI	23	69	5	0	0	3	100
1995	TLFDI	17	0	58	8	0	17	100
	LHFDI	22	11	0	67	0	0	100
	LTFDI	33	11	0	0	44	11	100
	EVFDI	45	27	0	9	0	18	100

Notes: Sample affiliates are restricted to those that existed in North America in both 1995 and 2001. The denominator is the total number of such affiliates in 2001, by FDI type in 1995. See also notes to Table 6.3.

Europe, HLFDI and TLFDI tend to turn out to be LLFDI, implying that localization is progressing among Japanese MNEs' procurement destinations in Europe. Fourth, in Asia, the changes from LHFDI/LTFDI to LLFDI have relatively large shares, indicating the localization of affiliates' sales destinations in Asia. Such localization of the sales destination might be due to the economic growth in Asia.

6.4   CONCLUDING REMARKS

This chapter classified FDI types of each Japanese MNE and discussed their motivation for investing and their impacts on performance at home.

Table 6.11   *Transition matrix of FDI type from 1995 to 2001: Europe (%)*

		2001						
		LLFDI	HLFDI	TLFDI	LHFDI	LTFDI	EVFDI	Total
	LLFDI	69	11	3	4	6	8	100
	HLFDI	26	49	7	3	3	11	100
1995	TLFDI	37	11	30	0	4	17	100
	LHFDI	10	2	1	57	8	21	100
	LTFDI	20	4	0	11	42	24	100
	EVFDI	9	9	2	15	9	57	100

Notes: Sample affiliates are restricted to those that exist in Europe in both 1995 and 2001. The denominator is a total number of such affiliates in 2001, by FDI type in 1995. See also notes to Table 6.3.

Table 6.12   *Transition matrix of FDI type from 1995 to 2001: Asia (%)*

		2001						
		LLFDI	HLFDI	TLFDI	LHFDI	LTFDI	EVFDI	Total
	LLFDI	59	17	0	0	3	21	100
	HLFDI	15	56	6	0	0	23	100
1995	TLFDI	13	21	38	0	8	21	100
	LHFDI	50	0	0	50	0	0	100
	LTFDI	31	8	0	0	46	15	100
	EVFDI	8	23	3	0	15	53	100

Notes: Sample affiliates are restricted to those that exist in Asia in both 1995 and 2001. The denominator is a total number of such affiliates in 2001, by FDI type in 1995. See also notes to Table 6.3.

Our main findings are as follows. First, most of the Japanese FDIs are based on the market-seeking motive and follow the horizontal production structure. Second, ASEAN countries serve as export bases to the world in the textile and precision machinery sectors, while China serves as an export base to Japan in the textile sector. In addition, in both ASEAN and China, there are a large number of efficiency-seeking VFDI firms in the electrical, IT and precision machinery sectors. Third, while both sales and procurement destinations tend to become local over time in North America, localization is progressing in procurement destinations in Europe and sales destinations in Asia.

NOTES

1. This chapter is the extended version of Matsuura et al. (2009).
2. In this chapter, East Asia means ASEAN countries plus China and NIEs, and Asia means East Asia plus South Asian countries such as India.
3. The figures in this paragraph are derived from Matsuura and Hayakawa (2008).
4. See, e.g. Navaretti and Venables (2004).
5. Recently, to explore the mechanics of setting up multiple affiliates, FDI theories have been reconstructed in the framework of a three-country, not the traditional two-country, setting (Yeaple, 2003; Grossman et al., 2006; Baltagi et al., 2007; Ekholm et al., 2007; Matsuura and Hayakawa, 2008).
6. As mentioned above, firms perform HFDI when shipping costs are high enough. Thus the HFDI increases the production quantity of products for the host country because firms no longer need to incur such high shipping costs.
7. An overseas affiliate of a Japanese firm is defined as follows: a foreign affiliate in which a Japanese firm has invested capital of 10 percent or more, a foreign affiliate in which a 'subsidiary' is funded more than 50 percent by a Japanese firm has invested capital of more than 50 percent, and a foreign affiliate in which a Japanese firm and a subsidiary funded more than 50 percent by a Japanese firm have invested capital of more than 50 percent.

REFERENCES

Baltagi, Badi H., Peter Egger and Michael Pfaffermayr (2007), 'Estimating models of complex FDI: are there third-country effects?', *Journal of Econometrics*, **140**, 260–81.

Ekholm, Karoline, Rikard Forslid and James Markusen (2007), 'Export-platform foreign direct investment', *Journal of the European Economic Association*, **5** (4), 776–95.

Feinberg, Susan and Michael Keane (2006), 'Accounting for the growth of MNC-based trade using a structural model of U.S. MNC', *American Economic Review*, **96** (5), 1515–58.

Grossman, Gene, Elhanan Helpman and Adam Szeidl (2006), 'Optimal integration strategies for the multinational firm', *Journal of International Economics*, **70**, 216–38.

Matsuura, Toshiyuki and Kazunobu Hayakawa (2008), 'Complex vertical FDI and firm heterogeneity', manuscript, Research Institute of Economy, Trade and Industry.

Matsuura, Toshiyuki, Kazunobu Hayakawa and Ayako Obashi (2009), 'Japanese firms' overseas activities and international division of labor', *Economy, Trade and Industry Statistics Studies*, **36** (4), 65–78.

Navaretti, Barba, Davide Castellani and Anne-Celia Disdier (2006), 'How does investing in cheap labour countries affect performance at home? France and Italy', CEPR Discussion Paper no. 5765.

Navaretti, Barba and Anthony J. Venables (2004), *Multinational Firms in the World Economy*, Princeton, NJ: Princeton University Press.

Yeaple, Stephen (2003), 'The complex integration strategies of multinationals and cross country dependencies in the structure of foreign direct investment', *Journal of International Economics*, **60** (2), 293–314.

APPENDIX

Table 6A.1   Country list

North America	Asia	Europe
Canada	Bangladesh	Austria
USA	China	Belgium
	Hong Kong, China	CIS
	India	Czech Rep.
	Indonesia	Denmark
	Korea, Rep.	Finland
	Malaysia	France
	Myanmar	Germany
	Pakistan	Hungary
	Philippines	Ireland
	Singapore	Italy
	Sri Lanka	Netherlands
	Taiwan	Poland
	Thailand	Portugal
	Vietnam	Romania
		Russian Federation
		Slovakia
		Spain
		Sweden
		Switzerland
		Turkey
		UK
		Yugoslavia

7. Production networks in East Asia: evidence from a survey of Japanese firms

Hiromichi Ozeki

7.1 INTRODUCTION

7.1.1 Background

A large amount of Japanese foreign direct investment (FDI) went to East Asia. After the Plaza Accord, many Japanese firms established manufacturing affiliates in ASEAN countries, as well as in China. The series of production processes is sliced and located in different countries to obtain cost advantages; the manufacturing process of parts and components, which is relatively capital intensive, remains in Japan, and the assembly process, which is relatively labor intensive, can be beneficially located in East Asian countries with low labor costs. Sometimes this is called production network or production fragmentation. Ando and Kimura (2005) pointed out that a sophisticated production network had been developed in East Asia where a complicated procurement link that includes third countries plays an important role. Japanese multinational firms have developed links among overseas affiliates and with their headquarters in Japan by trading in intermediate goods. The trade volume in parts and components expanded and its share of total trade increased in East Asia.

However, one question remains: will such a production network continue to expand in the future or shift to another mode? Some recent statistics show two different features. One is a rapid expansion in the total value of intermediary trade or international procurement. The other is an indication that Japanese manufacturing affiliates seem to shift their procurement activities to local purchases rather than cross-border purchases from Japan or other countries in Asia. The share of local procurement within host countries has increased while the share of procurement from Japan has decreased. Some changes appear to have occurred in affiliates' behavior, which might be caused by the affiliates themselves or their surrounding environments.

In this chapter, we examine whether the production network in East Asia is still expanding or changing its trends, by focusing on purchasing activities. If there is a change in the trend, we try to identify what causes such a change; in other words, what are the determinants of Japanese affiliates' purchasing activities. This helps us to consider the future development of the production network in East Asia.

7.1.2 Related Research

There is some literature on the production network or vertical specialization. Hummels et al. (2001) assessed the level of vertical specialization in OECD countries by means of an input–output table. They focused on the imported contents in exports as an index of vertical specialization. Hanson et al. (2005) examined the determinants of vertical specialization in US multinational firms. They assumed that the share of imported intermediate inputs from the home country (in this case, the USA) over total production costs indicated the level of vertical specialization and carried out a regression analysis based on the microdata of US affiliates in 1994. The results showed some interesting features: for instance, that low transportation costs, low wage levels of unskilled labor and a low corporate tax rate had a positive influence on vertical specialization.

With regard to Japanese firms, some studies have been done, although they focused on local purchasing of intermediate inputs rather than imports from the home country. Belderbos et al. (2001) examined determinants of local content for Japanese electronics affiliates by means of regression analysis based on microdata for 1992. The study showed that local content was influenced by some corporate characteristics such as ownership and length of operation, as well as country characteristics like the quality of infrastructure and the size of local supporting industries. Kiyota et al. (2008) reconsidered the determinants of the local procurement ratio based on affiliate-level panel data for 1994–2000. They found that the experience of the affiliates, which is measured by duration of operation, had a positive impact on local procurement for affiliates in Asia, but not on affiliates in developed countries. Ando and Kimura (2005) recalculated sales and purchases of Japanese multinationals based on microdata and found that the share of intermediate inputs from Japan, whose intra-firm ratio is high, decreased while that of local purchasing in the host country, whose intra-firm ratio is low, increased. One characteristic of Asia is that purchasing from third countries in the region, but not only in a bilateral relationship, plays an important role. Fukao and Ito (2006) analyzed the effects by means of progress in local procurement against corporate profitability.

Compared to previous literature, this chapter has two new aspects. The first is that it includes purchasing from third countries in consideration. The previous studies on determinants of procurement, which are based on microdata from multinational firms, concentrate on purchasing from the home country or a host country (Figure 7.1). There is a need to study purchasing from third countries because, especially in the case of Japanese affiliates located in Asia, intraregional purchasing plays an important role. This means that a comprehensive study, which deals with all purchasing origins, from home country, host country and third countries, may be required to further understand the production network in Asia.

The second consideration is the difference in purchasing behavior between intra-firm and inter-firm (arm's-length) transactions, an aspect that is not dealt with clearly in previous research. Although Hanson et al. (2005) conducted an additional analysis of intra-firm transactions of US affiliates, it was merely a robustness check of the total amount. No analysis was made for Japanese affiliates in this respect. So it seems that intra-firm and arm's-length purchasing activities need to be examined more closely, at least for Japanese affiliates.

In this chapter, we conduct a comprehensive study, which deals with all purchasing origins, from the home country, host country and third countries, paying attention to the difference between intra-firm and arm's-length transactions.

7.1.3   Structure of this Chapter

The next section explains the sources of data and provides a preview of Japanese overseas affiliates and their purchasing activities, based on aggregated statistics. In section 7.3, the determinants of purchase activities are examined by utilizing affiliate-level microdata. Section 7.4 provides some conclusions.

7.2   OVERVIEW OF JAPANESE AFFILIATES

7.2.1   Data Sources

We use both aggregated statistics and the firm-level microdata[1] of Kaigai Jigyou Katsudou Kihon Chousa (Basic Survey on Overseas Business Activities, hereinafter referred to as 'the survey') (METI, various issues). This is the survey on the business activities of overseas Japanese affiliates[2] as well as parent companies, which is conducted by the Japanese Ministry of Economy, Trade and Industry (METI). The survey is conducted annually, with a detailed survey containing additional questions

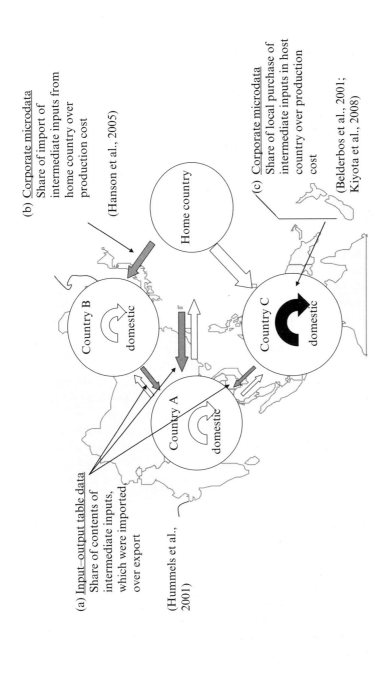

(b) Corporate microdata
Share of import of
intermediate inputs from
home country over
production cost

(Hanson et al., 2005)

(c) Corporate microdata
Share of local purchase of
intermediate inputs in host
country over production
cost

(Belderbos et al., 2001;
Kiyota et al., 2008)

Home country

Country B
domestic

Country C
domestic

Country A
domestic

(a) Input–output table data
Share of contents of
intermediate inputs,
which were imported
over export

(Hummels et al.,
2001)

Source: Compiled by the author.

Figure 7.1 Data and aspects of previous literature

127

being conducted every three years. The objective of the survey is to understand the actual conditions concerning the overseas business activities of Japanese firms and to serve as a basis for future policy planning.

The survey is very useful because it contains a wide range of essential information. Main survey items include brief information on the parent company (such as industrial classification, amount of capital, number of employees and sales figures) and more detailed information on individual affiliates (such as the host country, industrial classification, year of establishment, amount of capital, the Japanese investment ratio, number of employees, sales and purchasing figures, wage expenses, rental expenses, amount of depreciation, profits, R&D expenses and so on). This survey, in particular, is the only available source of information regarding sales and purchasing volumes with a regional breakdown by sales destinations and purchasing origins. Statistics on the main items are published, with a breakdown of the industrial sector and/or affiliate's location.

On the other hand, the survey also has certain weak points. Not all the companies responded to the survey because it is not mandatory, but voluntary. The latest response rate to the survey (conducted in July 2007) was 73.5 percent. This implies that some of the corporations that responded may be different and change in each research year. Furthermore, some of the columns in the questionnaire are not filled in by the respondents, and so some of the aggregated statistics are estimations based on assumptions. Therefore a recalculation based on panel data as well as screening of valid samples may be required for more detailed analysis.

Another point is that the volume of sales (and purchases) is not classified into intermediate goods and final goods. For example, products by an electric machinery manufacturer may be sold to consumers as final products or may be sold to another manufacturer as intermediate inputs. In this chapter, purchasing by a manufacturing affiliate is classified as intermediate inputs (like parts and components), although there are other possibilities.

7.2.2 Activities of Japanese Affiliates

We start with an overview of the activities of overseas Japanese affiliates, based on the statistics mentioned above.

Deployment
The total number of overseas Japanese affiliates in the world is 15 850, of which manufacturing affiliates amounted to 8048 in 2005 according to the survey and 67.7 percent (5449 companies out of 8048) of manufacturing affiliates are located in Asia, followed by North America (16.2 percent or 1306 companies) and Europe (10.9 percent or 877 companies). With

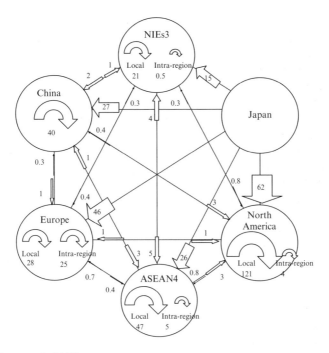

Note: Amounts in $ billion.

Source: METI (2005).

Figure 7.2 Purchases by Japanese manufacturing affiliates (2004)

regard to sales and purchases,[3] total sales and purchases are 185.0 and 146.8 trillion yen respectively, 87.4 and 64.8 trillion of which are due to manufacturing. Asia has a share of 41.4 percent and 42.9 percent of manufacturing sales and purchases, respectively. Those figures suggest that Asia is an important area for Japanese overseas production. In Asia, ASEAN countries and China are the main locations. That means that the column 'Asia' in the survey actually refers to East Asia, on which this chapter focuses. With regard to the industrial sector, electric machinery and transport machinery are two leading sectors.

Purchasing activities
Let us briefly consider the world flow of purchases by Japanese manufacturing affiliates (Figure 7.2). We use data from 2004, which contain a detailed breakdown for Asia (namely ASEAN4, NIEs3 and China).[4] Most Japanese overseas affiliates are located in Asia, North America

and Europe, as mentioned above. Some characteristics can be observed in purchasing activities: it is common that the major source of procurement is affiliates across regions purchasing from both host and home countries. However, there seem to be different tendencies with regard to purchasing from third countries. In North America, local purchases are dominant, followed by purchases from Japan; purchases from third countries are very limited. This implies that a series of production activities is conducted in two places: the home country and the host country. In Asia, local purchases and purchases from Japan are large, which means that host and home countries are big production bases, as in North America. However, the difference from North America is that purchases from third countries are also moderate in volume, compared to local purchases. We note that ASEAN4, NIEs3 and China are linked by procurement and that, also within ASEAN4, intermediate goods are procured among member countries. This suggests that a series of production activities involves three or more production locations across Asia, and so we should consider the third country factor when analyzing production networks in Asia.

Historical development

We now examine the historical development of purchasing origin, focusing on affiliates located in Asia. Figure 7.3 shows the long-term development in the value of corporate purchasing by Japanese manufacturing affiliates in Asia, with a regional breakdown by origin.[5,6,7] The Japanese manufacturing affiliates have increased their purchases from each region in terms of value, with a tentative decline due to the Asian financial crisis. In particular, the purchasing values from the host country increased tremendously, as well as purchases from Japan, and the purchasing from third countries in Asia also increased, although the value thereof is less than local purchases.

Next, we pay attention to the share of each origin. One important fact is that the share of imports from third countries in Asia increased until the mid-1990s (Figure 7.4). This means that the production network became more sophisticated, involving not only the home or host country, but also third countries. Another interesting fact is that the share of third countries remained almost at the same level after the mid-1990s and the share of local purchase increased after the late 1990s, while conversely the share of imports from Japan declined. The recent shares are: local 50 percent, Japan 30 percent, other countries in Asia 15 percent. It seems that the production network expanded by involving third countries until the mid-1990s and then started to shift from purchasing from Japan to local procurement. One interpretation is that the Asian financial crisis triggered the change in the affiliates' behavior, for example shrinking imports from

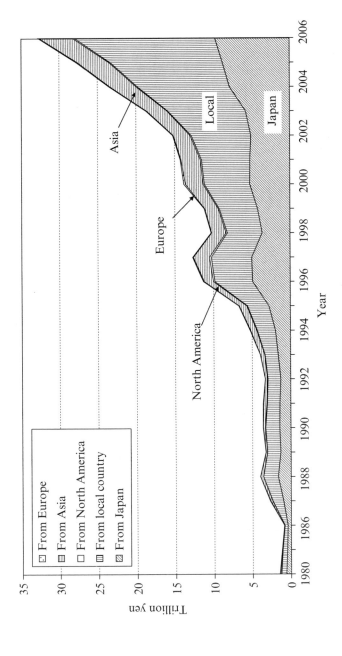

Note: Nominal basis.

Source: METI (various dates).

Figure 7.3 Purchases by Japanese manufacturing affiliates in Asia (value)

131

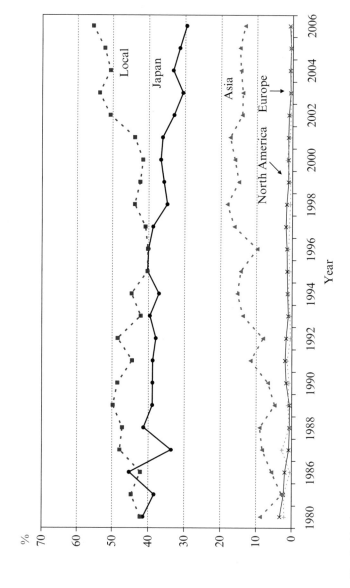

Note: Nominal basis.

Source: As for Figure 7.3.

Figure 7.4   Purchases by Japanese manufacturing affiliates in Asia (share)

Japan because of a rapid increase in the price of parts and components due to the exchange rate of the yen, and shifting to local purchases to avoid further exchange risks. However, we should bear in mind that there may be double counting and overvaluing of local purchases of intermediate goods among Japanese affiliates located in the same country.

Are such features the same across industrial sectors? Next, we check the differences among industrial sectors. If we focus on the two leading sectors, namely electric machinery and transport machinery,[8] which represent a large share of manufacturing purchases, we find a significant contrast in the regional structure of purchasing origins between them. In the case of electric machinery, the most striking feature is that the share of purchases from third countries has gradually increased, which suggests that the supply of parts and components has expanded across the countries in Asia (Figure 7.5). On the contrary, in the case of transport machinery, almost all the supply comes from Japan and the host country. In particular, the recent share of local purchase shows a drastic increase (Figure 7.6). What causes such a difference? Transportation costs and coordination/adjustment are thought to be involved. One possibility is that electric parts can be imported from neighboring countries because the transportation cost thereof is moderate due to their relatively small size and weight. On the other hand, automobile parts are bulky, heavy and expensive. It is logical that assemblers will purchase these from suppliers in host countries. Another possibility is that parts manufacturers are required to be located near the assembler for coordination and adjustment of manufacturing in the automobile industry, because the parts and components are specific rather than standardized for individual models. Also, procurement from suppliers in the host country is convenient for reducing the stocks of parts and components, as in a just-in-time system.

7.3   DETERMINANTS OF THE PRODUCTION NETWORK

7.3.1   Observations on Recalculated Statistics

Change according to the period of operation

We start with a consideration of the factors that affect purchasing behavior, especially factors concerning time flows. The most evident of these is the duration of the period of operation. How does the regional breakdown change according to time factors such as the period of operation? This relationship is examined by using microdata. Figure 7.7 shows the average purchasing share from each area and the number of years that

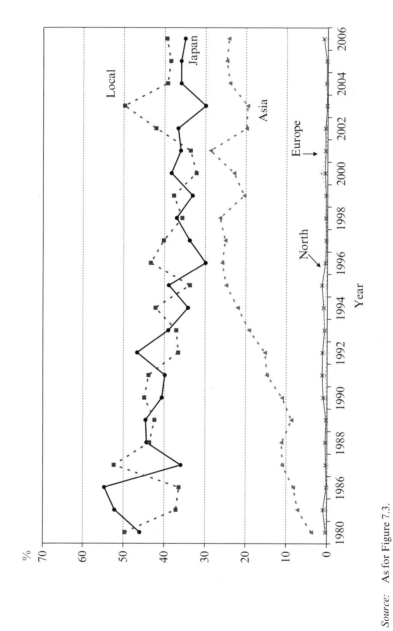

Source: As for Figure 7.3.

Figure 7.5 Purchase share of Japanese affiliates in Asia (electric machinery)

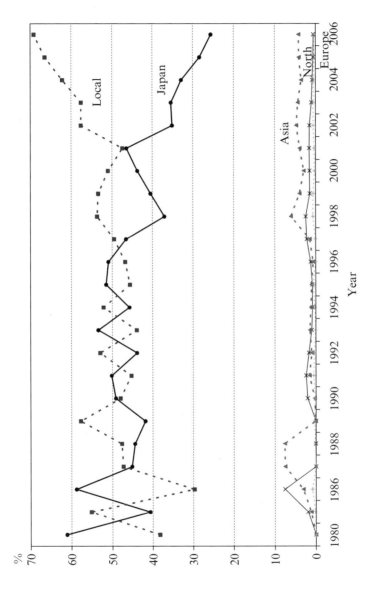

Source: As for Figure 7.3.

Figure 7.6 Purchase share of Japanese affiliates in Asia (transport equipment)

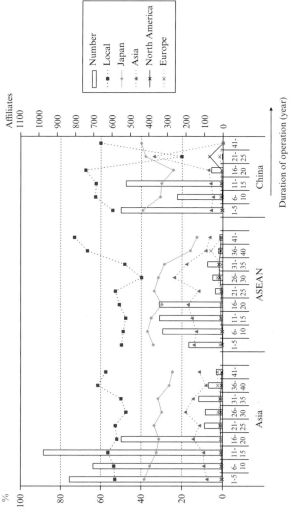

Notes:
1. Research conducted in 2006 (Asia: 3486, ASEAN: 1404, Chuna: 1425 affiliates).
2. Share is calculated on basis of corporate average.

Source: METI (2006).

Figure 7.7 Share of purchase origin and operation year of Japanese affiliates (manufacturing)

manufacturing affiliates have been operating in Asia, as at 2005. Affiliates located in ASEAN countries and those in China are calculated separately because their behavior may be different. The bar graph indicates the number of affiliates, which means that many affiliates were established after the Plaza Accord (operating period is less than 20 years). We can observe the share of purchases from Japan decreasing gradually with the duration of operation. On the contrary, the purchase share from third countries increased up to a certain stage (around 20 or 30 years) and then decreased after that. In the case of local purchase, the movement is not so clear across Asia. However, an upward trend is clear for affiliates in China, most of whom have been operating for less than 20 years.

Historical development by panel data
Next, we examine the development of purchasing origins by balanced panel data. The recalculation is based on the same manufacturing affiliates who responded to the questionnaire consistently and validly for the period 1995–2005. Although the number of samples is limited (239 in Asia), the responding affiliates were stable over the years and the figures should be reliable. Figure 7.8 shows that the share of local purchases increased together with a decreasing share of purchases from Japan. The basic trend is the same as the published and aggregated statistics. The movement is very clear and rapid, especially in China. It seems that the production network tends to shift to localization as the length of operation increases. Another possibility is that this change is caused by severity of global competition and not by period of operation. For further consideration, the effects by specific year can be controlled by regression analysis, which we attempt in the next section.

7.3.2 Empirical Analysis

There are many candidates as potential determinants of purchasing activities, including the duration of the period of operation, which we examined above. An empirical study has been conducted on the microdata of individual affiliates.

Model
Referring to Hanson et al. (2005) and Kiyota et al.(2008), we start with the cost function of a foreign affiliate i in industry j located in country c, as $C_{ijc}(\mathbf{p}_{ijc}, y_{ijc})$, where y_{ijc} represents the output of the affiliate and $\mathbf{p}_{ijc}$ is the vector of factor prices. We assume the cost function is in translog form. The output is produced by a set of factors n ($n \in N$). The second-order Taylor's series approximation in the log of cost function is:

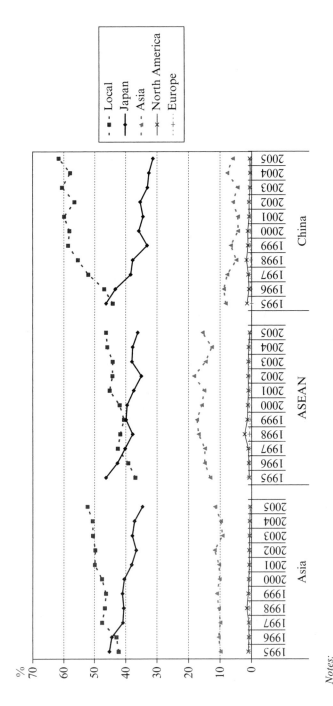

Notes:
1. Calculated on data of affiliates which responded to the questionnaire for all the years (Asia 239, ASEAN 109, China 52 affiliates).
2. Average of affiliates.

Source: METI (various dates).

Figure 7.8 Share of purchase origin by Japanese overseas affiliates (manufacturing)

$$\ln C_{ijc} = \ln \alpha_0 + \sum_{n \in N} \alpha_n \ln p_{ijc}^n + \frac{1}{2} \sum_{n \in N} \sum_{m \in N} \beta_{nm} \ln p_{ijc}^n p_{ijc}^m$$

$$+ \alpha_y \ln y_{ijc} + \frac{1}{2}\alpha_{yy}(\ln y_{ijc})^2 + \sum_{n \in N} \beta_{ny} \ln p_{ijc}^n \ln y_{ijc} \qquad (7.1)$$

By calculating the first derivative with respect to factor prices and employing Shephard's Lemma, the share of factors in the total cost is expressed as follows:

$$\frac{\partial \ln C_{ijc}}{\partial \ln p_{ijc}^n} = \frac{p_{ijc}^n}{C_{ijc}} \cdot \frac{\partial C_{ijc}}{\partial p_{ijc}^n} = \frac{p_{ijc}^n x_{ijc}^n}{C_{ijc}} = \alpha_n + \sum_{m \in N} \beta_{nm} \ln p_{ijc}^m + \beta_{my} \ln y_{ijc} \quad (7.2)$$

where

$$\sum_{n \in N} p_{ijc}^n x_{ijc}^n = C_{ijc}$$

We assume affiliate i uses five inputs: K (capital), L (labor), D (intermediate inputs from host country), J (intermediate inputs from home country, Japan) and R (intermediate inputs from third countries in the same region).[9] As mentioned above, the third country portion R is added because it plays an important role in Asia. The share of local purchases against cost is:

$$s_{ijc}^D = \beta_0 + \beta_{DL} \ln p_{ijc}^L + \beta_{DK} \ln p_{ijc}^K + \beta_{DD} \ln p_{ijc}^D + \beta_{DJ} \ln p_{ijc}^J$$
$$+ \beta_{DR} \ln p_{ijc}^R + \beta_{Dy} \ln y_{ijc} + \gamma Z_{ijc} + \mu_{ijc}^D \qquad (7.3)$$

where p_{ijc}^L, p_{ijc}^K, p_{ijc}^D, p_{ijc}^J, p_{ijc}^R are prices of L, K, D, J, R respectively. Z_{ijc} indicates the other control variables and μ_{ijc}^D is the error term. We can also get s_{ijc}^J and s_{ijc}^R in the same way. In this chapter, we estimate each of three material input shares ($s_{ijc}^D, s_{ijc}^J, s_{ijc}^R$) to compare their determinants. The meaning of each variable is outlined below.

Cost share
The cost shares are our dependent variable to be estimated. We estimate three different shares (s_{ijc}^D: share of intermediate inputs from host country, s_{ijc}^J: that from Japan, s_{ijc}^R: that from third countries in the same region) with the same set of independent variables to compare their determinants. The cost share of each input (s_{ijc}^D, s_{ijc}^J, s_{ijc}^R) is calculated as input value divided by total cost. The total cost is defined as the sum of all material input purchases, wages, interest, rental expenses and depreciation.

Prices of input factors

Equation (7.3) has five variables of input prices (prices of labor, capital, intermediate inputs from host country, that from Japan and that from third countries in the region: P^L_{ijc}, P^K_{ijc}, P^D_{ijc}, P^J_{ijc}, P^R_{ijc} respectively). The first of the five, the price of labor, can be calculated from the survey data. It is defined as the average wage of Japanese affiliates by the matrix of industry (14 sectors), host country (20 countries) and year (11 years). The average wage is deflated by each country's GDP deflator to get real terms.

The problem is obtaining the other input prices. In the previous work, Hanson et al. (2005) assumed the price of input from the USA (the home country) depending on the import tariff and transport costs, which can be calculated by using valuable US trade data by Feenstra (1996). I tried to calculate the trade cost as the rate dividing the c.i.f. (cost, insurance, freight) value of the importer by the f.o.b. (free on board) value of the exporter of each combination of countries, but the trial calculation produced some misleading results or discrepancies (sometimes, the rate was less than unity), so this method was abandoned. With regard to the price of capital and that of local input, it is also difficult to obtain information. They were submitted to the parent-industry dummy in Hanson et al. (2005) and the affiliate dummy in Kiyota et al. (2008). So, although there is the possibility of price change, we simplify the model and assume that the prices of capital and purchases from the host country, home country and third countries are affiliate-specific and fixed across years in this chapter.

Output

We use the sales value as the output of an affiliate. The values are deflated by each country's GDP deflator to get real terms, as in the case of the average wage.

Other variables

We tested some other variables, which included the capital amount per worker (*capwork*), the Japanese capital ratio over total investment (*jcapratio*), the number of total affiliates owned by the same parent company (*groupcom*), the duration of operation (*period*), the rate of R&D expenses against total sales (*rdrate*), the share of local sales against total sales of the affiliates (*sl*), and the number of Japanese affiliates of the same industrial sector in the same host country during the same year (*jcompany*). Some of these are included in the excellent work of Kiyota et al. (2008). Table 7.1 shows the list of variables.

Among these, the following three variables are the most important. The first is the period of operation because the change according to time factor is important when considering future development. Kiyota et al.

Table 7.1   List of variables

Variable	Explanation
lnP_L	log of price of labor (wage rate)
ln$Y$	log of output
capwork	log of capital per worker
jcapratio	Japanese capital ratio
groupcom	log of number of affiliates owned by same parent company (same group)
period	log of operation period
rdrate	ratio of R&D expenses to total sales
sl	share of local sales against total sales
sj	share of sale to Japan against total sales
sintra	share of sales to third country in the region against total sales
jcompany	log of number of Japanese companies in same industrial sector in host country
lmva	log of manufacturing value added in host country

Note: Nominal values are deflated by GDP deflator.

(2008) show that the period of operation has a positive impact on the local purchasing share in Asia. If so, what happens regarding purchases from the other origins, such as Japan or third countries in the region? Another interesting variable is the number of Japanese affiliates, which is a proxy for agglomeration of Japanese parts suppliers. The number of Japanese manufacturing affiliates has almost doubled during the last decade in Asia, which might affect purchasing activities. And the third is the share of the sales destination.

Data specification
We used the affiliate-level microdata from the Basic Survey on Overseas Business Activities, an outline of which was explained in the previous section. We also use country data from World Development Indicators (WDI) by the World Bank.

The target industry is manufacturing, which comprises 14 sectors, including electric machinery, transport machinery, general machinery, precision machinery, chemicals, iron and steel, textiles and so on. The target countries are the major countries in East Asia, North America and Europe: Indonesia, Malaysia, the Philippines, Singapore, Thailand, China, Korea, the USA, Canada, Austria, Denmark, Finland, France, Germany, Greece, Ireland, Italy, Spain, Sweden, Portugal and the UK. The sample period was 1995–2005.

We had to screen and drop some incomplete data. The conditions of eligibility are: (a) the affiliate was operating in the research year; (b) all required information was answered (capital, number of employees, Japanese investment ratio, wages, rentals, depreciation etc.); (c) data of purchases (sales) breakdown were correctly provided, which meant that the total amount equaled the sum of local purchase plus Japan plus Asia plus North America plus Europe plus others.

We also dropped some data from affiliates, which had only one eligible sample during the period, because we introduced an affiliate dummy.

As the result of data screening, the number of samples was reduced. The eligible sample numbers and the other basic statistics are presented in the Appendix.

7.3.3　Results

7.3.3.1　World manufacturing

We estimated world production (20 main countries in Asia, North America and Europe). We then estimated for Asia, to be compared with the results of the other regions. Table 7.2 shows the regression results for all manufacturing affiliates in the world. We checked the three variables regarding our primary interests first.

With regard to the variable period, its coefficients are significantly positive for a share of local purchases and significantly negative for those from Japan and third countries in the region. Kiyota et al. (2008) concluded that the experience of affiliates, measured by the duration of operation, has a positive impact on local procurement in Asia, and our result is consistent with this. The sales share of the local market, sl, has a positive impact on local purchases and a negative impact on both purchases from Japan as well as from third countries in the region. The last variable, *jcompany*, indicates the level of gathering of Japanese affiliates, in a sense an agglomeration of Japanese suppliers. Its effect is positive for local purchases and negative for purchases from Japan and third countries. Those three factors, *period*, *sl* and *jcompany*, give the same effects, positive for local purchases and negative not only for purchases from Japan, but also for the third country in the region. This suggests that such factors lead to a shift from vertical specialization or the production network, which is characterized by international procurement, to a local production linkage.

We look at the other variables one by one. The coefficients of $\ln P_L$ are significantly negative for all three purchase origins (local, Japanese and third country purchases). This is unexpected because the signs should be different between local purchases and purchases from Japan. However, it implies that the share of material input (regardless of origin) is smaller

Table 7.2   Estimation results

Independent variables	Dependent variables		
	Local purchase/ total cost	Purchase from Japan/total cost	Purchase from third country in the region/ total cost
$\ln P_L$	−0.005*	−0.010***	−0.003*
	(−1.93)	(−4.52)	(−1.89)
$\ln Y$	0.031***	0.026***	0.006***
	(12.16)	(11.49)	(4)
capwork	−0.005**	0.008***	0.001
	(−2.29)	(4)	(1.02)
jcapratio	−0.026**	0.028**	−0.012
	(−2.06)	(2.51)	(−1.46)
groupcom	0.007	−0.014***	0.005
	(1.12)	(−2.71)	(1.44)
period	**0.040***	**−0.054***	**−0.010***
	(4.68)	**(−7.18)**	**(−1.89)**
rdrate	0.021	−0.122***	0.050
	(0.41)	(−2.63)	(1.49)
sl	**0.120***	**−0.034***	**−0.086***
	(17.69)	**(−5.74)**	**(−19.68)**
jcompany	**0.029***	**−0.025***	**−0.007***
	(5.28)	**(−5.32)**	**(−1.9)**
Number of obs.	26824	26824	26824
R^2	0.7524	0.7953	0.7266

Notes:
1. Dummies for affiliates and years are used.
2. ***, ** and * indicate statistical significance at the 1%, 5% and 10% levels, respectively.
3. Figures in parentheses indicate *t*-statistics.

because the share of labor is larger due to a higher wage rate.[10] On the contrary, the coefficient of the next variable, $\ln Y$, is significantly positive for all three purchase origins. One interpretation is that the share of material input becomes larger because the shares of labor and capital become smaller as a result of economies of scale; ten times the number of semiconductors is needed for ten computers, but not necessarily ten times the amount of capital or number of workers.

The next variable, *capwork*, is a proxy for capital intensity. The result shows that the capital intensity of affiliates has a significantly negative impact on local purchases and a significantly positive impact on purchases from Japan. The variable *jcapratio* represents the strength of control by the Japanese parent company. Affiliates with stronger parent company control seem to have fewer local purchases and more purchases from Japan. The variable *groupcom* indicates the degree of overseas deployment of the parent company. More overseas deployment has a significantly negative impact on purchases from Japan. In the case of the next variable, *rdrate*, which indicates the intensity of R&D activities, R&D intensity of affiliates has a significantly negative impact on purchases from Japan.

Sales destination   We can already see that the sales share of the local market, *sl*, has a positive impact on local purchases. What about the sales share in other markets? Next, we examine the relationship between the sales destination and the purchase origin by replacing the independent variable *sl* (sales share of local market in total sales) with *sj* (sales share in Japan) or *sintra* (sales share of third countries in the region). Table 7.3 shows the results. The coefficient of *sj* is significantly positive for purchases from Japan, and that of sales to third countries in the region is also significantly positive for purchases from third countries in the region. The purchase origin is reflected by sales destination.

Agglomeration of parts suppliers   With regard to agglomeration, the number of Japanese companies has a positive effect on local purchases. What about companies other than Japan? Is it necessary for the companies to be Japanese? We replace the variable *jcompany* (number of Japanese affiliates) by another variable, *lmva* (value added by the manufacturing sector in the host country), which includes domestic as well as Japanese manufacturers). Table 7.4 shows that the coefficient of value added by local manufacturing is significantly positive. We cannot draw a firm conclusion;[11] however, there is a possibility that local manufacturers can also play an important role in the production network of Japanese companies.

Difference by industrial sectors   We have seen the estimates for total manufacturing. What about the difference among industrial sectors? Table 7.5 shows different results for two major sectors: electric and transport machinery. It is a little surprising that the coefficients of such factors as the period of operation, share of local sales and number of Japanese manufacturers are not very sensitive, and signs are even opposite in the case of transport machinery, which is contradictory to previous results for total manufacturing. The coefficient of the *period* for local purchase is not statistically significant, and the signs of *jcompany* may even be opposite, although they are not significant. On the other hand, the coefficients for

Table 7.3   Estimation results with alternative estimators of sales destination

Independent variables	Dependent variables			
	Purchase from Japan/ total cost		Purchase from third country in the region/ total cost	
$\ln P_L$	−0.010***	−0.010***	−0.003*	−0.004**
	(−4.52)	(−4.45)	(−1.89)	(−2.12)
$\ln Y$	0.026***	0.026***	0.006***	0.006***
	(11.49)	(11.77)	(4)	(3.59)
capwork	0.008***	0.007***	0.001	0.001
	(4)	(3.92)	(1.02)	(1.08)
jcapratio	0.028**	0.026**	−0.012	−0.010
	(2.51)	(2.4)	(−1.46)	(−1.26)
groupcom	−0.014***	−0.014***	0.005	0.005
	(−2.71)	(−2.67)	(1.44)	(1.27)
period	−0.054***	−0.053***	−0.010*	−0.011**
	(−7.18)	(−7.05)	(−1.89)	(−2.09)
rdrate	−0.122***	−0.128***	0.050	0.053
	(−2.63)	(−2.77)	(1.49)	(1.59)
sl	**−0.034***		**−0.086***	
	(−5.74)		**(−19.68)**	
sj		**0.090***		
		(10.94)		
sintra				**0.134***
				(27.29)
jcompany	−0.025***	−0.026***	−0.007*	−0.006*
	(−5.32)	(−5.36)	(−1.9)	(−1.68)
Number of obs.	26824	26824	26824	41.63
R^2	0.7953	0.7961	0.7266	0.6617

Notes: As for Table 7.2.

electric machinery are relevant to the results we checked earlier. One interpretation is that transport manufacturers, which rely on parts suppliers being located near factories, maintain a high level of local procurement from the outset and their attitude is sustained during operation.

7.3.3.2   Regional differences by location of the affiliate

We have examined the behavior of Japanese affiliates in the entire world. Now, we check the behavior of affiliates in Asia and compare this with behavior in other regions. An estimation was done individually for

Table 7.4   Estimation results with alternative estimator of agglomeration

Independent variables	Dependent variables Local purchase/total cost	
$\ln P_L$	−0.005*	−0.009***
	(−1.93)	(−3.43)
$\ln Y$	0.031***	0.029***
	(12.16)	(11.63)
capwork	−0.005**	−0.005**
	(−2.29)	(−2.35)
jcapratio	−0.026**	−0.025**
	(−2.06)	(−1.97)
groupcom	0.007	0.010*
	(1.12)	(1.65)
period	0.040***	0.036***
	(4.68)	(4.16)
rdrate	0.021	0.019
	(0.41)	(0.37)
sl	0.120***	0.118***
	(17.69)	(17.38)
jcompany	**0.029***	
	(5.28)	
lmva		**0.098***
		(7.88)
Number of obs.	26824	26824
R^2	0.7524	0.7528

Notes: As for Table 7.2.

affiliates located in each region. Almost two-thirds of the world's samples come from Asia. Table 7.6 shows the estimation results for Asia, North America and Europe. With regard to our most important three variables (*period, sl, jcompany*), the behavior in Asia is the same as those shown internationally; however, this is not necessarily true in North America or Europe. In Asia, *period* (period of operation) has a strong effect on purchasing activities from every origin: significantly positive for local, significantly negative for Japan and third countries. In Europe, the results are similar to those in Asia. However, in the case of North America, none of the coefficients is significant at all. These results are consistent with Kiyota et al. (2008). The next variable, *sl* (share of local sales), has almost the same significant influence across the locations of affiliates. The signs are the same as those of international results. The only exception is purchasing from Japan by affiliates in North America and

Table 7.5   Estimation results by industrial sector

	Local purchase/ total cost		Purchase from Japan/total cost		Purchase from third country in the region/ total cost	
	Electric machinery	Transport machinery	Electric	Transport	Electric	Transport
$\ln P_L$	0.005	0.026***	−0.007	0.004	−0.005	−0.006*
	(0.88)	(4.23)	(−1.28)	(0.64)	(−1.12)	(−1.82)
$\ln Y$	0.023***	−0.005	0.031***	0.027***	0.012***	−0.002
	(4.94)	(−1.02)	(7.19)	(4.9)	(3.25)	(−0.67)
capwork	−0.007*	−0.122***	0.005	0.009*	0.005	0.002
	(−1.86)	(−4.08)	(1.33)	(1.91)	(1.58)	(0.68)
jcapratio	0.047*	0.018	−0.020	0.146***	−0.050**	−0.027*
	(1.83)	(1.24)	(−0.83)	(5.38)	(−2.4)	(−1.68)
groupcom	0.020	0.059***	−0.039***	−0.027**	0.005	−0.003
	(1.6)	(2.83)	(−3.35)	(−2.11)	(0.52)	(−0.43)
period	**0.036****	**0.179**	**−0.070****	**−0.063 ***	**−0.011**	**0.014**
	(2.17)	**(1.44)**	**(−4.47)**	**(−3.32)**	**(−0.84)**	**(1.25)**
rdrate	−0.101	0.115***	−0.104	−0.033	0.046	−0.023
	(−1.39)	(6.48)***	(−1.52)	(−0.3)	(0.77)	(−0.34)
sl	**0.124****	**0.037***	**−0.022****	**−0.021**	**−0.107****	**−0.092****
	(10.48)	**(1.77)***	**(−2.01)**	**(−1.28)**	**(−11.24)**	**(−9.62)**
jcompany	**0.106****	**−0.012**	**−0.063****	**−0.033***	**−0.050****	**0.015**
	(7.08)	**(−0.71)**	**(−4.48)**	**(−1.75)**	**(−4.11)**	**(1.29)**
Number of obs.	6917	4143	6917	4143	6917	4143
R^2	0.7156	0.7307	0.7872	0.7663	0.7289	0.583

Notes: As for Table 7.2.

Europe, which is not significant. The coefficients of the variable *jcompany* (number of Japanese companies in a host country) are significant in Asia, but not necessarily in North America or Europe. This implies that local agglomeration of Japanese affiliates is one of the leading factors for the production network in Asia.

We find some other interesting results. The variables *capwork* (capital intensity) and *jcapratio* (Japanese share of capital) are significantly positive for purchases from Japan in the case of affiliates in Asia, but not in North America or Europe. The variable *groupcom* (number of affiliates in the world belonging to the same parent) is significantly negative for purchases from Japan in the case of affiliates in North America and Europe, but not in Asia. The variable *rdrate* (R&D expenses against total sales) has a significantly positive effect on local purchases in the case of affiliates in North America, but not in Asia or Europe.

Table 7.6　Estimation results by location of affiliates

Dependent variables	Local purchase/total cost			
Location of affiliates	World	Asia	North America	Europe
Independent variables ↓				
lnP_L	−0.005*	−0.005	−0.014	−0.021***
	(−1.93)	(−1.4)	(−1.61)	(−2.75)
ln$Y$	0.031***	0.027***	0.050***	0.041***
	(12.16)	(8.47)	(9.36)	(5.33)
capwork	−0.005**	−0.005	−0.003	−0.002
	(−2.29)	(−1.54)	(−0.78)	(−0.3)
jcapratio	−0.026**	−0.025	−0.039*	−0.004
	(−2.06)	(−1.57)	(−1.67)	(−0.10)
groupcom	0.007	0.012	−0.007	0.044**
	(1.12)	(1.5)	(−0.66)	(2.49)
period	**0.040*****	**0.035*****	**−0.008**	**0.050****
	(4.68)	**(3.11)**	**(−0.50)**	**(2.04)**
rdrate	0.021	−0.175	0.195***	−0.073
	(0.41)	(−1.23)	(2.62)	(−0.97)
sl	**0.120*****	**0.139*****	**0.102*****	**0.079*****
	(17.69)	**(15.39)**	**(7.26)**	**(5.47)**
jcompany	**0.029*****	**0.019*****	**0.005**	**−0.008**
	(5.28)	**(2.83)**	**(0.35)**	**(−0.51)**
Number of obs.	26824	17635	6030	3159
R^2	0.7524	0.7425	0.7798	0.7505

Notes:　As for Table 7.2.

7.3.3.3　Intra-firm and arm's-length

We have examined affiliate behavior in relation to total amount. However, differences may exist among intra-firm and arm's-length transactions, which we consider in this section. The detailed survey questionnaire (performance for 1995, 1998 and 2001) included such a breakdown of purchasing activities and we used the data for these three years. As mentioned earlier, the survey is not mandatory and some respondents did not reply to some questions. The number of respondents to this specific question is limited. We regard the blank answers to mean zero in this analysis. We divide purchases from each origin into two types of transaction (intra-firm and arm's-length), which means that we have eight production factors instead of five: intra-firm local purchases, arm's-length local purchases, intra-firm purchases from Japan, arm's-length purchases from Japan and so on.

Purchase from Japan/total cost				Purchase from third country in the region /total cost			
World	Asia	North America	Europe	World	Asia	North America	Europe
−0.010***	−0.013***	−0.004	−0.023***	−0.003*	−0.008***	0.001	0.008
(−4.52)	(−3.85)	(−0.57)	(−3.15)	(−1.89)	(−2.99)	(0.27)	(1.38)
0.026***	0.030***	0.014***	0.018**	0.006***	0.007***	0.001	0.012**
(11.49)	(10.67)	(3.3)	(2.52)	(4)	(3.22)	(0.55)	(2.13)
0.008***	0.011***	0.003	0.002	0.001	0.000	0.001	0.007*
(4)	(3.94)	(1)	(0.49)	(1.02)	(0.04)	(0.72)	(1.83)
0.028**	0.026*	0.015	0.037	−0.012	−0.010	−0.019*	−0.011
(2.51)	(1.84)	(0.83)	(1.06)	(−1.46)	(−0.93)	(−1.95)	(−0.40)
−0.014***	−0.012	−0.017**	−0.037**	0.005	0.007	0.004	0.009
(−2.71)	(−1.64)	(−2.09)	(−2.29)	(1.44)	(1.22)	(0.93)	(0.7)
−0.054*	**−0.061***	**0.003**	**−0.076***	**−0.010*	**−0.022***	**0.008**	**0.001**
(−7.18)	**(−6.06)**	**(0.24)**	**(−3.34)**	**(−1.89)**	**(−2.85)**	**(1.16)**	**(0.06)**
−0.122***	−0.224*	−0.125**	−0.091	0.050	0.117	−0.002	0.074
(−2.63)	(−1.75)	(−2.08)	(−1.3)	(1.49)	(1.21)	(−0.07)	(1.31)
−0.034*	**−0.054***	**−0.007**	**0.002**	**−0.086***	**−0.096***	**−0.076***	**−0.063***
(−5.74)	**(−6.74)**	**(−0.61)**	**(0.11)**	**(−19.68)**	**(−15.76)**	**(−12.99)**	**(−5.88)**
−0.025*	**−0.020***	**−0.038***	**0.024***	**−0.007*	**−0.010**	**0.005**	**−0.004**
(−5.32)	**(−3.21)**	**(−3.51)**	**(1.71)**	**(−1.9)**	**(−2.08)**	**(0.85)**	**(−0.34)**
26824	17635	6030	3159	26824	17635	6030	3159
0.7953	0.7684	0.8573	0.8257	0.7266	0.7082	0.6887	0.7803

Table 7.7 shows the contrast in these results. Some determinants have different effects on intra-firm versus arm's-length purchasing activities. The coefficients of *period* are significantly positive for local purchases for both intra-firm and arm's-length transactions. The coefficients of the *period* are significantly negative for intra-firm purchases from Japan. In the case of sales share of local market, the coefficients are significantly negative for arm's-length purchases, regardless of their origin (local, Japan, third countries) and significantly positive for local and Japanese intra-firm purchases. With regard to gathering Japanese manufacturers, the coefficient of *jcompany* is significantly negative for intra-firm purchases from Japan and third countries and significantly positive for arm's-length purchases, which implies intra-firm procurement from Japan being replaced by arm's-length purchases from local suppliers, as mentioned in Ando and Kimura (2005).

Table 7.7   *Estimation results for intra-firm and arm's-length transactions*

	Local purchase/ total cost		Purchase from Japan/total cost		Purchase from third country in the region/total cost	
	Intra-firm	Arm's-length	Intra-firm	Arm's-length	Intra-firm	Arm's-length
$\ln P_L$	−0.004	−0.012	−0.029***	0.006	−0.010**	0.001
	(−0.74)	(−1.22)	(−2.86)	(0.63)	(−2.14)	(0.17)
$\ln Y$	−0.007*	0.036***	0.022***	0.013*	0.001	−0.001
	(−1.74)	(4.67)	(2.73)	(1.68)	(0.21)	(−0.17)
capwork	0.003	−0.005	0.010	−0.003	0.007**	−0.006
	(1.03)	(−0.87)	(1.61)	(−0.56)	(2.3)	(−1.61)
jcapratio	0.023	0.008	0.031	−0.062	−0.001	−0.036
	(1.03)	(0.2)	(0.74)	(−1.57)	(−0.06)	(−1.48)
groupcom	0.009	0.004	0.032*	−0.059***	0.001	−0.003
	(0.91)	(0.24)	(1.7)	(−3.36)	(0.1)	(−0.24)
period	**0.024***	**0.043***	**−0.058***	**−0.026**	**0.004**	**−0.016**
	(1.7)	**(1.65)**	**(−2.12)**	**(−1.04)**	**(0.29)**	**(−1.03)**
rdrate	0.163	−0.327*	0.040	−0.080	0.106	0.157
	(1.59)	(−1.74)	(0.2)	(−0.43)	(1.13)	(1.39)
sl	**0.136***	**−0.089***	**0.112***	**−0.093***	**−0.035***	**−0.040***
	(10.14)	**(−3.63)**	**(4.33)**	**(−3.85)**	**(−2.88)**	**(−2.68)**
jcompany	**−0.012**	**0.034***	**−0.039***	**0.020**	**−0.016***	**0.014**
	(−1.28)	**(1.96)**	**(−2.17)**	**(1.2)**	**(−1.86)**	**(1.34)**
Number of obs.	4084	4084	4084	4084	4084	4084
R^2	0.6261	0.7893	0.724	0.5719	0.7896	0.6016

Notes: As for Table 7.2.

7.4   CONCLUSION

This analysis examined the trends in, and attempted to identify the determinants of, purchasing activities by Japanese affiliates. First, the results indicated that the total purchase amount as well as those from each area has increased, but the breakdown of its share has recently shifted to localization. Second, some determinants are identified that seem to make procurement shift to localization from international purchases. This chapter examines the effects on purchasing from host country, home country and third country in the region separately, which is new to the previous literature. The local share of procurement is higher with the duration of operation and agglomeration of Japanese affiliates belonging to the same industry in a host country. On the contrary, the share of purchasing from third countries in the region as well as that from Japan is negatively affected by these. Furthermore, the share of local sales in total sales has a positive influence on local purchases and a negative influence on purchases from third countries and from Japan. This implies that localization of purchasing will advance in Asia in the future. In that process, this chapter shows not only that the share of purchasing from Japan but also that the share of purchasing from third countries will be reduced. Another finding is that there is a shift between intra-firm and arm's-length transactions. The direction of the effect depends on the determinant. In the case of agglomeration of Japanese affiliates, intra-firm purchases from Japan seem to be replaced by arm's-length purchases from the host country.

What do these findings imply for production networks in Asia? We should be aware of two different levels: the behavior of individual affiliates (micro level) and aggregated movements (macro level). For individual affiliates, production appears to become independent of intermediate inputs from home or third countries (sometimes also transferring between arm's-length and intra-firm transactions) with length of operation and some other factors. Regarding aggregated movements, the trade of intermediate goods in Asia has expanded even though individual affiliates have shifted to local purchase, partly because of the expansion of total production and partly because of the establishment of new affiliates. In Asia, many Japanese affiliates have been established in recent decades. At the initial stage, such affiliates may be less experienced and may not find qualified parts suppliers or a sufficient size of market in the host country. The analysis suggests that newly established affiliates, especially affiliates located in countries where there are few Japanese companies and the market is small, are more likely to rely on purchasing from Japan or third countries rather than local purchasing. Even if one specific affiliate may shift to local purchasing along with length of operation, other affiliates (sometimes in new countries) may start operation and actively purchase from Japan or third countries rather than the host country as and when new affiliates are actively established in Asian countries one after another. This may consistently explain the expansion in trade of intermediate goods and corporate attitudes toward localization, with implications for the future.

For future study, the most important amendment to consider is the price factors for each purchase origin. A strong assumption on prices was made in this chapter because of data availability, but the previous work indicates that transport cost is very influential on purchasing activities. An improved model is expected to be considered in future.

NOTES

1. The use of microdata is subject to government permission.
2. Overseas affiliates include subsidiaries (in a sense, child companies) and sub-subsidiaries (in a sense, grandchild companies). They are defined as: (1) an overseas affiliate in which (a) Japanese corporation(s) has invested capital of 10 percent or more (subsidiary); (2) an overseas affiliate in which a subsidiary, funded for more than 50 percent by (a) Japanese corporation(s), has invested capital of over 50 percent (sub-subsidiary); or (3) an overseas affiliate in which a Japanese corporation(s) and a subsidiary, funded for more than 50 percent by (a) Japanese corporation(s), have invested capital of over 50 percent (sub-subsidiary).
3. Purchases only include material inputs such as parts and components, but do not include wages.
4. Those regional groupings are based on published statistics. ASEAN4 includes Indonesia, Malaysia, the Philippines and Thailand. NIEs3 includes Korea, Singapore and Taiwan. North America includes Mexico and the USA.
5. The research on regional breakdown of sales/purchases started in 1980, followed by research in 1983 and 1986. It has been conducted annually since 1987.
6. Some estimation has been done in recently published statistics. For example, as some respondents reply to total sales but do not give a regional breakdown (nor an accurate one), the regional figures for sales are estimated by multiplying: (1) the total sales using all replies by (2) the regional share, which is calculated using only replies containing both the total amount as well as an accurate regional breakdown. For data up to 1995, I attempted a similar estimation, using published statistics.
7. Some affiliates manufacture intermediate inputs such as parts and components. The total sales/purchases may involve double counting of intermediate goods. This suggests that the share of local sales or purchases is overestimated if affiliates in the same country supply intermediate inputs among themselves.
8. Because of the historical continuity of data, electric machinery includes information and communication equipment, although those two sectors are separated out in the present statistics.
9. Strictly speaking, third countries (other than host or home) include both countries in the same region and those in other regions. In this chapter, we divide these and only pay attention to intra-regional procurement because the characteristics of these regions may differ and the share of the other regions is only a few percent.
10. Similar estimations for both the shares of labor and capital have been made, merely for reference. In the case of the independent variable $\ln P_L$, the coefficient for the share of labor is significantly positive and in the case of the independent variable $\ln Y$, both coefficients for the shares of labor and capital are significantly negative. These results support the interpretation.
11. Actually the variable, *lmva*, is correlated with another variable, *jcompany*.

REFERENCES

Ando, Mitsuyo and Fukunari Kimura (2005), 'Two-dimensional fragmentation in East Asia: conceptual framework and empirics', *International Review of Economics and Finance*, **14** (3), 317–48.

Belderbos, Bene, Giovanni Capannelli and Kyoji Fukao (2001), 'Backward vertical linkages of foreign manufacturing affiliates: evidence from Japanese multinationals', *World Development*, **29** (1), 189–208.

Feenstra, Robert C. (1996), 'U.S. imports: data and concordances', NBER Working Paper Series 5515.

Fukao, Kyoji and Keiko Ito (2006), 'Determinants of the profitability of Japanese manufacturing affiliates in China and other regions: does localization of procurement, sales, and management matter?', RIETI Discussion Paper Series 07-E-001.

Hanson, Gordon, Raymond Mataloni Jr and Matthew Slaughter (2005), 'Vertical production networks in multinational firms', *Review of Economics and Statistics*, **87** (4), 664–78.

Hummels, David, Jun Ishii and Kei-Mu Yi (2001), 'The nature and growth of vertical specialization in world trade', *Journal of International Economics*, **54** (1), 75–96.

Kiyota, Kozo, Toshiyuki Matsuura, Shujiro Urata and Yuhong Wei (2008), 'Reconsidering the backward vertical linkages of foreign affiliates: evidence from Japanese multinationals', *World Development*, **36** (8), 1398–414.

Ministry of Economy, Trade and Industry (METI), Japan (various dates), Kaigai Jigyou Katsudou Kihon Chousa (Basic Survey on Overseas Business Activities). (In Japanese.)

World Bank (2007), World Development Indicators 2007 (CD-ROM).

APPENDIX

Table 7A.1 Number of samples, by country

WDI country	1995	1996	1997	1998	1999	2000	2001	2002	2003	2004	2005	Total
Austria	1	1	1	1	1	1	1	2	2	2		13
Canada	27	39	41	37	52	45	38	44	45	39	45	452
China	166	258	401	484	576	609	553	678	830	887	886	6328
Denmark	2	2	1	1	2	2	1	1	2	3	1	18
Finland	2	1	2	2	2	2	3	3	4	3	3	27
France	24	30	40	47	52	51	44	47	54	51	47	487
Germany	60	73	77	73	84	100	80	89	87	77	72	872
Greece	1		1	1	1	1		2	2	2	1	12
Indonesia	87	98	120	166	193	226	194	217	220	215	222	1958
Italy	11	14	16	24	24	24	19	20	20	22	19	213
Korea, Rep.	94	104	116	134	139	149	139	143	151	139	136	1444
Malaysia	112	127	157	186	214	243	221	229	224	225	210	2148
Philippines	30	45	71	81	95	110	94	117	113	110	109	975
Portugal	4	6	7	8	8	10	7	12	10	9	8	89
Singapore	118	135	134	144	159	160	146	153	157	164	154	1624
Spain	16	20	25	25	23	22	19	25	27	24	19	245
Sweden	3	5	4	5	5	7	5	5	7	6	7	59
Thailand	157	175	210	233	291	314	305	358	374	369	372	3158
UK	83	84	93	111	117	121	90	108	120	102	95	1124
USA	359	411	445	486	541	540	523	593	608	537	535	5578
Total	1357	1628	1962	2249	2579	2737	2482	2846	3057	2986	2941	26824

Table 7A.2 *Number of samples, by industry*

	1995	1996	1997	1998	1999	2000	2001	2002	2003	2004	2005	Total
Food	65	77	74	88	118	121	113	122	127	100	107	1112
Textile	101	117	182	192	205	211	155	187	198	167	173	1888
Woods	9	27	23	29	42	37	38	52	58	59	55	429
Chemical	145	161	188	227	264	284	279	337	335	301	286	2807
Petroleum	9	10	9	7	13	16	9	8	10	11	11	113
Ceramic	39	50	50	60	78	87	69	63	66	65	72	699
Iron and steel	26	47	61	66	88	99	98	85	76	69	59	774
Non-ferrous metal	31	40	51	57	71	77	68	77	71	76	83	702
Metal products	43	46	64	67	91	97	76	90	102	114	103	893
General machinery	135	175	217	253	307	315	263	315	327	325	317	2949
Electric machinery	355	442	509	599	659	696	611	699	780	796	771	6917
Transport machinery	215	229	284	332	350	368	403	459	494	501	508	4143
Precision machinery	45	47	67	65	82	106	95	98	118	106	113	942
Others	139	160	183	207	211	223	205	254	295	296	283	2456
Total	1357	1628	1962	2249	2579	2737	2482	2846	3057	2986	2941	26824

Table 7A.3   Basic statistics

Variable	Obs.	Mean	Std Dev.	Min.	Max.
pcl	26 824	0.375	0.300	0.000	0.999
pcj	26 824	0.289	0.291	0.000	0.998
pcintra	26 824	0.077	0.183	0.000	0.998
$\ln P_L$	26 824	−0.192	1.320	−4.322	5.654
$\ln Y$	26 824	7.492	1.652	0.980	14.240
capwork	26 824	1.131	1.527	−7.131	10.128
jcapratio	26 824	0.822	0.247	0.100	1.000
groupcom	26 824	2.217	1.399	0.000	5.889
period	26 824	2.405	0.623	0.000	4.477
rdrate	26 824	0.005	0.034	0.000	0.991
sl	26 824	0.616	0.396	0.000	1.000
sj	26 824	0.210	0.336	0.000	1.000
sintra	26 824	0.125	0.247	0.000	1.000
jcompany	26 824	5.203	1.517	2.387	7.434
lmva	26 824	4.112	1.156	0.000	6.246

Table 7A.4 *Correlation matrix*

	pcl	pcj	pcintra	lnwage	lnoutput	lncapwork	jcapratio	lngroupcom	lnperiod	rdrate	sl	sj	sintra	lnjcompany	lnlmva
pcl	1.000														
pcj	−0.654	1.000													
pcintra	−0.312	−0.188	1.000												
lnwage	−0.058	0.018	−0.049	1.000											
lnoutput	0.031	0.040	0.126	0.282	1.000										
lncapwork	−0.028	0.035	−0.074	0.359	0.038	1.000									
jcapratio	−0.206	0.150	0.047	0.228	0.101	0.183	1.000								
lngroupcom	−0.031	0.003	0.139	0.027	0.387	0.057	−0.047	1.000							
lnperiod	0.012	−0.051	0.055	0.247	0.320	−0.052	0.053	0.071	1.000						
rdrate	0.009	−0.067	−0.022	0.092	0.012	0.057	0.035	0.028	−0.012	1.000					
sl	0.106	−0.038	−0.157	0.300	0.041	0.212	−0.101	0.058	0.066	−0.030	1.000				
sj	0.000	0.058	−0.055	−0.368	−0.196	−0.219	0.037	−0.174	−0.135	0.023	−0.709	1.000			
sintra	−0.173	0.011	0.301	0.020	0.140	−0.030	0.099	0.102	0.042	−0.019	−0.471	−0.186	1.000		
lnjcompany	0.087	0.007	−0.231	0.323	0.077	0.275	0.128	−0.031	−0.037	0.079	0.261	−0.102	−0.238	1.000	
lnlmva	0.043	0.081	−0.118	−0.149	0.062	−0.043	0.034	−0.025	−0.119	0.012	0.004	0.093	−0.123	0.450	1.000

Note: Some relationships exist among shares of purchase origins (local, Japan, intra-regional) as well as sales destinations (local, Japan, intra-regional).

8. The spatial structure of production/distribution networks and its implication for technology transfers and spillovers

Fukunari Kimura

8.1 FIRM HETEROGENEITY, THE SPATIAL STRUCTURE OF NETWORKS, AND TECHNOLOGY SPILLOVERS

Multinational firms (MNEs) play a primary role in the formation of international production/distribution networks. Typically, one firm or a small number of MNEs either upstream or downstream of a value chain deliberately design, operate and manage a network of production and distribution with production-process-wise international division of labor. In this process, MNEs exploit various opportunities to establish relations with other firms, including those in less-developed countries (LDCs). The firm-specific nature and characteristics are thus naturally influenced in the process of network formation. As a result, there is a wide variety of production/distribution networks, even in the same industry or in the same product line. Firm heterogeneity is an essential basis of international production/distribution networks.

The sophisticated combination of intra-firm and arm's-length (inter-firm) transactions in production/distribution networks links with the recent proliferation of various business models. Until the 1980s, the most admired companies were giant MNEs, such as IBM, with intra-firm total integration of value chains from upstream to downstream. However, this type of giant total integration model has been critically reviewed since the 1990s. Currently, firms are trying to enhance their productivity and profitability by concentrating their resources on their core competences and outsourcing other tasks to other firms.[1] The formation of international production/distribution networks in East Asia has advanced together with the innovative construction of inter-firm relationships.

International trade theory has struggled to incorporate firm-specific aspects in formal theoretical models. Neither a perfect competition setting in traditional comparative advantage models nor a horizontal product differentiation model in new international trade theory captures the richness in the variety of corporate firms; the demand for model tractability necessarily oversimplifies firm-specific characteristics. The 'new' new international trade theory led by a group of young scholars, including Mark Melitz and Pol Antras, makes a breakthrough by explicitly introducing firm heterogeneity in the general equilibrium setting.[2] However, the base setting of their models is still too simplistic to analyze the current East Asian economy; firms with high productivity simply become bigger and internalize more activities such as export activities and foreign operations through foreign direct investment (FDI). A crucial missing element is inter-firm relationships. The leading firms today are able to concentrate on their own competences because they can outsource some activities to other firms. Some firms prefer to concentrate on work outsourced by other firms. 'The bigger, the better' no longer holds true because sophisticated inter-firm relationships have been developed.

This chapter claims that rich firm heterogeneity supported by sophisticated inter-firm relationships is an essential element in understanding the mechanics and spatial structure of international production/distribution networks in East Asia. Geographical distance is a crucial factor in the choice of transaction. When a firm needs close communication with (or close monitoring over) a counterpart, a short-distance transaction is chosen, and vice versa. The mechanics of production/distribution networks generate four layers of transactions in the case of machinery industries in East Asia. With various information obtained from fieldwork as well as some statistical data, this chapter explores the relationship between various types of transactions and the spatial structure of international production/distribution networks.

In addition, the development of production/distribution networks certainly alters the mechanism of technology transfers and spillovers between MNEs and local firms. In the era of globalization, it does not make sense to foster local firms for all sorts of activities; some activities may naturally be taken care of by MNEs. However, policymakers in LDCs naturally still wish to nurture some local firms and entrepreneurs, and so a possible mechanism of technology transfers and spillovers in international production/distribution networks is important.

The fragmentation theory suggests that although value-added slices may initially be thin, technology itself can move to LDCs much more easily than before. MNEs have a certain degree of freedom in how to cut out production blocks and how to establish technological links among them. Furthermore, the formation of industrial agglomeration based on active vertical linkages among firms generates a number of opportunities for technology transfers and spillovers from MNEs to local firms/ entrepreneurs and accelerates local human capital accumulation. In a competitive economic environment open to international competition, some MNEs have a strong incentive to facilitate technological transfers to local firms/entrepreneurs. Although the implication of the augmented fragmentation theory for technology transfers and spillovers has not yet been fully discussed, this chapter provides a preliminary analysis of the connection between technological transfers/spillovers and the augmented fragmentation theory, and tries to establish links with the literature on empirical technology spillovers.

The chapter is organized as follows: the next section provides an overview of a wide variety of outsourcing in East Asia, with reference to the framework of two-dimensional fragmentation. The third section proposes the concept of four layers of transactions in production/distribution networks. The fourth discusses factors that affect the choice of layers in transactions with the framework of two-dimensional fragmentation. The fifth section examines the relationship between the spatial structure of production/ distribution networks and technology transfers/spillovers from MNEs to local firms. The sixth section discusses the implication of the nature of production/distribution networks for new development strategies, particularly on technology transfers and spillovers. The last section concludes.

8.2   THE FORMATION OF PRODUCTION/ DISTRIBUTION NETWORKS IN EAST ASIA

Although international production/distribution networks in East Asia began forming from the beginning of the 1990s, Jones and Kierzkowski (1990) made an early start in developing the theory of fragmentation. The theory pointed out fundamental differences between industry-wise division of labor and production-process-wise division of labor or between finished-products trade and intermediate-goods trade, particularly in the flexibility of a firm's decision-making in cutting out and relocating production blocks, considering the existence of service link costs to connect remotely located production blocks.

Figure 8.1 illustrates the original idea of fragmentation. Suppose that a large factory initially exists in the electronics industry that takes care of all upstream and downstream production processes. Such a factory is capital and human-capital-intensive as a whole and thus is likely to be located in a developed country. However, a closer look at the factory may reveal

Before fragmentation

Large integrated factory

After fragmentation

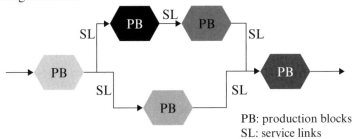

PB: production blocks
SL: service links

Source: Compiled by the author.

Figure 8.1   The original idea of fragmentation

a variety of production processes. Some processes are human-capital-intensive and require close monitoring by researchers and technicians. On the other hand, some are purely labor-intensive, and a mass of unskilled labor may suffice. Alternately, some processes need 24-hour operations to accelerate capital depreciation. Hence, if we can fragment production processes into several production blocks and locate them in appropriate places with different location advantages, total production costs may be reduced. This is fragmentation.

Fragmentation of production processes makes sense when: (i) the saving in production costs *per se* in production blocks is large; and (ii) incurred service link costs to connect remotely located production blocks are small. Firms can cut out production blocks so as to exploit differences in location advantages in remote areas. On the other hand, service link costs, including not only transport costs but also various coordination costs, should not be too high. In East Asia, differences in location advantages such as wage levels are very large, which potentially generates large saving in production costs *per se*. However, in order to take advantage of differences in location advantages, service link costs must be low. Tremendous efforts to develop logistic infrastructure and logistic services as well as trade facilitation have supported the formation of international production networks in East Asia.

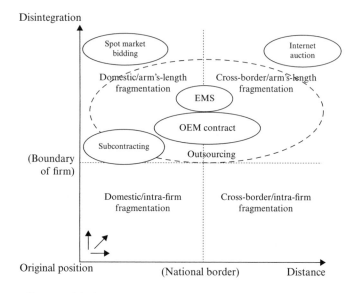

Source: Kimura and Ando (2005).

Figure 8.2   Fragmentation in a two-dimensional space

Kimura and Ando (2005) propose an expanded version of the framework called two-dimensional fragmentation. Figure 8.2 illustrates the basic concept. The horizontal axis depicts fragmentation along the axis of geographical distance, which is the traditional fragmentation, while the vertical axis represents fragmentation along the axis of disintegration or uncontrollability, which indicates whether intra-firm or arm's-length fragmentation is chosen. The sophisticated nature of international production/distribution networks arises from a complicated combination of two kinds of fragmentation. In the East Asian context, fragmentation along the disintegration axis is particularly important.

An important aspect of two-dimensional fragmentation is the spatial implication of disintegration-type fragmentation. Service link costs in arm's-length transactions, in other words 'transaction cost' in Oliver Williamson's conceptualization, are highly sensitive to geographical distance. Geographical proximity reduces search costs for new business partners, monitoring costs for quality and delivery timing, and troubleshooting costs when an unexpected event occurs. The close relationship between disintegration-type fragmentation and geographical proximity is one of the major sources of agglomeration forces. In East Asia, fragmentation and agglomeration have proceeded together.

Although it is very difficult to comprehend intra-firm and arm's-length transactions in official statistics, the data of foreign affiliates of Japanese firms collected by METI (Kaiji Chosa) provide useful information. By-destination sales and by-origin purchases of affiliates of Japanese firms in East Asia, particularly in machinery industries, present a clear-cut pattern of intra-firm and arm's-length transactions. Transactions with Japan are predominantly intra-firm while those in the host country's market are mostly arm's-length. Transactions with other East Asia countries fall in between (Ando and Kimura, 2008). This is important evidence that confirms the intimacy between disintegration-type fragmentation and geographical proximity.

We observe a wide variety of disintegration-type fragmentation in production/distribution networks. East Asia has a number of prototypes for arm's-length transactions. The *Shitauke* system in Japan, subcontracting in Taiwan, and Hong Kong–Guangdong operations are examples of these. Some of the arm's-length transactions in East Asia are a direct extension of these prototypes in the international setting. Furthermore, the abundance of opportunities for exploiting differences in location advantages and firm-specific assets in East Asia results in the proliferation of outsourcing. Examples include original equipment manufacturers (OEM), original design manufacturers (ODM), electronics manufacturing services (EMS), and foundries. The designers or managers of networks are also varied, not necessarily downstream assemblers; vendor-managed inventory (VMI) services are examples in which logistic companies play a crucial role.

The recent technological and managerial innovation in corporate management is clearly supporting the proliferation of various business models in East Asia. As mentioned above, the evolution of business models, particularly in the computer industry, from vertically integrated giants to firms concentrating on core competences is one of the crucial changes in the mindset of corporate managers. Another significant trend is the development of a lean production method, a just-in-time system, value (supply) chain management, and cash flow management. Furthermore, the deepening of the product architecture argument, namely modular versus integral, is also crucial to the development of various business models.

The next task for research is to investigate the spatial structure of production/distribution networks.

8.3   FOUR-LAYER SPATIAL STRUCTURE

Currently, machinery industries are dominant players in East Asian networking, in both quantity and quality. Because machines typically consist

Table 8.1   Four layers of transactions in production/distribution networks

	1st layer (local)	2nd layer (sub-regional)	3rd layer (regional)	4th layer (world)
Lead time	Less than 2.5 hours	1 to 7 days	1 to 2 weeks	2 weeks to 2 months
Frequency	Once or more per day	Once or more per week	Once per week	Once per week
Transport mode	Trucks	Trucks/ships/ airplanes	Ships	Ships
Trip length	Less than 100 km	Less than 1500 km	Less than 6000 km	Longer

Source: Compiled by the author.

of a large number of parts and components, fragmentation with delicate coordination is naturally pursued. Short product life cycles result in active R&D and frequent reshuffling of value chains. Machinery industries therefore present the most sophisticated form of production networking in the globalizing world, and so we can derive important economic logic that is largely applicable to other industries.

Although it is difficult to capture by official statistics, numerous factory visits as well as interviews with businessmen reveal the pattern of inventory management with the geographical layered structure of transactions in production networks, largely common to subsectors in machinery industries including electric appliances, printers, computers, hard-disk drives automobiles and others, as well as upstream and downstream companies across firm nationalities. To my knowledge, the literature in new economic geography has not yet directly examined the geographical extension of industrial agglomerations, but it is extremely important, particularly for drawing policy implications, to conceptualize the geographical structure of transactions within and between industrial agglomerations.

An assembly plant in the machinery industry uses a large number of parts and components, and the procurement of parts and components and the sales of products are typically stratified into four layers, primarily in terms of gate-to-gate lead time (Table 8.1). Other criteria in Table 8.1, namely frequency of transactions, transport mode and trip length, are supplementary; lead time and other criteria do not always hold one-to-one correspondence. For convenience, let us call these 'the first layer (local)', 'the second layer (sub-regional)', 'the third layer (regional)', and 'the fourth layer (world)', each of which represents qualitatively different transactions. Weights over four layers are different across subsectors in machinery industries, but their basic characteristics are common.

The first layer covers transactions with a gate-to-gate lead time of less than 2.5 hours and a delivery frequency of once or more per day. Most of these transactions are handled by trucks and are predominantly arm's-length. The geographical area of these transactions corresponds to what we call 'industrial agglomeration' in which a tight just-in-time system with frequent deliveries and monitoring is operated. Transactions with business partners that are new, small, and not entirely trusted are conducted mostly within this geographical boundary. Here, an integral interface is possible, and penetration by local firms/entrepreneurs into production networks as well as technological transfers/spillovers may occur. Congestion effects in the form of wage hikes, increases in land prices, traffic jams and others also occur in such geographical areas.

Examples of geographical areas where first-layer transactions occur with dense vertical links include the Bangkok–Eastern Seaboard area in Thailand, Selangor and Penang in Malaysia, and the Pearl River Delta and the backyard of Shanghai in China. Figure 8.3 is a map of the Bangkok–Eastern Seaboard area in Thailand with major industrial estates. A circle with a 100-km diameter, centered in east Bangkok, covers most of the industrial estates in this area. This is exactly the geographical area in which Toyota sets up a tight just-in-time system for more than 80 percent of parts and components; Toyota plants only hold less-than-two-hour inventories for most parts and components. The Pearl River Delta is almost the same geographical size and so this type of agglomeration may develop. The distance of 100 km corresponds to Tokyo–Takasaki, Tokyo–Mishima, Nagoya–Iwata, Osaka–Suzuka and Osaka–Akoh; thus a circle with a 100-km diameter roughly covers the greater Tokyo, Nagoya and Osaka metropolitan areas, respectively.

The second layer includes transactions with a lead time of 1 to 7 days and a delivery frequency of once or more per week. Transport modes vary; these can be trucks, ships or airplanes. For intra-firm transactions, the second layer covers transactions between plants held by the same large MNEs. For arm's-length transactions, parts and components with a modular interface comprise a large portion; trade in computer modules and transactions with EMS (electronics manufacturing service) firms are typical examples. Some transactions have an integral-type interface; in these cases, parts and components producers often have a sound reputation and negotiating power, so they do not follow a downstream firm's request for relocation. In addition, plant-level economies of scale are sometimes crucial in this type of transactions.

An example of a geographical area in which second-layer transactions are

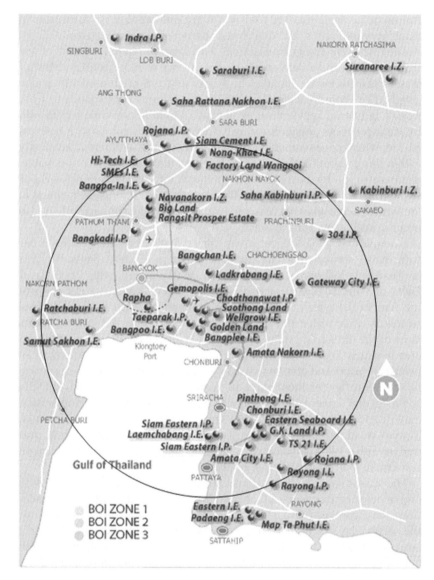

Note: Circle is added by the author.

Source: Board of Investment, Thailand.

Figure 8.3   The Bangkok–Eastern Seaboard Area and industrial estates

conducted is the North–South corridor between Bangkok and Singapore. The distance between these two cities is roughly 1500 km, which is equivalent to the length of Honshu Island in Japan. This is the longest distance for second-layer transactions. Figure 8.4 presents daily traffic on highways in the ASEAN region, and the arrow denotes a distance of 1500 km. The traffic connection between Singapore and Malaysia is known to be dense, with multiple bridges and high-grade highways. In addition, cross-border operations between Thailand and Malaysia are developing gradually, accompanied by an improvement in customs clearance at the border and the mutual acceptance of trucks without reloading. Figure 8.5 depicts the locations of major ports and their annual cargo handling in the ASEAN region. We can conceive that a large portion of second-layer transactions are among industrial agglomerations. Figure 8.6 shows the frequency of regular air flights between ASEAN airports. Again, the importance of the North–South corridor between Bangkok and Singapore is confirmed. Air transportation represents a large share of cross-border trade in electronic parts and components, which have high values per weight or volume. With the improvement of customs clearance, a within-24-hour just-in-time system becomes possible among three countries by air. It is also important that businessmen can make a round trip within a day along this North–South corridor.

If we draw a circle with a 1500 km diameter, it covers the core of the whole of Southeast Asia or the flat region of mainland China. However, second-layer transactions are not yet observed everywhere. The second-layer transactions can extend to a distance of 1500 km only when industrial agglomerations have grown at both ends simultaneously with the development of transport infrastructure, logistic industries and trade facilitation.

The third layer includes transactions with a lead time of one to two weeks, and a typical delivery frequency is once per week. The corresponding geographical area covers the whole of East Asia region; transactions between Japan and China/ASEAN fall into this category. Actually, the size of North America is about the same, and Europe is slightly smaller than East Asia. Because transactions are allowed to have some flexibility in their delivery timing, marine transportation is a major mode. Air transportation is used additionally in urgent situations. Intra-firm transactions between parent firms and affiliates are included in this layer. This is the geographical area in which the regionalization of economies has developed.

The fourth layer includes transactions covering the entire world. The lead time is typically two weeks to two months, and the frequency of delivery is, say, once per week. The predominant transport mode is marine

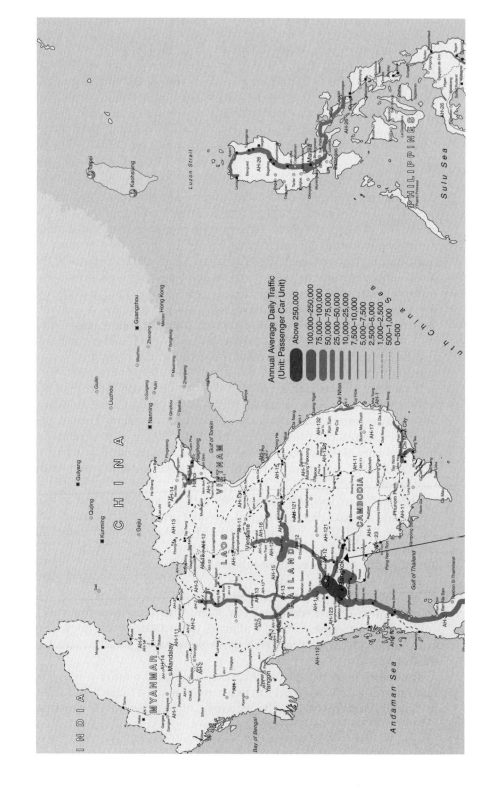

Annual Average Daily Traffic
(Unit: Passenger Car Unit)

Above 250,000
100,000–250,000
75,000–100,000
50,000–75,000
25,000–50,000
10,000–25,000
7,500–10,000
5,000–7,500
2,500–5,000
1,000–2,500
500–1,000
0–500

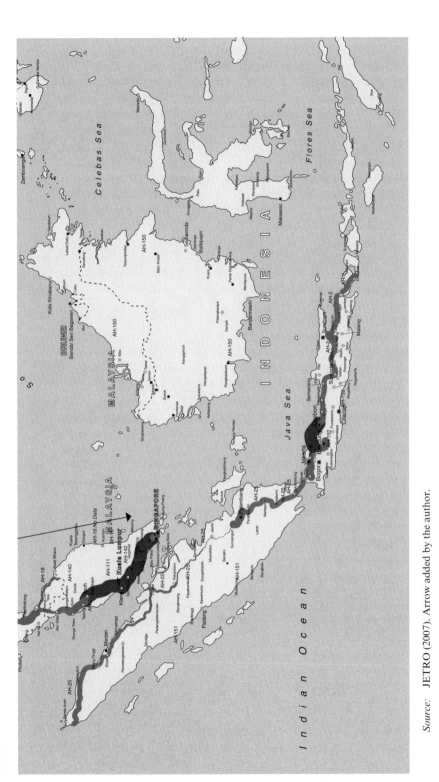

Source: JETRO (2007). Arrow added by the author.

Figure 8.4 Daily traffic on ASEAN highways

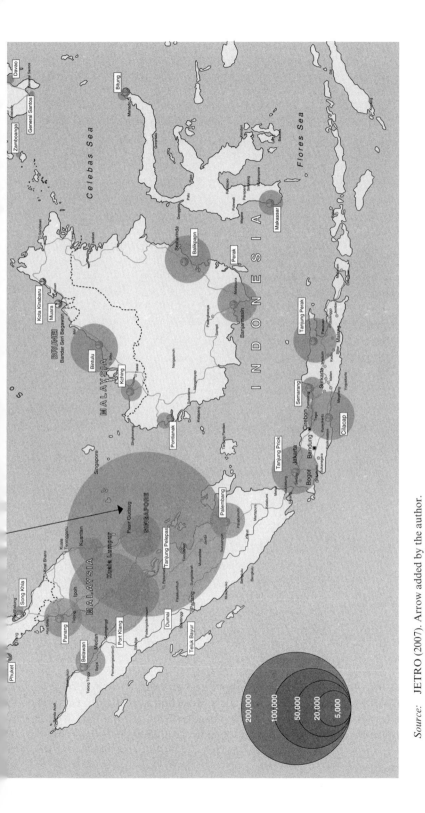

Source: JETRO (2007). Arrow added by the author.

Figure 8.5 Major ports and their cargo handling in ASEAN

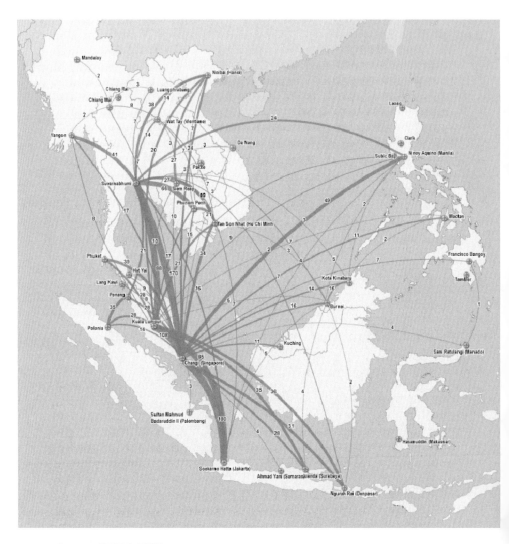

Source: JETRO (2007).

Figure 8.6   Frequency of air traffic in ASEAN

transportation with containers using regular shipping routes. Although air transportation is sometimes used, the proportion is relatively small. For machinery producers located in East Asia, markets outside East Asia are still important, although market shares are gradually decreasing due to the development of the East Asian market itself (Ando and Kimura, 2008).

8.4 FACTORS AFFECTING THE CHOICE OF TRANSACTION LAYERS

By returning to the framework of two-dimensional fragmentation, we can list major factors that affect which transaction layers are chosen, as in Table 8.2.

In the economic logic in fragmentation along the distance axis, there are three kinds of costs to be considered: (i) network set-up costs or relocation costs; (ii) service link costs; and (iii) location advantages to save production costs *per se*. When network set-up costs or relocation costs are low, shorter-distance transactions are better, and vice versa. When service link costs including transport costs are high, shorter-distance transactions are preferred, and vice versa. When differences in location advantages are significant, long-distance transactions are permitted and vice versa. When plant-level economies of scale are salient, long-distance transactions may be warranted.

As for fragmentation along the disintegration axis, the relationship between transaction costs and geographical proximity is crucial. If the intimacy or trust between business partners is high, the geographical distance in transactions can be long, and vice versa. Therefore arm's-length transactions are predominant in the first layer while intra-firm transactions occupy a large share in the third layer. For arm's-length transactions, when credibility is weak (strong), the first layer (second layer) is chosen. When the power balance between upstream and downstream firms is unbalanced, the first layer is chosen. When the power of upstream and downstream firms is balanced, the second layer can be selected. In addition, the architecture of the inter-firm interface is important. When a modular interface is selected, transactions can be in the second layer or third layer. On the other hand, when the interface is totally integrated, the first layer is predominantly chosen.

The list of factors in Table 8.2 is useful for understanding differences in the spatial structure of production networking across industries and product lines. Production networks for personal computers consist of the first layer for production-supporting services, the second layer for modules, and the third and fourth layers for procurement through Internet auction and product distribution. HDD (hard-disk drive) assembly spans the first and second layers. It requires close communication between upstream and downstream firms. On the other hand,

Table 8.2 *Factors affecting transaction choices*

	1st layer (local)	2nd layer (sub-regional)	3rd layer (regional)	4th layer (world)
Re: fragmentation along the distance axis				
Network set-up cost/relocation cost	small ——————→		large	
Service link cost (esp. transport cost – cost, lead time, quality)	large ———————————————————→			small
Location advantages (esp. production conditions, economies of scale)	small ——————→		large	
Re: fragmentation along the disintegration axis				
Intimacy of inter-firm relationship				
Intra-firm vs arm's-length (capital holdings)	arm's-length ——————→		intra-firm	
Credibility	weak ←——→ strong			
Power balance	unbalanced ←——→ balanced			
Architecture of inter-firm interface				
Modular vs integral	integral ——————→		modular	

Source: Compiled by the author.

parts and components are light to carry, and both parts producers and assemblers are strong and oligopolistic. The automobile industry primarily utilizes the first layer with tight just-in-time systems, while some parts with economies of scale such as spark plugs are in the second layer. Production networks with an OEM/ODM contract or EMS firms are in the first and second layers. By assessing the weights of these factors, we can explain the choice of transaction layers, applicable even across subsectors in machinery industries.

The application of this framework to industries other than machinery industries would require some cautious empirical work because the technological and managerial setting could be different. However, fundamental factors that determine the spatial structure of production networks seem to share factors across industries. For example, garment and footwear industries usually have much slower transactions in production networks than machinery industries because location advantages, namely cheap labor, are particularly important. Chemical industries do not typically have tight just-in-time system, which can be explained by strong economies of scale in production and transportation. Outsourcing in software development between the USA and India may look like quite different, but credibility and intimacy seem to be crucial in the nature of transactions, whether they require frequent interactions for fine-tuning or consist of simply labor-intensive works.

8.5 THE LINK WITH TECHNOLOGY TRANSFERS AND SPILLOVERS

International production/distribution networks provide various opportunities for MNEs and local firms in developing countries to compete and cooperate with each other. Such interactions between MNEs and local firms are much more varied and intense than in a world with a relatively simple industry-wise North–South division of labor. This in turn implies that the nature of technology transfers and spillovers has certainly evolved in the enhanced economic dynamism.

What would be the implication of production fragmentation for technology transfers and spillovers? In comparison with the relocation of whole operations to LDCs, an MNE has a degree of freedom in how to cut out production blocks, which generates much larger flexibility in the location pattern. This means that an MNE can relocate some activities to LDCs with much smaller commitments than in the case of the relocation of entire activities. The consequence is that some production processes in industries, the relocation of which have not even been considered in the past, actually move to LDCs with technology. From the viewpoint of hosting LDCs, weaker policy intervention such as the improvement of special economic zones and logistics services would be necessary to induce such FDI than in the case of the relocation of the entire industry in the form of import-substituting FDI.

The physical movement of technology and managerial know-how to LDCs would provide more opportunities for local firms or entrepreneurs to enjoy technology transfers or spillovers. However, a possible difficulty comes from thin slices of value chains. Particularly at the early stage of development, fragmented production blocks do not typically engage in transactions with neighboring firms, which limits the linkage channel of technology transfers/spillovers. In addition, technology absorptive capacity is one of the crucial determinants for what sort of production processes will be located in LDCs, whether vertical linkage is developed, and whether technological spillovers occur. LDCs at the initial stage of industrialization typically suffer from low technology absorptive capacity.

Once LDCs reach the stage of formulating industrial agglomeration, the perspective of technology transfers and spillovers is drastically improved. In industrial agglomeration, vertical division of labor by means of arm's-length transactions is actively conducted. Initially, such transactions tend to be among upstream and downstream MNEs. However, under severe competitive pressure, MNEs start seeking local firms to procure parts and components at lower prices. Some MNEs may even be keen to transfer technologies to local firms/entrepreneurs in order to obtain a supply of parts and components at satisfactory prices, quality and delivery timing. Technology absorptive capacity of local firms and entrepreneurs again becomes an important determinant of the extent of technology transfers and spillovers. A key difference from the traditional import substitution strategy with heavy trade protection is competitive pressure from international markets, which provide efficiency in the operation of MNEs.

The spatial structure of production networks is an important geographical consideration regarding technology transfers and spillovers. At least in the case of machinery industries with major just-in-time systems, arm's-length transactions almost always occur in geographical proximity. When a novice local firm enters international production networks, this most often occurs as a first-layer transaction. This geographical extension is also equal in size to one industrial agglomeration. It coincides with the geographical extent in which human resources can travel daily. Cross-border arm's-length transactions by local firms, i.e. transactions in the second or third layer, are rare except in cases where the firm has already established a strong reputation.

In industries other than machinery, some adjustments are necessary. In the garment industry, for example, the speed and frequency of transactions are typically lower than in the machinery industry, and thus longer-distance transactions between MNEs and local firms may be possible. In the software industry, the geographical distance in transactions may be less crucial, although credibility remains important. In both cases, technological links with MNEs are vital to the quality of work.

8.6   NEW DEVELOPMENT STRATEGIES AND TECHNOLOGY TRANSFERS/SPILLOVERS

The formation of international production/distribution networks in East Asia induces fundamental revision of development strategies for LDCs. New development strategies claim that participation in international production/distribution networks is the key to accelerating economic development in an era of globalization.[3]

The concept of four layers of transactions has a profound policy implication. In the context of East Asia, developing countries at the early phase of economic development try to participate in international production networks by hosting production blocks pushed out of congested industrial agglomeration in the neighborhood. During this phase, transactions by invited production blocks occur mostly in the second layer. On the other hand, developing countries that have reached a higher phase of economic development should try to formulate efficient industrial agglomeration; in this phase, transactions in the first layer become important. Alternatively, in the context of developing economies outside East Asia, long-distance transactions such as those in the third layer become important. Required policies as well as demand for hard and soft infrastructure are certainly different, depending on what types of transactions are expected.

The development of international production/distribution networks in East Asia also presents a new perspective on technology transfers and spillovers. Hosting FDI generates both positive and negative effects on local firms and entrepreneurs. Negative effects stem from enhanced competition in local markets of products and labor where technological dominance by MNEs may adversely affect the performance of local firms. On the other hand, positive effects derive from easier access to technology and managerial know-how for local firms and entrepreneurs. Technology transfers or spillovers may occur in the form of imitation or reverse technology, spin-off of engineers, and most notably vertical links to upstream/downstream MNEs.

A traditional development strategy utilizing import-substituting FDI intends to establish vertical links between local firms and MNEs and explore the possibility of technological upgrading of local firms and entrepreneurs. Such attempts often fail because the size of the local market is small and compensating incentives for MNEs such as import restrictions degrade the competitive environment. Under discretionary incentive schemes, MNEs typically have a weak incentive to make technology transfers to local firms and entrepreneurs.

Another development strategy that utilizes export-oriented FDI does not provide a notable outcome in technology transfers and spillovers in so far as the activities of MNEs are geographically segregated in narrow export processing zones (EPZs). MNEs in EPZs are exposed to international competition and pursue maximum efficiency. However, value-added slices that MNEs bring in are often very thin and limited to purely labor-intensive activities, and the enclave nature of EPZs becomes a serious obstacle to technology transfers and spillovers.

International production/distribution networks, particularly at the stage of development observed in East Asia today, present a new possibility for technology transfers and spillovers. East Asia proves that the sophistication of production fragmentation can achieve the formation of industrial agglomeration in which active technology spillovers may occur. In an internationally competitive environment, some MNEs are quite willing to transfer technologies. This is a new way of pursuing technology transfers and spillovers.

One problem is that not all countries can immediately attain such a stage of development. In order to participate in international production/distribution networks, a country must host the first wave of production blocks invested by MNEs. At this stage, the operation tends to be thin in value added, perhaps even thinner than in the case of traditional EPZ operations, and local vertical links are not yet established. This means that significant technology transfers or spillovers may not be expected for a while if the technology absorptive capacity is not well developed. Policymakers in LDCs must be patient until they are hosting a critical mass of FDI, rather than hastily introducing performance requirements for technology transfers. Once the seed of industrial agglomeration has been planted, local firms and entrepreneurs will have ample opportunities for penetrating into production networks, which will eventually accelerate technology transfers and spillovers.

Although these arguments require further theoretical elaboration and empirical support, they seem to be largely consistent with the literature on technology spillovers. The literature in particular suggests that vertical, input–output linkages between local firms and MNEs are the most powerful channel to accelerate technology transfers and spillovers.[4]

8.7 CONCLUDING REMARKS

This chapter explores the spatial structure of production/distribution networks in East Asia by introducing the concept of four layers of transactions. By further expanding the framework of two-dimensional fragmentation theory, a much clearer picture of spatial designs for production/distribution networks is revealed.

This chapter also presents preliminary thoughts on the implication of international production/distribution networks for technology transfers and spillovers. It seems obvious that well-developed production/distribution networks with industrial agglomeration generate massive technology transfers and spillovers. East Asia is presenting a novel development strategy in which fragmentation and agglomeration forces are effectively utilized. Further empirical studies using micro/panel data are expected to confirm our intuition.

NOTES

1. Berger (2005) provides an excellent argument on recent changes in corporate strategies.
2. See in particular Melitz (2003), Bernard et al. (2003), Helpman et al. (2004), and Antras and Helpman (2004).
3. Kimura (2004) discusses the decline in traditional development strategies and the emergence of new thinking in East Asia. Kimura (2008, 2009) strengthens the argument by connecting policy discussion with the extended fragmentation theory and the spatial structure of production/distribution networks.
4. For literature on microdata-based empirical studies on the impact of globalization, including technology spillovers, see Hayakawa et al. (2008).

REFERENCES

Ando, Mitsuyo and Fukunari Kimura (2008), 'Production fragmentation and trade patterns in East Asia: further evidence', presented at Ninth Global Development Network Conference, Research Workshop 'Emerging Trends and Patterns of Trade and Investment in Asia' (Brisbane, Australia, 1–2 February 2008).

Antras, Pol and Elhanan Helpman (2004), 'Global sourcing', *Journal of Political Economy*, **112**, 552–80.

Berger, Suzanne and the MIT Industrial Performance Center (2005), *How We Compete: What Companies around the World Are Doing to Make It in Today's Global Economy*, New York: Currency Books/Doubleday, Random House, Inc.

Bernard, A.B., J. Eaton, J.B. Jensen and S. Kortum (2003), 'Plants and productivity in international trade', *American Economic Review*, **93** (4), 1268–90.

Hayakawa, Kazunobu, Fukunari Kimura, and Tomohiro Machikita (2008), 'Firm-level analysis of globalization: a survey', ERIA Discussion Paper Series ERIA-DP-2008-01.

Helpman, E., M.J. Melitz and S.R. Yeaple (2004), 'Export versus FDI with hetero-geneous firms', *American Economic Review*, **94** (1), 300–316.

JETRO (2007), *ASEAN Butsuryu Network Map*, Tokyo: JETRO (in Japanese).

Jones, R.W. and H. Kierzkowski (1990), 'The role of services in production and international trade: a theoretical framework', in R.W. Jones and A.O. Krueger (eds), *The Political Economy of International Trade: Essays in Honor of R. E. Baldwin*, Oxford: Basil Blackwell, pp. 31–48.

Kimura, Fukunari (2004), 'New development strategies under globalization: foreign direct investment and international commercial policy in Southeast Asia', in Akira Kohsaka (ed.), *New Development Strategies: Beyond the Washington Consensus*, Basingstoke, Hampshire: Palgrave Macmillan, pp. 115–33.

Kimura, Fukunari (2008), 'The mechanics of production networks in Southeast Asia: the fragmentation theory approach', In Ikuo Kuroiwa and Toh Mun Heng (eds), *Production Networks and Industrial Clusters: Integrating Economies in Southeast Asia*, Singapore: Institute of Southeast Asian Studies, pp. 33–53.

Kimura, Fukunari (2009), 'Expansion of the production networks into the less developed ASEAN region: implications for development strategy', in Ikuo Kuroiwa (ed.), *Plugging into Production Networks: Industrialization Strategy in Less Developed Southeast Asian Countries*, Chiba and Singapore: IDE, JETRO and Institute of Southeast Asian Studies, ch. 2.

Kimura, Fukunari and Mitsuyo Ando (2005), 'Two-dimensional fragmentation in East Asia: conceptual framework and empirics', *International Review of Economics and Finance* (special issue on 'Outsourcing and Fragmentation: Blessing or Threat' edited by Henryk Kierzkowski), **14** (3), 317–48.

Melitz, M.J. (2003), 'The impact of trade on aggregate industry productivity and intra-industry reallocations', *Econometrica*, **71** (6), 1695–725.

9. International fragmentation in Laos:[1] patterns, progress and prospects

Keola Souknilanh

9.1 INTRODUCTION

The largest and fastest-growing component of world trade since World War II has been the exchange of manufactures between the industrialized economies (Ethier, 1982). It is a well-known fact that increasing interconnectedness of production processes in vertical trading chains that stretch across many countries, with each country specializing in particular stages of an item's production sequences, is one of the most important changes in the nature of international trade in the last few decades (Hummels et al., 2001). Cross-border production sharing, horizontal/vertical specialization and international fragmentation are among the many terms that have been used to refer to different aspects of this phenomenon (Deardorff, 1998; Hummels et al., 2001; Hanson et al., 2003). This chapter has adopted 'international fragmentation' as a term to refer to all variations of the above phenomenon led by location strategies of regional and global multinational enterprises (MNEs).

Since the 1960s, Asian newly industrializing economies (NIEs), namely, Hong Kong, Singapore, South Korea, the Taiwan region (henceforth 'Taiwan'), and founding members of the Association of Southeast Asian Nations (ASEAN) such as Malaysia, together with Thailand, also began participating in global production networks by becoming local production bases for Japanese, American and European MNEs. Realizing how effective FDI (foreign direct investment), in manufacturing industries in particular, could be for industrialization and economic development, Cambodia, Laos, Myanmar and Vietnam (henceforth CLMV), also chose to reproduce these Asian NIEs and founding ASEAN members success' stories.

However, as of late 2008, the performance in attracting external investments has been quite different among CLMV, with Vietnam outperforming the others. Vietnam has attracted most of the foreign direct investment in manufacturing industries flowing into CLMV, in terms of both numbers and value. Of course, a simple comparison among these countries may not make much sense. Being new members of ASEAN and transition econo- mies are only a few characteristics that CLMV share. Population size, a prime factor of the home market effect, varies largely, from approximately 6 million in Laos, 14 million in Cambodia to 50 million in Myanmar and more than 80 million in Vietnam. Infrastructure developments such as the availability of electricity and communications are far better in Vietnam than in the other countries, while Myanmar is even lagging behind the much-smaller Cambodia and Laos, despite its relatively high potential. Vietnam also outperformed the others in the Human Development Index (HDI), a possible determinant of competitiveness, compiled by the United Nations Development Program. All of these differences, together with border-related barriers such as culture, language, currency etc., should have been translated into different broadly defined transport costs that define the attractiveness of these countries as destinations for interna- tional fragmentation and therefore might be the cause of their variable performances.

Nevertheless, CLMV have made more or less progress in attracting FDI. On the one hand, Vietnam somehow seems to be reproducing what happened in Asian NIEs and founding members of ASEAN. It managed to attract multinational and regional firms in the first and higher tiers of cross-country production networks in various industries, and from both global and regional sources of FDI. On the other hand, FDI in Cambodia occurred mostly in the garment industry, with China and Taiwan as the main source country and region, respectively. As of 2008, the garment industry is estimated to be employing more than 350000 workers nation- ally and accounts for more than 80 percent of Cambodia's exports. It is obvious that most of these garment factories are in Cambodia to enjoy better access to major markets for clothing products such as the EU and the USA. The same phenomenon also happened in Laos, but on a much smaller scale, and with Thailand as the main source country. The garment industry is now the largest manufacturing industry in Laos, employing around 30000 workers or about one-tenth that of Cambodia. Although this does not account for as large a percentage as in Cambodia, garments were also one of the country's major exports, together with electricity generated by many hydroelectric power plants. In the case of Laos, FDI in the electronics and automotive sectors, mostly by Japanese affiliates in Thailand, can also be observed since the late 1990s, but on a much smaller scale. As for Myanmar, much of its potential to become a manufacturing base for MNEs has not materialized, for many reasons including internal conflict, sanctions by the USA and EU, and relatively underdeveloped infrastructure.

The purpose of this chapter is to investigate the patterns, progress and prospects of international fragmentation, based on possible motivations that may have caused MNEs to expand their production networks to Laos, being an example of a small country.

This chapter is organized into six sections. The next section will summarize possible determinants for FDI firms engaging in international fragmentation from related literatures and works, which will then be used as a framework for categorization of patterns or international fragmentation. The third section is dedicated to the historical background of FDI in Laos and the fourth section categorizes international fragmentation in Laos into patterns according to section 9.2 and provides details of what has happened in each. Section 9.5 will show the progress made, especially in reducing broadly defined transport costs, as well as the progress made in international fragmentation itself, in Laos. Finally, section 9.6 summarizes Laos' advantages and certain policy implications that it may implement to enhance its participation in global production network.

9.2 THEORETICAL FRAMEWORKS

For related concepts and possible definitions of international fragmentation, Deardorff (1998) explained fragmentation as the splitting of a production process into two or more steps that can be undertaken in different locations but that lead to the same final product. Hummels et al. (2001) discussed vertical specialization as production processes that involve a sequential, vertical trading chain stretching across many countries, with each country specializing in particular stages of the production process. Re-export of processed goods using imported inputs was offered to distinguish vertical from horizontal specializations. Hanson et al. (2003) defined vertical production networks as a form of 'vertical FDI' by which multinationals spread across different locations and the various activities they perform, such as R&D, input production and input processing.

This chapter focuses on the fragmentation of production processes between two or more different countries and those that are carried out by MNEs. Therefore, whether or not processed goods are exported or sold locally need not be determined. This chapter uses 'international fragmentation' to mean the splitting of production processes between countries. Unless otherwise stated, international fragmentation as is used in this chapter refers to those by MNEs.

Next, many papers provide possible explanations for the determinants of international fragmentation. Puga and Venables (1997) showed that a discriminatory trade policy raises the profitability of firms located within preferential arrangement areas, and therefore attracts industry into them. Fujita et al. (1999) showed in various models that a combination between wage differences and a decrease in broadly defined transport costs between the core and periphery to certain levels will cause factories in the core to move to the periphery. Hanson et al. (2003) found that lower trade costs, lower wages for less-skilled labor and lower corporate income tax rates increase demand for imported inputs and therefore international fragmentation. Trade costs were defined by Anderson and Wincoop (2004) as all costs, other than the marginal costs of producing the goods themselves, incurred in getting goods to final consumers. From these related works, international fragmentation can be regarded as measures by firms to maximize their profits under many predefined conditions, from discriminatory trade arrangements, high tariff rates, to differences in factor endowments, such as wages, infrastructure etc.

Although their work is not directly related to the above research, Suzuki and Keola (2005) advocated a policy recommendation report to the effect that attracting labor-intensive processes from several thousand Japanese and other foreign direct investments in Thailand could be an industrialization option for a small country like Laos. This is called a sub-regional industrialization strategy. Hiratsuka et al. (2008) conceptualized this idea and showed that reducing border-related costs plays a determinant role, because parts, semi-finished products, as well as finished products, need to be moved back and forth across borders each time, with at least one export and one import procedure. They also provided a case study where a factory successfully reduced the import–export procedure time and managed to expand in terms of the number of workers.

Grouping many factors to broadly defined transport costs or concentrating on specific components of it, as in the related works above, is one of the many ways of understanding the nature of determinants and therefore obtaining possible answers on how to promote cross-border fragmentation. However, these factors may be looked at from a different point of view. While they may cause international fragmentation to increase or decrease, they are completely different in one respect: on the one hand, preferential trade arrangements and tariff rates are measures imposed by certain governments or countries for the intended policies' objectives and, on the other hand, differences in the availability of wage rates or infrastructure are generally not intended, and are mostly targets of improvement or eradication.

Based on this view, determinants or motivations of international fragmentation can be regrouped into two types: those aimed at overcoming intended policies by authorities; and those that arise because of differences between available factor endowments such as wages, infrastructure etc. The former can then be further divided into two types: (i) driven by preferential trade arrangements, involving lowering of barriers to certain countries or regions; (ii) driven by tariff barriers, which heighten barriers to certain group of products; and (iii) driven by factor endowments, which refers to relocation of fragmented production processes in order to benefit from existing differences in terms of resources.

9.3   THE HISTORICAL BACKGROUND OF FDI IN LAOS

Because international fragmentation, in this chapter, is limited to cases related to cross-border operations in manufacturing sectors, whether or not FDI is possible in a country becomes extremely important. In order for foreign investment to occur, the consent of both source and host countries is required. FDI that may be regarded as international fragmentation, in the context of this chapter, is a relatively new trend in global trade, and started about a decade after the end of World War II. Laos, on the other hand, was effectively not open for FDI until 1989. The big wave of factory relocation to developing countries by industrialized nations started in the 1960s when Laos was undergoing a fierce armed struggle. The war ended in 1975, with the establishment of the Lao People's Democratic Republic, but with attempted nationalization of the national economy, FDI was not possible for several years, either legally and practically. After a few years of severe economic downturn and amid decreased assistance from the East, Laos adopted the so-called 'new economic mechanism policy'[2] at the 4th general congress of the People's Revolution Party in 1986 and began many processes to transform the economy to a market-oriented one (Joiner, 1988). The reform was first attempted domestically with the introduction of socialist business accounting for existing state-owned enterprises, and privatization of domestic investors, but the moves quickly proved to be not viable due to a lack of sufficient local funds and capable investors (Stuart-Fox, 1989). The geographically nearest regional economic powerhouse of Thailand was where the authorities turned to as the next available option. While the new economic mechanism policy brought about many changes, such as diversification of external assistance and a sharp increase in foreign tourists, in terms of industrial policies the main reforms in the transition were, in practice, privatizations and opening up to FDI. However, it took the authorities nearly two years to issue an administrative decree on FDI, which, for the first time, provided legal grounds for direct investment in Laos.

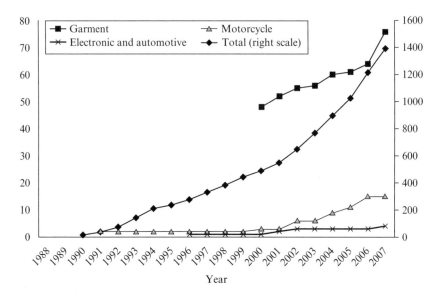

Source: Compiled by the author based on statistics provided by Department of Domestic and Foreign Investment, Ministry of Planning and Investment.

Figure 9.1   Cumulative number of approved FDI applications in Laos

Figure 9.1 depicts the cumulative number of approved FDI applications, between 1989 and 2007, with the focus on those that can be categorized as international fragmentations. About 1400 applications, averaging 77 per year, were approved during this period. There were nearly 80 export-oriented garment factories during the entire period. According to the latest figures from the Association of Lao Garment Factories, there were around 60 export-oriented garment factories, close enough to the approved figure above. Investment approvals for Japanese,[3] Korean[4] and Chinese[5] motorcycle brands started with two in the early 1990s and grew to more than ten in the 2000s. Approval of applications for direct investments in the electronic and automotive sectors occurred later, from 1997 onwards, and only about five had been approved by 2007.

Three characteristics in terms of sources, sectors and value of investments according to approval figures can be summarized as follows. First, in terms of sources, one can notice the relatively large influence of Thailand in FDI in Laos (Figure 9.2). Approximately 40 percent of approvals issued from 1988 to 1995 were attributed to Thai nationals. Thai influence was reduced after the Asian financial crisis in 1997, but still remained at nearly 20 percent of annual approved numbers. China and

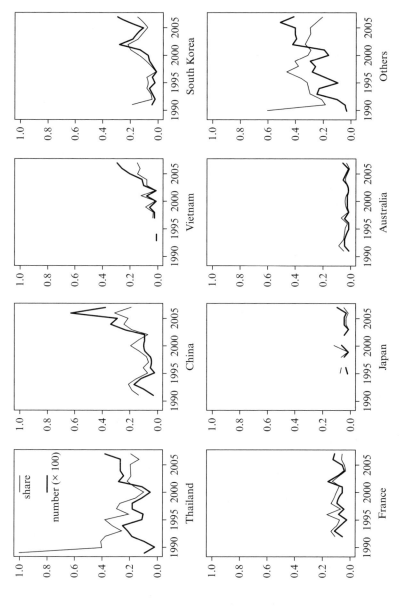

Figure 9.2   Share of the number of direct investment approvals by major source countries

Vietnam have begun to catch up with Thailand since the mid-1990s and the early 2000s, respectively. These three countries have been the biggest source of direct investments in Laos in recent years, with each accounting for around 20 percent of total approvals in 2007. However, Thailand is currently by far the biggest in term of factories in operation. According to a survey of business establishments in the manufacturing sector in 2005, nationally 56 of 909 establishments are from or joint-ventured with Thailand, almost twice the figure of 33 from or with China, in second place. The number of those from Thailand could actually be higher, as I have been able to confirm that many investments that were labeled as local were in fact from Thailand.

Second, in terms of industries, many more investment licenses were granted to companies in primary and tertiary industries. Approvals of investments concentrated on medium- to small-scale hotels and restaurants, together with trading and consultancy businesses. Approvals in the manufacturing sector engaging in cross-border production networks accounted for less than 10 percent (Figure 9.1). Lastly, in terms of investment values, a few hydropower and mining projects are already much larger than the rest.

9.4   PATTERNS OF INTERNATIONAL FRAGMENTATION IN LAOS

As discussed above, this chapter categorizes international fragmentation into three types, based on the motivation of investors, namely (i) driven by preferential trade arrangement, or more specifically by the generalized system of preferences in Laos's case, (ii) driven by tariff barrier and (iii) driven by factor endowment fragmentation. Varieties (i) and (ii) are location arrangements by firms in order to overcome policy measures or barriers such as high tariffs and restricted quotas. Type (iii) are those carried out by firms in order to maximize profits according to differences in factor endowments over places.

Information from field surveys has been used to categorize FDI in different industries into the above three categories. I had an opportunity to conduct a field survey on FDI in Laos during Macroeconomic Policy Support phases 1 and 2, between 2001 and 2004, a joint project between the government of Laos and Japan International Cooperation Agency, where I was responsible for submitting joint reports on FDI and state-owned enterprises' reforms. From 2006, I continuously visited several foreign affiliated factories every year, as a member of many research groups in the Institute of Developing Economies, mostly on economic integration. Most recently, I conducted a field survey on nearly all foreign-invested factories in the electronic and automotive industries in late 2008.

First, I found that type (i) were mainly foreign-affiliated garment factories, which have been established since the early 1990s. To date, this type has also been the largest international fragmentation in terms of number in the country. These garment factories mostly manufacture clothes to be exported, first to the EU, then to the USA from 2005, and more recently to Japan. Nationally, there were around 60 garment factories in 2007 and these were largely factories that crossed the border into Laos in order to overcome high tariffs and quota limits imposed on imported garments from developing countries by the EU, the USA and Japan.

Second, type (ii) were mainly factories that assemble motorcycles for the local market, which moved or split to Laos to overcome extremely high import tariffs imposed on finished motorcycles by the Laos authorities. Nonetheless, both types (i) and (ii) have occurred in Laos since the beginning of the 1990s.

Third, I found that a few electronic and automotive (rather than motorcycle assembly) factories existed by late 2008. They were generally of the type (iii), or those that relocated or split factories to Laos as a result of non-policy factors. They were still small in number and were mainly established after 2000.

9.4.1 Type (i)

Multi-fiber arrangements are preferential trade arrangements that have advanced international fragmentation in Laos in 1990s. These were an imposition of high import tariffs by the EU, between 1974 and 2004, on garment products imported from developing countries, exceeding certain predefined amounts. The measure was meant to protect producers in the EU from being overwhelmed by the importation of garments from developing countries, but generally with exceptions for the less-developed countries (LDCs), including Laos. In other words, under this arrangement, Laos was treated as if were on the same side, for instance as the EU, against other more developed countries such as China, Thailand, Malaysia etc. on the other side of this policy barrier. This preferential arrangement has been the main driving force for international fragmentation in Laos since the 1990s, in all respects. The value of total exports of finished garment products was nearly US$240 million in 2007, more than ten times that of non-garment products (Figure 9.3).

Figure 9.4 depicts the content of policy barriers created by the multi-fiber arrangement. In this arrangement, garment producers will gain 0 percent tariff and no-quota access to the EU markets by relocating certain

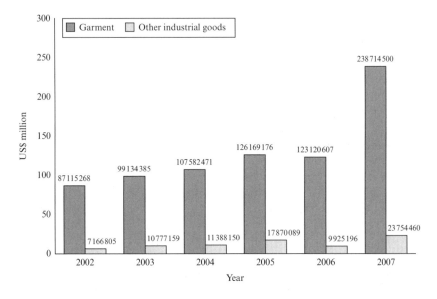

Source: Compiled by the author based on statistics on Ministry of Industry and Trade website, http://www.moit.gov.la.

Figure 9.3 Laos export values of garment and non-garment goods

processes to Laos. Foreign garment producers, especially those in neighboring Thailand and China, and some from final product major markets, were quick to get approval to operate garment factories in Laos, or almost immediately after the country reopened its doors to foreign investors in 1988 (Figure 9.5). Garment-exporting factories increased sharply from two to 54 between 1990 and 1994 (Bouthsivongsack, 1999). Although the value added in Laos by these garment factories was mostly limited to wages paid to workers, the industry grew quickly to become the number one exporter in terms of total value, exporting goods to the value of more than US$100 million in just a few years. The total number of workers in garment factories engaging in exports had increased from zero to more than 25 000 people by 2004 (Phounmalay, 2007). The number of garment factories and workers employed was unprecedented in the history of the manufacturing sector in modern Laos. The level of 1000 workers, as were employed in some big garment factories, was comparable to the total national workforce in the entire manufacturing industry[6] at any point in Laos's modern history.

The effects of preferential trade arrangements on relocation, or division of garment factories into Laos, were rather obvious. I came across

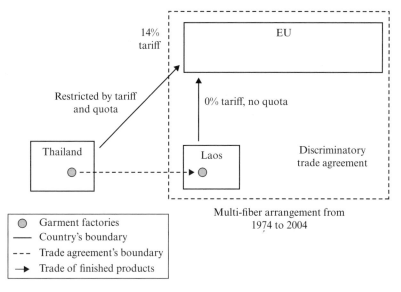

Source: Author.

Figure 9.4   Preferential-trade-arrangement-driven international fragmentation

only one foreign manager denying that GSP (the Generalized System of Preferences) was the reason why his factory was in Laos, from dozens interviewed between 2001 and 2008. Furthermore, many garment factories shut down in 1995, when Laos discovered that the EU's GSP for garment products from Laos was subjected to application, and the fact that the Lao government failed to do so prior to 1995 would result in a fine of the same amount of exempted import tariffs (Bouthsivongsack, 1999). After the first wave of garment factory establishments that had had the EU as their main market since the 1990s, a series of advances in Japanese-related socks, shoes and shirts followed in the early 2000s, or after Japan started to give similar preferential treatment to these products from LDCs, including Laos (Figure 9.5). Relocation of Japanese-related garment factories began later because, at first two processing steps were needed to certify that the products originated in Laos.[7] This rule was obviously not viable for LCDs, where few finished products and generally no supporting industries exist. The problem was resolved by authorities from both countries in 2006, after which the rules were changed to one processing step in Laos's case. The number of approvals to establish garment factories in Laos increased sharply in 2007 (Figure 9.5).

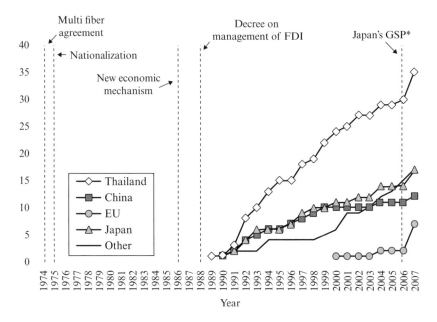

Source: Compiled by the author based on statistics provided by Department of Domestic and Foreign Investment, Ministry of Planning and Investment.

Figure 9.5   Cumulative number of applications to establish export-oriented garment factories in Laos

The first wave of garment factories came to Laos even before any major cross-border infrastructure developments, such as friendship bridges between Laos and Thailand, or the introduction of trade facilitation measures. For garment factories in the capital, raw materials and finished garment products still had to be imported and exported to and from Laos via a simple ferry across the Mekong River before 1994,[8] by which time there were over 60 garment factories. The workers in garment factories in Laos are said to be first-generation factory workers. Although to a lesser extent, many foreign factory managers are still complaining about the high turnover of workers during agricultural plantation and harvest seasons.[9] In other words, even with all these disadvantages, the advantages of moving garment factories to Laos should have been greater than the costs these factories had to bear. It is, however, easy to understand that the 14 percent difference in import tariffs and the relatively large EU market for garment products were the reasons for this.

Figure 9.6 provides further evidence of the above claims, showing Laos' input materials needed to manufacture into finished garments from nearby

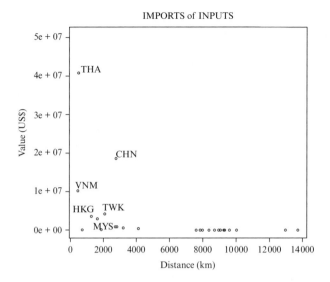

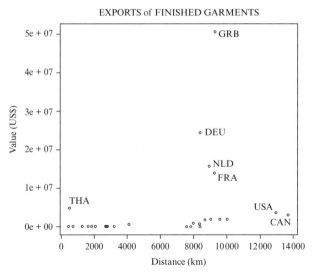

Figure 9.6   Laos imports of raw materials and exports of finished garments by source and destination countries or regions (fiscal 2005)

countries and export finished products to relatively developed nations. The main destination for garment products from Laos is still the EU and European countries, which were the only major global markets that had given Laos a practical preferential trade status in 2005. Exports to the

USA, which had just granted Normal Trade Relations (NTR) in 2005, was equal to only 2.5 percent that of the EU and European countries. The proportion of garment products from Laos to the USA is obviously too low, given the size of the market. This could, however, easily be explained by the fact that Laos had not received preferential treatment from the USA after the establishment of the new regime in 1975. Until it received NTR in February 2005, Laos was one of the few states subject to economic sanctions by the USA. Still, preferential treatment according to NTR is far behind the status of GSP (Generalized System of Preferences). To date, Laos's efforts to obtain GSP status from the USA has not borne fruit. In other words, in the case of the USA, Laos is still outside the preferential trade arrangements. Japan's GSP to Laos has also proved effective so far, increasing the cumulative number of applications, as well as the actual establishment of garment factories, since 2006 (Figure 9.5).

9.4.2   Type (ii)

Setting high tariffs may be termed import substitution in a general sense. This chapter, however, sees this as a possible determinant of international fragmentations. It is worth noting that the objectives of these high tariffs imposed by the government were not always obvious in Lao cases. Saving scarce foreign currency, fostering local industries and securing revenue were among the speculative objectives. Nonetheless, it did induce a few assemblers of well-known Japanese motorcycles to move into Laos, almost immediately after Laos was opened to FDI.

In 1991 and 1992, or almost at the same time as the relocation of Thai garment factories into Laos, two assemblers of well-known Japanese motorcycles set up assembly factories in Laos. The motivation was to overcome high import tariffs for finished transport equipment, which ranged from 100 to 200 percent.[10] One was a direct investment by a Thai assembler of a Japanese-brand motorcycle in Thailand, while the other was a joint venture investment between a Japanese trading company in Thailand, a Thai company and a Lao partner. The business models of both were almost identical, which was the assembly of complete knock-down parts initially imported from Thailand. The slight difference was that Japanese-brand motorcycles assembled in one Lao factory were also exported to Vietnam, until direct investment was made by that Japanese maker in Vietnam a few years later.

According to Suzuki and Keola (2005), these two factories enjoyed 70 percent and 30 percent of the domestic market respectively until much cheaper Chinese motorcycles were imported into Laos in the 2000s. The combined market share for new motorcycles of both assemblers in newly

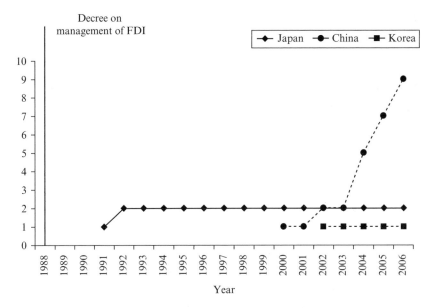

Note: Number of operating motorcycle assembly factories as of late 2008 was the same as the above figures for Japanese and Korean motorcycles. While only two were visited, the number of operating Chinese motorcycle assembly factories should be close enough to the above figure.

Source: Compiled by the author based on statistics provided by Department of Domestic and Foreign Investment, Ministry of Planning and Investment for number of investment application and Ministry of Public Works and Transportation for registered number of motorcycles.

Figure 9.7   Cumulative number of applications to establish motorcycle assembly factories and number of registered motorcycles in Laos

sold motorcycles reduced dramatically from 100 percent to just 1 percent in the early 2000s. The number of motorcycles sold per month by one factory that held 70 percent of the domestic market, in the period until the arrival of Chinese motorcycles, dropped from 1000 units to around 40 or 50 units. The growing trade volume, including these motorcycles, between China and Laos was said to be the result of the Laos government's policy of diversifying trade partners to reduce risks in the event of a crisis, a policy shift after the Asian financial crisis in 1997. In order to reduce economic dependence on Thailand, Laos signed bilateral trade agreements with China and Vietnam, making import tariffs on goods imported into Laos from these two countries about half of those from the rest of the world.

Table 9.1   Non-garment international fragmentation factories in Laos

Factory (year est.)	Products	Number of workers	Source country
A (1997)	Trigger coils, transformers for camera flash	700	Japan
B (2002)	Electric resistors	200+	Japan
C (2002)	Wire harness for automobiles	226	Laos
D (2008)	USB	80	Japan

Source: Author, based on interviews.

9.4.3   Type (iii)

It is important first to clarify what factor endowments or complementary production resources Laos has to offer to which potential foreign direct investors. In the manufacturing sector, obviously lower wage rates were among the few advantages, but for those from Thailand, Laos had much more to offer (Hiratsuka et al., 2008). Due to geographical and cultural proximities, there are virtually no language and currency barriers between Laos and Thailand. These naturally lower communication costs allow firms from Thailand to operate with low operation costs and almost without exchange rate risks.

International fragmentation of the factor endowment type happened on a relatively small scale in Laos, when compared with those to overcome policy barriers. Approximately one decade after foreign investors applied to establish a garment factory in Laos, an affiliate of a Japanese electronic components manufacturer decided to establish a supporting factory for its Thai factory in Laos. As of October 2008, there were four Japanese affiliate factories in Laos, mostly participating in international fragmentation by taking charge of certain processes to support the same Japanese affiliate factories in Thailand. Because no significant trade arrangements exist for these products, lower wage rates[11] and decreasing broadly defined transport costs are thought to be what drove them to Laos.

A very small amount of international fragmentation of this type makes it possible to discuss these in more detail. These four factories had so-called mother factories in Thailand, all of which were Japanese investments. Most of them have been operated by managers of Thai nationality, dispatched from corresponding mother factories. Workers in all four factories constantly received training from Thai trainers, in either Laos or Thailand.

The first investment of this type received permission to invest in Laos in 1997 and began operations in 1999 after two years of construction and test production. The processes that were fragmented from the Thai factory were manufacturing of trigger coils and transformers (of relatively older models). Besides its location in Laos, the group also had its headquarters in Japan and a factory in China. It imported all raw materials from Thailand, by both land and air, while exports were always done by air. The number of workers increased from 72 to more than 700[12] between 1999 and 2008. Although it was a Japanese investment, this factory has since the start of operations in 1999 been operated by a Thai manager with no Japanese expatriates (based on an interview[13]).

The second case was also a Japanese investment. The Lao factory was established in 2002, or 20 years after operation in Thailand. Compared to steady growth in the above case, this factory went through fluctuations of good and bad periods. After starting with about 100 workers, the number peaked at about 500, after which it declined to 200 plus, as of October 2008. This factory manufactures electrical resistors using materials imported from mother factories in Thailand. It was operated by a Thai manager until recently, when a Japanese manager took over (based on an interview).

The third factory, also established in 2002, was owned and run by a Lao national. This factory was one of many established by a former employee of the state-owned Electricité du Laos. Although there are no connections in terms of ownership or equity, the establishment of this factory that manufactures wire harnesses for Japanese-branded automobiles had been fully supported by the Japanese-affiliated mother company in Thailand (based on an interview). All raw materials were also imported from factories in Thailand, to which all processed products would be shipped back. The number of workers increased from 20 in 2002 to 226, as of October 2008.

The fourth international fragmentation of factor endowment type was a factory that started operating in late 2008. It was also a factory fragmented from a Japanese-affiliated factory in Thailand. It manufactures electronic components such as USB cables. During the initial phase of operations as of October 2008, about 80 workers worked under nearly ten Thai staff members, including managers and trainers.

It is still too early to assess whether or not type (iii) will prosper in Laos. However, it is clear from the discussion above that, from the late 1990s, or approximately a decade after international fragmentation of the policy-barriers-driven type was observed, at least four factories were identified during several field surveys since 2001. Two out of four managed to become ten times bigger in terms of number of jobs, compared to the time they started. Behind the fact that they have common characteristics as further advancement of Japanese affiliates in Thailand may be hints to how this type of international fragmentation could be promoted in Laos.

9.5   THE PROGRESS OF INTERNATIONAL FRAGMENTATION IN LAOS

Factory-based manufacturing in Laos has progressed significantly, with international fragmentation since 1988. This has at the same time brought about many changes to Laos. Modern regulations and laws have been promulgated to accommodate FDI, including those relating to international fragmentation.[14] The number of factory workers in Laos increased from virtually none[15] to more than 30 000 during the early 1990s. Tax revenues from modern factories have become a stable source of income for the government. Many institutional reforms, especially those related to cross-border trade facilitations, have been carried out as a result of interactions between authorities and these factories. In terms of internal fragmentation, the following developments have been observed.

9.5.1   Spillover to Local Entrepreneurs

This has probably been most obvious in the garment sector. While the number of FDI garment factories has been stable at around 60 since the late 1990s, the number of local supporting factories has increased from ten in 1998 to almost 60 in 2007. 'Local supporting factories' here refers to small subcontractors to whom foreign-invested garment factories outsource part of their middle processes. By not being directly involved in import and export, they participate only indirectly in a global production network. These local supporting factories are mostly small-scale, with just dozens of workers that are loosely hired by lower wage rates. Salaries at local supporting factories are said to be often set at the lowest possible level at the time of low or no orders at all.

Although these factories are called supporting factories locally, they must not be confused with supporting industries that many developing countries are making desperate efforts to foster. They are not, as many of their local parent factories are, using local inputs other than cheap labor. The only difference is they are mostly owned and run by Lao nationals.

With few exceptions, most international fragmentation factories in Laos are owned and operated by foreign managers. Due to language similarities, many of them are Thai. On the other hand, local supporting factories are mostly locally owned and therefore run by local managers. These managers range from ex-workers of foreign-affiliated factories, to local capitalists or even civil servants. If operations by foreign-affiliated garment factories are labeled 'international fragmentation', these local supporting garment factories are participating in that through local fragmentation.

From Laos's perspective, this is definitely progress. International fragmentation, particularly in the garment industry, has certainly contributed to the fostering of entrepreneurship in the country. Started by FDI since 1988, international fragmentation in the garment sector has moved to the next stage, where local entrepreneurs are beginning to play a significant role.

9.5.2   Moving Up the Production Stream

The activities of garment and motorcycle manufacturing industries in the early stages were concentrated at the lower point of the production stream, that is, the assembling process, and so in most cases did not lead to an increase in locally generated value added. There is, however, evidence that some local factories started to engage at the upper levels of production processes such as the production of parts and materials, and thus have successfully 'moved up' the production stream. Figure 9.8 depicts how international fragmentation progressed up the production stream between 1992 and 2008. Although this change was brought about by external factors such as fierce competition, with new entries and new boundaries for discriminatory trade arrangements, it did lead to higher competitiveness of the factory, both as a local assembler and as a production group in the regional market.

This Japanese motorcycle assembly factory, to be more specific, was established in Laos in 1992 to bypass high import tariffs on finished motorcycles by assembling them locally. It began with 100 percent assembly, or complete knock-down (CKD) parts imported from Thailand. It enjoyed substantial local demand and near-monopoly status, with only one other Japanese motorcycle assembly factory in the country. The situation suddenly changed with the entry of much cheaper motorcycles from China from the beginning of 2000s. Sales of this factory, together with those of other Japanese motorcycle assemblers, dropped sharply to just a few motorcycles per day at the beginning of the 2000s. This assembly factory then began making efforts to cut costs by shifting from CKD to incomplete knock-down (IKD) parts, on which lower import tariff rates were imposed. The recovery of this factory did not happen until it shifted to cheaper IKD from Vietnam, which signed a bilateral trade agreement with Laos to exempt some and reduce most import tariffs on goods between Laos and Vietnam to 50 percent of original rates.

This factory had been at the same stage of the production chain up to this point. Its operation since 2006 is the focus of this section. The factory invested quite heavily, by Lao standards, by procuring modern press

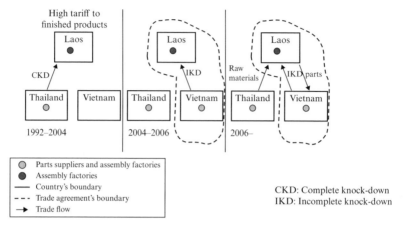

Source: Author, based on interview.

*Figure 9.8   Evolution of operations of an international fragmentation
            factory in Laos*

machines in order to partly transform itself into a parts supplier. Since 2006, or about 14 years of assembling motorcycles for local markets, it began export of processed motorcycles parts from raw material in Thailand to assemblers in Vietnam and Cambodia. This made it more competitive as a local assembler due to lower local wage rates, and also enabled its parts supplier in Thailand to supply cheaper parts to Vietnam by carrying out some of the processes in Laos, which has a discriminatory trade arrangement with Vietnam.

Progress like this rarely happens in existing international fragmentation in Laos. The case study was one of only two cases that I came across during field surveys in Laos, where partial localization of inputs could be confirmed. It is nonetheless a progress worth noting as regards international fragmentation in this country.

9.5.3   Reducing Investment Costs

Reducing investment costs does not represent progress in international fragmentation, but rather the progress of one of its determinants. Laos has made much progress in reducing investment costs since 1990s. First, time needed to get approval for an application for direct investments decreased drastically from months or sometimes a year[16] in the 1990s to days[17] in 2007. This was largely possible because of a series of institutional reforms. In the 1990s, every direct investment application was discussed at a weekly meeting attended by ministers. The meetings were often canceled or cut short due to the generally tight schedules of these high-ranking officers. Many investment incentives were subjected to case-by-case negotiations, and most of the time with different ministries. These were changed to examinations of investment applications by lower-ranked officers and with predefined incentives, drastically reducing the time needed to accept or reject filed applications.

Second, broadly defined transport costs, a possible crucial determinant of international fragmentation, have been reduced substantially during the last two decades, especially between Laos and Thailand. After examining Laos's broadly defined transported costs and a few case studies, Hiratsuka et al. (2008) concluded that border-related barriers could play crucial roles if Laos is to participate in global production networks. Import and export processing times for most international fragmentation factories, which used to be weeks and sometime months until the late 1990s, were as short as two days in 2008. Physical transport costs have also been reduced by means of many bridges that were constructed on the Mekong River to connect Laos's major cities, mostly to the East to Thailand via on-land transport.

9.6   CONCLUDING REMARKS

Categorizing international fragmentation in Laos into the three types described in this chapter enables us to see the possible options that Laos may take to progress in participation in the global production network.

First, it was obvious that policy measures such as preferential trade arrangements and high tariff rates may drive international fragmentation to a certain country. The scale seemed, however, to depend heavily on the size of the market within the discriminatory trade arrangements. As had been confirmed in the Lao case, nearly 100 garment factories emerged in Laos because of large industrialized nations' markets such as the EU, while the number of motorcycle assembly factories was far smaller, obviously because of the much smaller Lao local market. Therefore, entering into discriminatory trade arrangements with larger markets is one policy implication, and is in line with recent efforts in Laos.

Second, making an effort to attract international fragmentation must take into consideration available local factor endowments. Cheaper wage rates, geographical proximities with Thailand and lower transport costs are the main reasons why few non-garment international fragmentations have been operating in Laos so far. While it is important to enhance these, making use of other factor endowments must also be considered. There are certainly good reasons why some regional enterprises and MNEs have been paying attention to Laos as a potential production base for agro-forestry and mineral manufacturing.

Lastly, a combination of the above should also be considered. It has been shown that international fragmentation has made progress as a result of both discriminatory trade arrangements and lower wage rates. Therefore the authorities could also play a role in attracting more international fragmentation by paying more attention to ensuring that local industries with factor endowment competitiveness are sufficiently covered by proper trade regimes.

NOTES

1. The official name is Lao People's Democratic Republic or Lao PDR.
2. Joiner used 'New Economic Management', but 'New Economic Mechanism' has been widely used as the translation for the original Lao term 'Konkai (Mechanism) Setthakit (Economic) May (New)'.
3. Two of the internationally renowned Japanese motorcycle brands, namely Honda and Suzuki. However, these were not direct investments by the Japanese makers themselves, as it is the Thai affiliate that assembles Honda motorcycles called 'New Chip Xeng' for Honda motorcycles, and a joint venture between the Japanese trading company, a Thai and a Lao partner named 'Santiphab Suzuki' for Suzuki motorcycles.
4. An investment by a Korean national that began assembling a local motorcycle called 'Kolao' after it successfully grew by selling second-hand Korean motorcycles in the local markets. The Kolao group grew prominent by conducting several businesses, including banking.
5. These refer to those assembled using parts imported from China that sell under local and imitated international brands.
6. Excluding family-based, small-scale manufacturing.
7. According to a field survey in 2005, a Japanese-bound sock manufacturer was refused a certificate of origin by the then Ministry of Trade (Laos) because it imported all raw materials from abroad.
8. The first Lao–Thai Friendship Bridge, wholly funded by a grant from the Australian government, was officially opened in April 1994.
9. Based on my field survey of several foreign invested factories since 2001.
10. Based on interviews.
11. According to a presentation of a Japanese wire harness manufacturer in Thailand that has a supporting factory in Laos, the biggest advantage of Laos was its lower wage rate compared to Thailand. The monthly salary in Laos averages US$50, around one-third to one-sixth of that in Thailand.
12. According to the Thai manager, the immediate future plan was to increase the number of workers to 1000.
13. Based on an interview with the Thai manager in October 2008.
14. A Decree on Management of Foreign Direct Investment was issued in 1988, two years before the constitution and many other decrees.
15. The workers in garment factories established in Laos since 1988 are called first-generation factory workers in many studies.
16. Suzuki and Keola (2005).
17. According to a presentation in an investment seminar, it took a Japanese-affiliated USB manufacturer only a few months to begin operation (2008) after it decided to invest in Laos.

REFERENCES

Anderson, James E. and Eric van Wincoop (2004), 'Trade costs', *Journal of Economic Literature*, **XLII**, 691–751.

ASEAN–Japan Research Institute Meeting (2003), Joint Study Report ASEAN–JAPAN Comprehensive Economic Partnership: Vision and Tasks Ahead, the Institute of Developing Economies, http://www.ide.go.jp/Japanese/Lecture/Sympo/pdf/e_report_all.pdf.

Bouthsivongsack, Onsy (1999) 'Situation of investments and production in export oriented garment industry in Lao P.D.R. (1990–2000)', Garment and Textile Group, Lao National Chamber of Commerce, No. 174.

Deardorff, Alan V. (1998), 'Fragmentation in simple trade models', presented in a session on 'Globalization and Regionalism: Conflict or Complements?', North American Economics and Finance Association, Chicago, IL.

Ethier, Wilfred J. (1982), 'National and international returns to scale in the modern theory of international trade', *The American Economic Review*, **72** (3), 389–405.

Fujita, Masahisa, Paul Krugman and Tomoya Mori (1999), 'On the evolution of hierarchical urban systems', *European Economic Review*, **32**, 209–251.

Hanson, Gordon H., Raymond J. Mataloni, Jr and Matthew J. Slaughter (2003), 'Vertical production networks in multinational firms', NBER Working Paper no. 9723, http://www.nber.org/papers/w9723.

Hiratsuka, Daisuke, Souknilanh Keola and Motoyoshi Suzuki (2008), 'Industrialization through vertical production networks: can Laos participate?', in Daisuke Hiratsuka and Fukunari Kimura (eds), East *Asia's De Facto Economic Integration*, Basingstoke: Palgrave Macmillan.

Hummels, David, Jun Ishii and Kei-Mu Yi (2001), 'The nature and growth of vertical specialization in world trade', *Journal of International Economics*, **54**, 75–96.

Joiner, Charles A. (1988), 'Laos in 1987: new economic management confronts the bureaucracy', *Asian Survey*, **28** (1), 95–104.

Phounmalay, Noulack (2007), 'Coping with restrictive policies and maintaining competitiveness: Lao PDR', Regional Dialogue on Restrictive policies on the Textiles and Clothing Trade in Asia and the Pacific CEIBS, Shanghai, 9–10 April 2007, http://www.unescap.org/tid/mtg/weaving_lao.pdf

Puga, D. and A.J. Venables (1997), 'Preferential trading arrangements and industrial location', *Journal of International Economics*, **43**, 347–68.

Stuart-Fox, Martin (1989), 'Laos in 1988: in pursuit of new directions', *Asian Survey*, **29** (1), 81–8.

Suzuki, Motoyoshi and Souknilanh Keola (2005), 'Sub-regionally complementary industrialization strategy for Laos under economic unity', *Macroeconomic Policy Support for Socio-Economic Development in the Lao PDR, Phase 2*, Main Report Volume 1, pp. 25–42.

Index

Amiti, Mary 4
Anderson, James E. 92, 184
Ando, Mitsuyo 1, 125, 149, 162, 163
Antras, Pol 159
Arndt, Sven W. 14
ASEAN Free Trade Area 70
Asian international input–output tables (AIO) 16–20, 43
automobile industry 42
  multinational enterprises (MNEs) 69–70

Baier, Scott L. 84, 92, 93
Belderbos, Rene 5, 85, 86, 125
Bergoeing, Raphael 84
Bergstrand, Jeffrey H. 84, 92, 93
Blanchard, Olivier 16
Blonigen, Bruce A. 72, 85, 86, 93, 94

Cambodia 182
Carr, David L. 71
chemicals sector 2, 4, 27
  fragmentation index 35
China 23
  electronics industry 67–8
  fragmentation index 35
  input trade 44
  vertical specialization 25, 27, 31
competition 159

Davies, Ronald B. 72
Deardorff, Alan V. 4, 14, 183
discriminatory trade policy 184

Ekholm, Karoline 5, 117
electronics industry 3, 4, 27, 31
  fragmentation index 35
  multinational enterprises (MNEs) 66–9

patterns of international
  fragmentation in Laos 196–8
production networks 125
Ethier, Wilfred J. 14
European Union (EU) 189, 191

Feenstra, Robert C. 84, 92, 140
Feinberg, Susan 108
food industry 42
foreign direct investment (FDI) 85, 86, 88, 90–91, 94, 97, 100, 103–4, 124, 159, 177–8, 181, 182
  complex FDI in Japanese
    multinationals 107–8, 120–21
  empirical analysis 112–20
  Laos 185–8
  types 109–12
fragmentation theory 11, 159–60, 160–61, 173, 183–5, 201–2
  fragmentation index 3, 32–4, 37
    concept 34–5
    East Asia 35
  patterns of international
    fragmentation in Laos 188–9
    type (i) 189–94
    type (ii) 194–5
    type (iii) 196–8
  progress of international
    fragmentation in Laos 198
    moving up production stream 199–200
    reducing investment costs 200–201
    spillovers 198–9
free trade 84
Fujita, Masahisa 184
Fukao, Kyoji 125

Generalized System of Preferences (GSP) 191